Psychological Concepts
and
Dissociative Disorders

Psychological Concepts and Dissociative Disorders

Edited by

Raymond M. Klein
Benjamin K. Doane
Dalhousie University

LEA LAWRENCE ERLBAUM ASSOCIATES, PUBLISHERS
1994   Hillsdale, New Jersey   Hove, UK

The cover art is adapted from a line drawing by
Gail LaBossiere and is reproduced here, and in this form,
with permission, from the collection of Dr. George Fraser.

Copyright © 1994 by Lawrence Erlbaum Associates, Inc.
All rights reserved. No part of this book may be reproduced
in any form, by photostat, microform, retrieval system, or any
other means, without the prior written permission of
the publisher.

Lawrence Erlbaum Associates, Inc., Publishers
365 Broadway
Hillsdale, New Jersey 07642

Library of Congress Cataloging-in-Publication Data

Psychological concepts and dissociative disorders / edited by Raymond
    M. Klein, Benjamin K. Doane.
        p.   cm.
    Includes bibliographical references and index.
    ISBN 0-8058-0516-8
    1. Dissociative disorders--Congresses. I. Klein, Raymond M.
    II. Doane, B. K. (Benjamin K.)
    [DNLM: 1. Dissociative Disorders--congresses. 2. Multiple
    -Personality Disorders--congresses. WM 173.6 P974]
    RC553.D5P78 1993
    616.85'23--dc20
    DNLM/DLC
    for Library of Congress   92-48976
                                                         CIP

Books published by Lawrence Erlbaum Associates are printed
on acid-free paper, and their bindings are chosen
for strength and durability.

Printed in the United States of America

10 9 8 7 6 5 4 3 2 1

This book is dedicated to
the intellectual legacy of
D. O. Hebb.

Conference Participants at the Dalhousie University Club
Left to right, bottom to top:

1-Benjamin Doane, 2-Raymond Klein, 3-Susan Bryson
4-Gordon Bower, 5-Richard Kluft, 6-Kenneth Bowers,
7-John Barresi, 8-Campbell Perry, 9-Brian Doan, 10-Mary-Jo Nissen,
11-John Connolly, 12-John Curtis, 13-Pierre Flor-Henry,
14-Frank Putnam, 15-Herbert Weingartner, 16-George Fraser

Contents

Preface

In clinical psychiatry, no diagnostic group has engendered more controversy in recent years than the *dissociative disorders*. Most scepticism relating to this group of illnesses has focused upon one form of dissociative disorder—namely, *multiple personality disorder* (Dell, 1988). It is nevertheless true that a lack of scientific understanding of the nature of dissociation of consciousness in its varied forms has contributed to a lack of confidence on the part of some professionals, not only in the validity of current concepts of dissociative behavior, but also in therapeutic techniques employed in treatment. (For a description of various dissociative manifestations, see chapter 4 by G. Fraser, this volume.)

This book is based on a symposium that was held at Dalhousie University, Halifax, Nova Scotia. The symposium was inspired by the late Donald O. Hebb, who, in his latter years while an Honorary Professor in the Department of Psychology at Dalhousie, became very interested in the phenomenon of multiple personality and other dissociative states. Hebb was troubled by the lack of understanding of dissociative behavior and, through his discussions with basic science and clinical colleagues in psychology and psychiatry, he became convinced that the subject would be a figurative gold mine for psychological theory and experimentation.

Hebb did not share the scepticism shown by many in the fields of psychology and psychiatry with regard to the validity of multiple personality disorder or other dissociative states. He recognized, however, that much of this scepticism stemmed from the facts: (a) that some of these disorders have such dramatic qualities that they inspire disbelief; and (b) that, in their diagnosis and management, hypnosis, itself poorly understood from a scientific point of view, is frequently used. Nevertheless, Hebb admired the experimental work on hypnosis done by his old friend Ernest Hilgard (Hilgard, 1977; see Hebb, 1978) and saw in this work clear indications for sound scientific theorizing that, together with extensions of Hebb's own cell assembly theory (Hebb, 1949), gave promise of fruitful experimental hypotheses for work on multiple personality and related dissociative disorders. The key, according to Hebb, was to get well-trained experimentalists to turn their talents on these clinical phenomena. The editors, together with Hebb and other colleagues, conducted a series of lunchtime meetings and seminars. We discussed the possibility of holding an interdisciplinary symposium at which Hebb's enthusiasm for the topic could be disseminated to major clinical and basic research scientists. Hebb passed away before we could hold the symposium, so when we did hold it, we dedicated it to his memory. The symposium was entitled: "Psychological Concepts and Dissociative Disorders: Reverberating Implications. A Symposium Stimulated by and Dedicated to D. O. Hebb."

Throughout most of his active career in psychology, Hebb was not greatly involved in clinical issues. His interests were in the basic principles of normal behavioral organization in brain function that, he would assert, must be well understood before pursuing knowledge of how disorganization of brain activity results in psychiatric disorders. He saw, however, in multiple personality and similar states, the existence of compelling phenomena that (while poorly understood) held the potential to lead to important findings relating to basic principles of brain organization and behavior.

It was Hebb's strongly held belief that psychology must not keep its head in the sand when its standard frameworks seem unable to account for a class of phenomena. Moreover, he argued that the application of the rigorous methods of experimental psychology and the rapidly developing theoretical frameworks of modern cognitive science to the dissociative disorders would produce a truly deeper understanding of memory, thinking, and consciousness. The purpose of the symposium was to bring together clinical and research scientists with interest and expertise in dissociative phenomena such as multiple personality disorder, hysteria, and hypnosis. This group would exchange ideas and findings, discuss theory, and lay the groundwork for an interdisciplinary research program into dissociative phenomena generally, and more specifically, into multiple personality disorder and its principal precipitating factor: physical and sexual abuse in children.

We believe that clinicians and clinical researchers with interest in dissociative disorders (including multiple personality disorder and some cases of post-traumatic stress disorder), hypnosis, somatoform disorders (including conversion disorders), and cognitive psychologists with interest in consciousness, amnesia, and hypnosis will find this book interesting. The chapters contained in this book should be well suited to interdisciplinary graduate or advanced undergraduate seminars.

We would like to acknowledge the financial assistance of the Natural Sciences and Engineering Research Council of Canada and the National Health Research Development Program (Canada) which made the symposium possible. We would also like to express our appreciation to the following graduate students at Dalhousie

University—Marissa Calianga, April D'Aloisio, Mary Farmer, Susan Hall, Heather Schellinck and Catherine Smith—for their insightful comments on the contributed chapters. Finally, we would like to thank Janet Lord, Debbie Naugler-Haugen, and Marilyn Klein for their assistance in the preparation of this volume.

REFERENCES

Dell, P.F. (1988). Professional skepticism about multiple personality. *The Journal of Nervous and Mental Disease, 176*, 528-531.

Hebb, D.O. (1949). *Organization of behaviour.* New York:Wiley.

Hebb. D.O. (1978). Review of E. Hilgard's Divided consciousness: Multiple controls in human thought and action. *American Journal of Psychology, 91*, 545-547.

Hilgard, E.R. (1977). *Divided consciousness: Multiple controls in human thought and action.* New York: Wiley.

R.M. Klein
B.K. Doane

Introduction: Demystifying Dissociative Phenomena

Raymond M. Klein
Benjamin K. Doane
John Curtis
Dalhousie University

D. O. Hebb is best known for his very influential book, The Organization of Behavior, in which is presented his neuropsychological "cell-assembly" theory (1949). Equally important, but less well appreciated, was Hebb's determination to see psychology attempt to illuminate cognitive processes which, during the first half of the 20th century, had been subjugated by the behaviorist zeitgeist (Klein, 1979).

As noted in the Preface, Hebb was very impressed by Hilgard's work on the "hidden observer" as described in Hilgard's book, Divided Consciousness (Hilgard, 1977). In his review of Hilgard's book, Hebb (1978) wrote:

This book is, I believe, of the greatest importance for all of us who are concerned with the study of human thought. It is about hypnosis, but not as a far-out state unconnected with ordinary experience; it is related rather to the divided attention or dual mental process that makes it possible to drive a car and argue politics at the same time...(p. 545)

In Hilgard's work, Hebb saw a programmatic attack by a sound experimentalist that not only brought respectability to the phenomenon of hypnosis, but also discovered and methodically explored a genuinely new dissociative phenomenon, which Hilgard called the "hidden observer." "What this amounts to," Hebb continues,

is that in at least a few highly hypnotizable subjects there are, in hypnosis, two distinct consciousnesses. One, in chief control of the subject's behaviour, verbal and nonverbal, is in turn controlled by the hypnotist's instructions; told that he or she is deaf or feels no pain, the subject's whole behaviour conforms with the instruction. But another conscious state or activity may include full awareness of the auditory world or of noxious stimulation and be able in certain circumstances to report it, for example by automatic writing. (p. 545-546)

Chapter 4 of this volume, by George Fraser, describes a number of behavioral phenomena that may involve brain mechanisms of dissociation as well as a commentary upon the clinically recognized group of dissociative disorders. This group of disorders, especially that which meets the criteria for multiple personality disorder, aroused Hebb's interest. He became enthusiastic about the possibilities for scientific advances that might be made through the application of rigorous experimental paradigms to such clinical entities as multiple personality disorder and other dissociative states.

In 1982 he wrote the following editorial for an issue of the Canadian MPD (Multiple Personality Disorder) Newsletter.

De-mystifying the multiple personality

It seems evident that the study of multiple personalities offers a fundamentally important, new line of attack on cognitive processes; if experimental analysis can be applied to the clinical phenomena. But it is important also to recognize that there is profound scepticism about the genuineness of the phenomenon. And it is essential to overcome that attitude. The study of hypnosis 50 years ago had to deal with the same thing. Perhaps not as severe, but still a barrier to research. It was dealt with by the accumulation of data, hard factual evidence, and the avoidance of romanticizing or making a mystery of the phenomena. The same approach is what is needed in the study of multiple personality. The ideal way to de-mystify is to provide a physiologically intelligible mechanism in terms of brain processes. Cell-assembly theory, a theory of brain activity in thinking, may serve the purpose. It has been applied to hypnosis to some effect, and in view of the evidently near relation between hypnosis and multiple personality, should be of value in the latter case as well. This is theory only, and there is no certainty that it is correct, but even if it turns out to be not sound, it may still have the value of helping to make the study of multiple personality take the appearance of a sober, factual, unromantic, nonmystical investigation. It is quite evident in talking to the patient that multiple personality is a disorder of the brain, not the result of witchcraft on the one hand, nor a vulgar put-up job in search of publicity on the other. The research won't flourish if everyone is skeptical of it. It will flourish if it is recognized as an important clinical problem and equally important, a new avenue to the study of the mind.

As Hebb notes in the foregoing passage, his interest in the scientific investigation of dissociative phenomena was reinforced by his perception that his own cell-assembly theory might provide a useful conceptual framework for at least a partial explanation of multiple personality states and similar disorders. At the same time, he was keenly aware that a rigorous and objective approach to the subject was needed to avoid the risk of merely re-designing or re-labeling old concepts of personality theory. Toward this end, our symposium was designed to explore the implications that dissociative phenomena might have for psychological theory and that cognitive theory might have for understanding dissociative phenomena.

The overall objective of the symposium was to facilitate interchange among experts in the clinical and experimental fields. We hoped that this might suggest to each group possible opportunities for interaction that could promote the scientific investigation of dissociative behaviors. Fulfillment of this objective would substantiate Hebb's belief in the value of such a symposium.

Several more specific objectives were in mind when the symposium was planned. One of these was to describe the various kinds of behavioral phenomena which fall within the clinical classification of dissociative disorders, especially for the benefit of the symposium participants whose work is outside the clinical field. Here, issues of symptomatology and classification, etiology, diagnosis, and treatment were to be addressed by experts. One question that might arise from presentation of such data is, for example, whether multiple personality disorder is, in itself, a truly unique condition or merely one form—perhaps an extreme variant—of much more common dissociative processes. Other questions for research come to mind when viewing the clinical presentations of dissociation: What are the cardinal symptoms of a dissociative disorder? Do any particular symptoms cluster together, or are any of them mutually exclusive? In terms of biological or cognitive processes, can we satisfactorily explain why it is that certain predisposing factors—such as patterns of early life trauma—result in the development of these behavioral anomalies? What are the similarities and differences between dissociative states of consciousness as a result of emotional trauma compared with neuro-physiological disturbances such as seizure disorders?

The symposium was also planned to examine important psychological phenomena that appear to be closely related to dissociation and important for understanding its mechanisms. Hypnosis was the focus of Hilgard's work on the division of conscious processes and the "hidden observer" which caught Hebb's interest, as noted in the Preface and earlier in this Introduction. Other important topics covered were studies of amnesia as it occurs in dissociative disorders and the relationship between memory and mood states. These, as well as the process of rapid switching of states of behavior or consciousness as seen in multiple personality and related disorders, would appear to be fruitful topics for research along with the study of cerebral physiology and pathology that can be found to correlate with them.

In looking ahead to future research on the mechanisms of dissociation, it is apparent that theoretical and conceptual frameworks in several areas of psychology might illuminate the phenomena under consideration as well as being illuminated by them. These would include: cognitive models (particularly of memory and consciousness), personality theory, and neuropsychological concepts. To serve the application of such conceptual models to research on dissociative processes, it is interesting to consider the kinds of experimental tools or procedures that might prove most useful. While some of these have already been employed in studies of dissociation and multiple personality, it seems certain that there is a potential for many new applications of techniques and methodology. The planning of new projects, which was one of the goals of this symposium, might well make use of applied psychological techniques such as hypnosis, tests of memory and cognitive ability, or other neuropsychological measurements, as well as personality inventories. Electrophysiological techniques including electroencephalography (EEG) and evoked potentials, as well as brain imaging, also would appear promising.

The Symposium had three main objectives:

1. Explore Hebb's proposal that dissociative disorders may be a fertile field for exploring basic psychological issues such as the nature of consciousness, self-concept and the relationships between mood and memory, and brain and behavior.

2. Explore the reverse proposition that recent advances in cognitive and neuropsychology may help illuminate dissociative disorders.

3. Develop a framework for basic research in this field.

REFERENCES

Hebb, D. O. (1949). *Organization of behavior.* New York: Wiley.

Hebb, D. O. (1978). Review of E. Hilgard's Divided consciousness: Multiple controls in human thought and action. *American Journal of Psychology, 91,* 545-547.

Hilgard, E.R. (1977). *Divided consciousness: Multiple controls in human thought and action.* New York: J. Wiley.

I
CLINICAL
ANALYSIS

1
Multiple Personality Disorder: Observations on the Etiology, Natural History, Recognition, and Resolution of a Long-Neglected Condition

Richard P. Kluft
The Institute of Pennsylvania Hospital

Multiple personality disorder (MPD) is a complex chronic dissociative psychopathology characterized by disturbances of identity and memory (Nemiah, 1981). These disturbances are rather consistent. They change relatively slowly over time in the absence of clinical intervention or major life changes, but may be altered over the passage of many years (Kluft, 1985a, 1991a). The ongoing coexistence of relatively consistent but alternating separate identities (called personalities) associated with recurrent episodes of memory distortion, frank amnesia, or both (episodes that correlate with the alternation of the separate identities) distinguish MPD from all other mental disorders (Kluft, 1985b, 1987a; Putnam, Loewenstein, Silberman, & Post, 1984).

Until recently, MPD was not a major subject of concern to the mental health disciplines, either clinical or academic. MPD was considered quite rare, and its legitimacy as a naturalistically occurring mental disorder was openly doubted. Many psychotherapists and researchers considered it a virtual psychiatric dinosaur, a syndromic relic of a more naive era left behind long ago. Stengel offered the most drastic statement of this nature when, in 1943, he declared the condition extinct.

Over the course of a decade, however, MPD has once again entered the mainstream of North American psychiatry, and cases are being recognized and treated in Europe, Asia, Africa, and Australia (Coons, Bowman, Kluft, & Milstein, 1991). Clearly, Stengel's obituary has proven somewhat premature.

It is the purpose of this chapter to comment briefly on the recent rise in recognition of MPD, and thereafter to offer a series of observations on the etiology, natural history, recognition, and resolution of this long-disregarded condition. These remarks are made from the perspective of a clinician-researcher who has worked with MPD patients for more than 20 years, interviewed over 2,000 patients who were under assessment for possible MPD, observed over 600 patients with this disorder, and treated over 140 patients to the point of integration. Consequently, they emerge from the more murky and roiled waters of clinical practice and lack the crisp and clean qualities of findings from the academic setting, in which the more detailed and controlled study of a smaller number of subjects can be carried forward. Hopefully, the loss in precision is somewhat compensated for by the likelihood that the sample that has been observed is much more representative of the overall population of MPD patients than a smaller series would be.

THE RECENT HISTORY OF MPD

The commonly accepted history of MPD is that a small number of cases were identified throughout the early and middle 19th century; that a good number of cases were reported in the era of Charcot and Janet and, in the United States, in the era of Morton Prince and Borus

Sidis; and that then relatively few additional cases were reported prior to the 1980s. Articles from the early parts of that decade generally stated that the world's literature consisted of approximately 200 to 300 cases. MPD was considered to be quite rare.

Unfortunately, this history is more than somewhat misleading. Fine (1988 and personal communication, 1986-1988) discovered that several large series of MPD patients in the French literature had remained unknown to most students of the condition, and there is reason to believe that experiences and databases of many European contributors of the last century continue to be unknown to contemporary scholars. It is dubious that MPD was terribly rare when clinicians were aware of it as a significant psychopathological entity. With the rise of Freudian concepts and with Bleuler's declaring MPD a form of schizophrenia, and with the predominance of behaviorism in academic psychology, interest in dissociation and the dissociative disorders waned for nearly two generations. Case reports were few. The publication of Thigpen and Cleckley's *The Three Faces of Eve* (1957) excited public interest in MPD, but the thrust of this account was that "Eve" was the only case of MPD recognized anywhere in the world. Hence, it did not create a higher index of suspicion for MPD among the mental health community. It is of interest that these authors, in near-total disregard of the contemporary literature, continue to insist that the condition is very rare and that they have seen only one additional genuine case (Thigpen & Cleckley, 1984).

With the publication of *Sybil* in the lay literature (Schreiber, 1973) and "The objective study of a multiple personality" (Ludwig, Brandsma, Wilbur, Bendfeldt, & Jameson, 1972), it became evident that a clinician knowledgeable about MPD could identify a number of contemporary cases. Cornelia B. Wilbur, whose successful treatment of "Sybil" was the basis for the popular book of that name, diagnosed several MPD patients, and became a valuable resource to an increasing number of mental health professionals who were confronting patients with MPD and looking for guidance as to how to proceed. Her influence is discussed in a recent text (Kluft & Fine, 1993). Ralph B. Allison reported experience with a series of over 30 MPD patients in the 1970s (Allison, 1974, 1978). Unfortunately, some of Allison's rather idiosyncratic ideas and unconventional conceptualizations have obscured the recognition that many of his clinical observations have proven very useful and sound.

Allison, in collaboration with Wilbur and other pioneers such as the late David Caul, organized the first American Psychiatric Association courses on MPD in 1978. These courses, which continue to the current day under the direction of Richard P. Kluft, and Bennett G. Braun, became a major resource for the education of mental health professionals about MPD; the faculty and students of these courses became major figures in spreading knowledge about this condition across the United States and Canada.

By the late 1970s, a rising interest in MPD could be noted and this was expressed by the publication of a number of important articles on MPD in the professional literature in 1980. Of these, George Greaves' 1980 study, "Multiple personality: 165 years after Mary Reynolds," is of particular significance. Greaves received over 6,000 requests for reprints. This astonishing response indicated that a large number of clinicians had reason to be interested in MPD. It also inspired Dr. Greaves to begin the ancestor of what has become the 2,800-plus member International Society for the Study of Multiple Personality & Dissociation. In the same year, DSM-III (American Psychiatric Association, 1980) listed MPD as a free-standing member of a new class of mental disorders, the dissociative disorders, and provided useful diagnostic criteria and descriptive text.

In 1984, several special journal issues on MPD were published (*American Journal of Clinical Hypnosis*, 26:2, Oct. 1983 [not mailed until 1984]; *Psychiatric Annals*, 14:1, Jan. 1984; *Psychiatric Clinics of North America*, 7:1, 1984; *International Journal of Clinical and Experimental Hypnosis*, 32:2, June 1984), and the foundation of a credible scientific literature on MPD had been established. An increasing number of articles on MPD entered mainstream psychiatric journals and, in 1988, Kluft and Fine began *Dissociation*, a journal dedicated to the study of dissociation and the dissociative disorders.

This increase in the discussion of MPD within scientific publications and forums was matched by a rise in the number of clinical reports of contacts with large series of such patients. Between 1974 and 1987, at least 11 investigators or groups had reported experience with 10 or more MPD patients (Kluft, 1987a), and as many large series again have been reported at the First through Fifth (1984 1988) International Conferences on Multiple Personality/ Dissociative States. A particularly significant series of 50 MPD patients was published by Coons, Bowman, and Milstein in 1988. This mounting number of reported cases led to the removal of the designation "rare" from the description of MPD in DSM-III-R (American Psychiatric Association, 1987). More recently additional large series have been reported by Ross, Norton, and Wozney (1989),Ross et al. (1990), and Schultz, Braun, and Kluft (1989).

It is appropriate to ask why this exponential increase in interest and reporting has occurred. Having demonstrated it, what drives it? Although many skeptics dismiss it as a faddish preoccupation, more substantial reasons may be offered. The following attempt to explain these upsurges is far from comprehensive, but it addresses several important considerations.

The progress of psychopharmacology and biological psychiatry has generated many powerful organic approaches to the understanding and treatment of mental disorders. With effective medications for so many major disorders, the patients who fail to respond to adequate treatment for the conditions that they first appeared to have often receive more careful scrutiny. A history of treatment failure for a major (and usually drug-responsive) mental disorder is a characteristic of the backgrounds of MPD patients. The phenomenologic orientation of the DSM-III and DSM-III-R, under the direction of Robert L. Spitzer, was instrumental in effecting a realization that MPD was not a form of hysteria, schizophrenia, or borderline personality disorder. Once correctly classified and adequately described (despite minor difficulties), a firmer foundation was laid for its clinical recognition and scientific study.

Historically, periods in which hypnosis is studied intensely are periods in which MPD is recognized and studied with greater frequency. Hypnosis has been enjoying a renaissance since the 1970s. This has been a mixed blessing, however. Many outstanding authorities in hypnosis have extrapolated from their own areas of expertise to reach pronouncements about MPD that are nearly devoid of connection to the clinical reality of the condition, and/or offered wide-reaching generalizations on the basis of quite limited data.

Lay attention to MPD has been extensive. It captures the imagination of the public. Often, the very drama of the condition has made it appear a subject more fit for soap opera than for science. Few long-standing television series have failed to exploit the sensationalistic aspects of MPD. It is a simple historical fact that MPD was rarely discussed in depth in the training programs of the mental health professions for over two generations, and still has not entered the curricula of the mental health disciplines in many areas. Consequently, until the last few years, the average mental health professional gained most of his or her vicarious knowledge about MPD from lay sources. Of these lay sources, *Sybil* (Schreiber, 1973) was the most influential. For better or for worse, the media has made MPD part of today's popular culture.

The striking, albeit preliminary descriptions of the psychophysiologic expressions of the several personalities, and of the differences among them, have attracted considerable attention. Here, the work of Putnam (1984, 1991a, 1991b) is most noteworthy. Despite the interest shown in Putnam's research, few have appreciated the cautions that Putnam has repeatedly expressed about the risks of overinterpreting his findings.

The efforts of dedicated teachers to spread information about MPD have been important. Before articles on MPD became readily accessible, it was the work of this relatively small group, many of whom were very charismatic individuals whose clinical expertise was readily apparent, who shared their knowledge with others and established what Kluft (1984a) described as the "oral literature" of work with MPD.

The two most important factors prior to 1984, however, are none of the aforementioned—they are feminism and the aftermath of Vietnam. Prior to feminism and the increasing importance of women in the mental health professions, one could speak of allegations of sexual abuse and incest as if they were the fantasies of hysterical females without encountering substantial challenge. In fact, this attitude was quite prevalent. It may be hard to realize today that, in the 1970s, major psychiatric texts were stating that the true incidence of incest was one in one million (e.g., Henderson, 1975). The consciousness raising of the feminists and the infusion of more women into the mental health disciplines have made it increasingly difficult to deny the unconscionable prevalence of the sexual abuse of women, and of children of both genders. Now it is appreciated that the true incidence of broadly defined incest is that close to 16% of female children are thusly affected (Russell, 1986), and that their allegations can be substantiated in the vast majority of cases (Herman & Schatzow, 1987). When one addresses an auditorium full of mental health professionals such as those who attended the Hebb Symposium that inspired this book, one does so in appreciating that one is likely to be addressing colleagues who are survivors of the very experiences that were discounted as fantasies not very long ago. Because MPD is largely a disorder of sexually victimized women, a new awareness of the prevalence of sexual abuse and a new freedom to discuss it have spurred a new acceptance of MPD.

Among the terrible legacies of Vietnam were a delayed but finally implemented study of posttraumatic stress disorder (PTSD) and a recognition that the capacity to commit atrocities is far from rare. As scientific investigators and clinicians struggled to learn about PTSD and to treat it, it became clear that many of the symptoms of PTSD are dissociative, and that dissociation is commonly associated with trauma. Putnam's masterful review (1985) clearly demonstrated the connection of dissociation with traumatic experiences, and Spiegel (1984, 1986a, 1991) was the first to publish what many were observing—that MPD is closely allied to and may be a form of PTSD. The cross-fertilization of progress in studying PTSD and MPD has been impressive. Many professionals who had no difficulty in accepting the PTSD findings but who were most skeptical about MPD became able to understand and accept MPD when they realized that its similarity to PTSD was compelling.

The factors just noted explain a large part of the rising interest in MPD that developed in the late 1970s through the mid-1980s. More recently, the major influences have included: (a) the fact that increasing numbers of clinicians, sensitized by the aforementioned, have encountered their first MPD patients or have learned that a respected colleague has done so; (b) the increasingly substantial and accessible literature in the field; and (c) the rise of cognitive psychology, which, with its interest in the mind's processing of information, finds many of its principles consistent with the clinical phenomenology of MPD.

THE ETIOLOGY OF MPD

On a clinical and descriptive level, MPD is, intrinsically, no more exotic than a brutalized child's whimpering in the night and wishing with desperate earnestness that he or she were someone else, somewhere else, and that what had befallen him or her had befallen someone else. Most parsimoniously put, MPD appears to be a dissociative posttraumatic condition of childhood onset (Kluft, 1987a, 1991B). Throughout any discussion of MPD it is important not to lose sight of the fact that most "fascinating" cases of MPD, like beautiful cultured pearls, no matter how lustrously they shine and how wondrous they are to behold, are the organism's attempt to wall off and survive a deliberately inflicted and totally unnecessary traumatic insult.

Over 90% of studied cultures have dissociative syndromes in which another entity takes over control of the body and behaves in a different manner. Some of these conditions appear related to unique social stressors within those societies, some to the life experiences of the victims. These syndromes are often described as *possession*, and MPD appears to be the secular expression of the Judeo-Christian possession state (Ellenberger, 1970). It is indeed ironic that those who have studied the literature on the witches and witchhunts indicate that one of the frequent "chief complaints" of those who were declared to be witches and later burned at the stake was that their father had lain with them. Because this was deemed to be impossible, or at least unlikely in a patriarchal society, the prevailing theory became that the devil or one of his minions had assumed the guise of the father and had lain with the woman. It was therefore assumed that she was possessed, and it naturally followed that she should be destroyed, and, pari passu, the threat to the social order that was posed by the woman's allegations was relieved (J. Goodwin, personal communication, 1985). A colleague who was raised in rural Jamaica, where the "multiple souls" syndrome was endemic, confided that all of the girls in his village who developed it were incest victims. In short, dissociative syndromes in which more than one entity are encountered have long been known in numerous cultures, and some observations, necessarily abbreviated and selectively illustrated in this context, suggest that, although some may emerge from the characteristic pressures and role demands in a given society, many are sequelae of circumstances that most would agree are traumatic to the individual who suffers them.

Both Putnam (in press) and Kluft (in press) have recently explored theories of the etiology of MPD. In summary, Putnam's critical review demonstrated that all available theories fall short of the mark because they fail to account for certain phenomena intrinsic to the disorder, that most are more descriptive than informative and predictive. Kluft acknowledged as much, but tried to illustrate such theories as are available. Clearly, most theories of the etiology of

MPD have been advanced by clinicians who had relatively little concern with the philosophical and logical underpinnings of scientific proof. Concepts such as *eliminative inductivism* and *falsificationalism* are not frequent visitors to the clinic or consulting room (for a fascinating study of these concepts in another context, see Edelson, 1983). Conversely, many authors who have represented themselves as working at a more academic or scientific level of discourse have been fairly remote from the clinical realities that they are trying to conceptualize.

Single-factor theories of the etiology of MPD have proven incomplete and unsatisfactory. Stern (1984) classified them into four groups: supernatural, physiologic, psychologic, and sociologic. The first, that MPD is a possession state of supernatural dimensions, claims few adherents. The second, the physiologic, is largely speculative. Braun (1984) attempted an admittedly speculative synthesis of information from many areas, which is fertile food for thought but sufficiently recondite to discourage all but the most intrepid readers. A flurry of interest in the possibility that MPD constitutes an ictal or paraictal phenomenon has not borne fruit. Loewenstein and Putnam's (1988) data soundly refute the posited connection.

Virtually every psychological theory has been applied to the etiology of MPD, with mixed results. Kluft (in press) summarized:

A list, modified and expanded from that of Stern (1984, p.151), would include ego weakness, personification (of the mental structures, wishes, impulses, and fantasies), conflicted identifications, conflicting and/or unhomogenized introjections, repression, primitive wish-fulfillment, the use of aspects of self as transitional or self-objects, splitting, ego state theory, and neodissociation models based more or less loosely on the work of Hilgard (1977) and his discovery of the "hidden observer". The sociologic theories have emphasized role-taking behaviors.

A small number of recent single-factor theories have wide currency. The most prevalent one holds that MPD is the direct consequence of child abuse. Certainly, abuse histories are found in as many as 97% of contemporary MPD patients (Putnam, Guroff, Silberman, Barban, & Post, 1986; Schultz, Braun, & Kluft, 1984), but nonabuse etiologies are known (Kluft, 1984a), and not all abused individuals develop MPD. Another theory is that MPD is caused by the (often unwitting) abuse of self-hypnosis (Bliss, 1986). Certainly, MPD patients are highly hypnotizable (when cooperative), but most highly hypnotizable individuals do not develop MPD, and there remains no proof that hypnosis can create stable MPD (although phenomena resembling it are easily induced). Many have postulated that MPD can be explained in terms of psychoanalytic concepts of development and object relations theory. Although these concepts may relate to the patients described by these authors, children with MPD have not shown the postulated dynamics (Kluft, 1984b, 1985c). It seems more plausible to infer "that the trauma response stands aside from, although it influences and is influenced by, other developmental lines" (Kluft, in press).

Three polyfactorial (in the loose sense of this term) approaches to the conceptualization of MPD are available. Stern (1984) offered what he called "a paradigmatic description of the etiology of a multiple personality" (p.152). He postulated that the typical MPD patient will have suffered child abuse or neglect and will have been exposed to at least one caretaker with severe psychopathology. The first split occurs in childhood in response to a sudden high level of stress associated with the behavior of at least one other person, and later splits may occur at any time. Splits may not become obvious until years later. Usually, but not inevitably, the child's environment will include strict religious or mystical beliefs; these may be used as the vehicle or rationalization for other factors (such as abuse). Most MPD patients believe that they have had parapsychological experiences. Physiological causes will be offered for amnesia, but the posited etiological events or phenomena will be found to have followed rather than caused it. Confusing messages about identity will result in identity diffusion. Intelligence will be average or higher. Personalities will have functions that may change over time, but their main function is to protect the main or host personality from others or from internal conflict.

Braun and Sachs (1985) advanced the *Three-P Theory* of MPD (Predisposing, Precipitating, and Perpetuating Factors) . They delineated two major predisposing factors: the inborn capacity to dissociate and exposure to severe overwhelming trauma. Other predisposing elements were a good working memory, above average intelligence, and creativity. They noted that MPD patients, in contrast to other abuse victims, had been subjected to frequent, unpredictable, and inconsistent abuse, a greater severity of abuse, and had also been shown some sort of love.

Their precipitating factors were most commonly overwhelming stressors, with child abuse preeminent.

The formation of an alternate personality occurs when a series of fragmented but defensively related episodes, linked by a common affective state, take on a life of their own . . . [using a computer analogy]. It is almost as if two separate memory systems are created. Memory System "A" contains information that forms the identity of the "host" personality. Memory System "B," which is split off from memory system "A," contains that information which system "A" was unwilling or unable to integrate. The structurally organizing theme of these previously fragmented episodes now gives the new entity an identity and purpose. (Braun & Sachs, 1985, p.49)

Then, perpetuating factors of a personal, interpersonal, and situational variety may come into play. The use of dissociation becomes self-reinforcing, and family dynamics and subsequent life experiences may be reinforcers as well. Stimulus generalization may occur, and numerous individuals are reacted to just as those who had played a role in the condition's etiology.

Kluft's four-factor theory was developed in 1979 and published several years later (1984a; 1986a). It stemmed from the failure of his efforts to reconcile MPD with psychoanalytic theory, and his conclusion that its etiology stood outside of classic developmental lines and was best understood as a posttraumatic condition. Furthermore, he became convinced on the basis of clinical experience that MPD was the final common pathway for a diverse number of etiological combinations, and was not a unitary condition. Briefly stated, his research demonstrates that the individual who develops MPD (a) has or develops the capacity for dissociation; (b) encounters life experiences that traumatically overwhelm the nondissociative defensive/adaptive capacities of the child's ego, compelling the use of dissociative capacities in the service of adaptation/defense; (c) the dissociative defense makes opportunistic use of the available substrates for dividedness (of which there are many); and (d) if he or she is not provided adequate protection (stimulus barriers) against further overwhelming experiences, appropriate consolation and soothing, the opportunity to express and process his or her hurt, and is not afforded sufficient restorative experiences, the transient multiplicity response is reinforced, remains adaptive, and a relatively stable dissociative pattern becomes established.

The four-factor theory seems reasonably robust as a descriptive framework. Much evidence, summarized elsewhere (Kluft, in press), supports or is consistent with it. In fact, however, because the Stern (1984) and Braun and Sachs (1985) theories are largely consistent with both the four-factor theory and the evidence marshalled in its support, that evidence does not indicate that one theory is superior to the others (although the evidence does indicate that Stern's paradigm is not universally applicable).

Factor 1, dissociation potential, was initially assumed equivalent to the biologic component of hypnotizability. It may well be that only the most hypnotizable individuals develop MPD, but it might prove that trauma increases dissociative potential or encourages the mobilization and utilization of whatever such capacity is present.

More recently, however, Kluft (1986a) postulated that there are several pathways into dissociation, and he views this factor as more complex than originally envisioned. More sophisticated studies have been offered by Carlson and Putnam (1990), and efforts to tease apart the contributions of hypnotizability and dissociativity are underway (Putnam, 1991a, 1991b).

Factor 2, the overwhelming of nondissociative defenses by life events with the consequent mobilization of dissociative potential for defensive purposes, is addressed more comprehensively by this theory than others, probably because its author had encountered a larger group of MPD patients and had had the opportunity to study patients whose MPD began without exposure to intentional abuse. Certainly, intentional abuse (sexual, physical, psychological), neglect, and idiosyncratic mistreatments and overwhelming experiences in highly deviant families that defy easy classification, are encountered in the vast majority of MPD patients. The lowest prevalence of such antecedents was 86% (Coons & Milstein, 1986). However, the experience of being overwhelmed is the universal dimension, rather than abuse per se.

Other overwhelming experiences include the death or loss of a loved one, actual exposure to the death of a significant other, or witnessing the deliberate destruction of a loved one (such as in murder or war). In some cases, exposure to the dead body of a loved one, or being forced to touch or kiss it, may be a precipitant. At times, the exposure to the death or injury of an unrelated individual or stranger, such as in an accident or war, may be sufficient. Severe threats to the integrity or survival of one's self, such as are experienced in severe sustained pain, severe debilitating illness, near-death experiences, or when threats of death, injury, or torture are made, are occasionally the instigators of defensive dissociation. Other causes are being caught in the midst of a natural or man-made disaster, cultural dislocation, being treated as if one were not of one's biological gender, brainwashing by embattled parents in the course of custody disputes, and excessive primal scene exposure.

The shaping influences and possible substrates of dividedness constitute Factor 3, and many of them are universal. The unity of the self is a subjective illusion (Hilgard, 1977), and it cannot be assumed that humans are born with a sense of unity. In fact, there is every reason to believe that the infant begins without a sense of continuity, and that this is achieved gradually (Putnam, 1988; Stern, 1985). The possible substrates and shaping influences include inherent mechanisms, inherent potentials, and extrinsic influences.

Among the inherent mechanisms is dissociation per se. As Spiegel (1986b) demonstrated, dissociation is a rule-bound process by which certain subsets of information are excluded from others and, as Braun and Sachs (1985) noted, dissociation is self-reinforcing. Also, a child who has recourse to dissociation from early in life may develop in a divided pattern that becomes personified. The frequent use of autohypnosis may facilitate a child's living in alternate realities (Bliss, 1986). Furthermore, a child exposed to emotional extremes may be inclined to build upon the phenomena of state- and mood-dependent memory (see Bower, this volume). In addition, some may be more predisposed than others to an organization into ego states, as described by Watkins and Watkins (1982). Also, the human potential to have multiple systems of cognition and memory (Hilgard, 1977) is a very intriguing possible substrate. Finally, the newer literature on states of mind and the development of the self, exemplified in the work of Stern (1985) and Emde, Gaensbaure, and Harmon (1976), brought into the literature of MPD by authors such as Putnam (1988) and Fink (1988), offer further possibilities.

There are several inherent potentials for psychodynamic dividedness that may be relevant to particular patients with MPD. Clearly, the vicissitudes of the various developmental lines—long-studied within the psychoanalytic literature—offer many models, among which are the libidinal, the narcissistic, the object-relational, the developmental, and others. Imaginary companionship, which may occur in as many as 65% of normal children (Pines, 1978), is an ideal substrate, involving a believed-in other that emerges in the service of the child's attempts to master developmental issues. Schultz, Braun, and Kluft (1985) found that 80% of MPD patients' imaginary companions had gone on to become alters. A major mechanism, probably first suggested by Freud (1961), involves the processes of introjection, internalization, and identification. It is rare to find a patient with MPD who does not have alters clearly related to these pathways. In essence, any pattern that the mind may take in experiencing severe conflict or a challenge to normal development has within it the potential for generating alternative mechanisms and structures. The reader may be puzzled that splitting, so often regarded as a mechanism for MPD, is not even mentioned specifically, but noted by implication due to its association with developmental and object-relations models. Space does not allow adequate discussion of how this term has been overused and misused in attempts to conceptualize MPD. The reader is referred to Young's (1988) critical review of this area.

Extrinsic influences on the form of MPD include, during childhood, the encouragement of role-playing and acting in children, their being exposed to contradictory parental demand and reinforcement systems, their having numerous caretakers, and their identifying with an MPD parent. As the child matures, the influences of society, culture, and their careers as patients may influence the form of their MPD. They absorb the values and stereotypes of their family, race, religion, ethnicity, and so forth. They are exposed to the media. The MPD patients of the past and present built their alters on the raw materials that were available to them. The MPD patient of the future will have personalities that reflect the influences that impacted upon them. Many childhood MPD patients today have alters based on television characters, for example. A girl who read J. R. R. Tolkien's "Ring Trilogy" (Tolkien, 1965a, 1965b, 1965c) reworked all of her alters in conformity with the characters of this fantasy masterpiece.

Factor 4, the inadequate provision of stimulus barriers and restorative experiences by significant others, requires little exploration.

Clearly, the first three factors will be found in the histories and assessments of many individuals who are never found to have MPD. Childhood MPD is a fragile condition that responds rapidly to treatment under ideal conditions (Kluft, 1984b, 1986a) and undergoes spontaneous remission in some children whose environmental circumstances improve. It only becomes more fixed when the child is further traumatized, not offered the opportunity to process his or her hurts, not given positive restorative experiences, and not given clear communication and permission to communicate clearly. As Spiegel (1986a) has demonstrated, double-bind theory has a valuable role in explaining the perpetuation of dissociative defenses and structures.

THE NATURAL HISTORY OF MPD

The delineation of the natural history of MPD is a very recent achievement. Working from the histories of 210 MPD patients and their presentations at different ages, Kluft (1985a) was able to trace this disorder from its childhood manifestations to its presentations in the older adult. The subject is complex, and it is reviewed in detail elsewhere (Kluft, 1984b, 1985a, 1986a, 1988, 1991a). Here an effort is made to offer a brief summary and then to study, by way of illustration, the longitudinal course of a single patient with MPD, whose history illustrates a number of the most salient points of concern.

Childhood MPD patients are rarely recognized. Clinicians' index of suspicion is low, and the children often are unable to appreciate and/or articulate their difficulties. Their symptoms overlap with those of many other conditions and normative behaviors. For example, if a child denies a behavior one has witnessed, and for which the child might reasonably expect an adverse response, such as a punishment, it is more parsimonious to assume that the child is lying than that he or she suffers a dissociative disorder. Also, the child may withhold data, having been previously disbelieved or punished for efforts to communicate his or her plight. Children can sometimes suppress alters whose emergence cause difficulties, and alters try to remain undetected or to pass as one single personality. Also, the alters of many patients with MPD do not firm up their identity or become narcissistically invested in separateness until adolescence.

In summary, the presentation of childhood MPD is often rather subtle. These children may be noted to be absent-minded or off in a trance, may fluctuate widely in abilities, age-appropriateness, or moods, may be intermittently depressed, hear voices, suffer passive influence experiences in which they feel their behavior is out of their control, and be noted to disavow witnessed behavior, especially if it is polarized (too good or too bad). They often are called liars. Their school behavior is inconsistent, but at times their grades are excellent, with teachers discounting occasional incidents of "going blank" or other sub-par performances. A number have excellent grades for the first few years, and then decline.

Usually, once the index of suspicion for MPD has been raised, it is easy to document repeated episodes of altered behavior and memory. These patients are quite responsive to treatment under ideal circumstances, but virtually impossible (or at least exceedingly difficult) to treat otherwise, because the dissociative defenses offer more security than does the proffered therapy (Kluft, 1986a).

Adolescents with MPD may either continue with the covert nature of the childhood form or become exceedingly flamboyant, but most fall into one of three patterns described by Kluft (1985a). In the first, most common in males, antisocial aggressive behavior is noted, and the patient is assumed to be psychotic, epileptic, borderline, and/or sociopathic. In the second, most common among females who, in general, are apart from their families or come from very chaotic families, there is flagrant adolescent turmoil and behavior thought to be characteristic of borderline personality disorder. Many were promiscuous, had been involved with drugs, had suffered rapes, and had sought refuge away from home with fringe social groups. Many had somatoform complaints. Most fluctuated rapidly and showed phenomena associated with switching, but did not openly admit that this was occurring. They often dissimulated when questioned directly until they trusted the interviewer. The passive influence experiences once thought characteristic of schizophrenia (Kluft, 1987b) are quite conspicuous. As a group, they had learned that no one believed them when they disavowed a disremembered behavior, so, out of despair and/or expeditiousness, they allowed their initial denials to crumble into false confessions of their being liars. This group usually was diagnosed as adjustment reaction of adolescence, borderline personality disorder, some variety of drug abuser, and so forth. The third group is withdrawn. Some are beginning to show the typical adult classical presentation: a neurasthenic and depleted host predominates, and acknowledges amnesias, headaches, and experiences of being confronted or regaining awareness in the midst of out of character behavior.

The adult picture of MPD is that of a polysymptomatic pleiomorphic presentation in which the episodes of altered memory and identity are discerned among a welter of psychopathologic manifestations. It is well described in recent reviews and texts (Kluft, 1987a,1987c; Putnam, et al., 1986; Ross, 1989), and illustrated elsewhere within this book. The presentation of MPD in the elderly has been described by Kluft (1985a, 1988).

Illustration

Jessie (pseudonym) is now a successful mental health professional of 42. She has been integrated for several years. Although details regarding her identity are altered freely to protect her confidentiality, her history is presented as accurately as possible. The format that is used is to present the known external landmarks of her life for particular periods, and follow them with a description of her actual history and inner circumstances.

Ages 0-5.

Jessie was the product of a normal pregnancy and delivery. Her father was a dominant and controlling man, her mother, a rather weak and passive woman, who relied heavily on her parents. Jessie's maternal grandparents were rigid and emotionally cold, highly religious individuals, who disapproved of their new son-in-law. Jessie's developmental landmarks were precocious, and her medical checks were uneventful until 3 1/2 when she was brought to a family doctor for genital irritation, presumed consequent to her compulsive masturbation. From then on, it was noted that she frequently regressed and appeared to be more babyish, and she seemed to be becoming quite a liar. On several occasions her family doctor, treating her for sore throats, noted erythematous lesions in her pharynx that he could not explain, and which did not seem to be infectious in origin. At age 5, Jessie, on a visit to the grandparents, masturbated publicly and approached her grandfather smilingly, and zipped down his fly. She was severely punished, and prayed over. Apparently her grandmother began to suspect that something was amiss. She questioned Jessie closely, and Jessie denied that anything was wrong. Not convinced, the grandmother arranged for the whole family to visit the family doctor. Although nothing specific was said, the family doctor suspected sexual abuse and questioned Jessie's father intensely. He denied everything, as did Jessie and her mother. Grandmother and grandfather sat through the session in stony silence, never voicing their suspicions.

Interviewed in 1984, the doctor confirmed that these memories of the session in his office, which Jessie had recovered under hypnosis, were accurate in all major respects. It was his impression, then and now, that the grandparents could not bring themselves to speak openly, that Jessie was terrified into silence, and that her parents were liars.

As Jessie later recalled in treatment, and her father admitted when confronted, Jessie was already an incest victim, having experienced oral, vaginal, and attempted anal intercourse. She had already developed several alters, including one who undertook to make her father happy by offering sex. This alter had approached her grandfather as well.

Ages 6-12.

Jessie was an excellent, if often daydreamy and distracted, student. She masturbated publicly in kindergarten and first grade, finally succeeding in suppressing this in the face of peer ridicule. She often complained of bellyaches. At times she was incontinent of feces. She often seemed in a daze in class, and was regarded as weird by her classmates. Occasionally, she cried for no apparent reason. At times she wandered into the classroom that had been her room in the grade before and sat down as if she belonged there. There were frequent absences. The school nurse suspected that she was being abused but could not obtain any documentation. Jessie would often make plans with people and then forget the plans; slowly, her circle of friends diminished. By junior high school she was a loner. Her grades were no longer uniformly excellent. At times she went blank and flunked tests, or seemed to have no awareness of the subjects under discussion. Once, in geography class, she was asked a question about the Eskimos, and responded that she thought that they were studying Hawaii. In fact, they had studied Hawaii a month before. Jessie was very aware that she lost time, and she heard voices in her head. Sometimes, she thought she could hear others talking to one another in her head.

During this time, which was reconstructed from Jessie's memory and from school records, she was being exploited by her father in child pornography and child prostitution. Furthermore, her father staged sex shows in which both she and her mother were exploited. Bestiality and homosexual relationships were forced on her. In one sex show scenario, she was dressed like a little princess all in white, and then sodomized, smeared with feces, and forced to perform coprophagia directly from the anus of a member of the audience, who would pay an additional price for this favor. This detail is given in lieu of hundreds of others that were recovered and worked through. As noted, Jessie's father admits his exploitation of her. Jessie's mother, long since divorced from her father, does not deny that such events occurred. She maintains, however, that electroconvulsive therapy for her depression has obliterated her memory of the past. In an unguarded moment in 1983, Jessie's mother admitted to Jessie that she does occasionally recall the events of those years, but each time that she does she requires hospitalization, and that her doctor has forbidden her to discuss the past with anyone for that reason. As this book was going to press, Jessie called the author and reported her mother, having reentered therapy, now recalls the past and confirms Jessie's accounts.

Ages 13-18.

Jessie was seen frequently by her family doctor for severe headaches, felt to be migraines, and for abdominal pains assumed to be menstrual. One doctor, noticing that her introitus was nonvirginal, chastised her at length. She struggled through high school and performed erratically. Several teachers were aware of her potential, and some inferred that she was being mistreated at home. Midway through this period her parents separated and divorced. She went to live with her grandparents, who were determined to "whip her into shape," and did. She became a compulsively good girl, who used no foul language and did not date until her senior year of high school. After each visit from her father she became disorganized and severely depressed. Occasionally, her grandparents would hear that she had behaved in some inappropriate way, or a teacher would observe her in some out-of-character behavior, which she would deny. Although increasingly in pain within, her behavior was generally that of a "good girl" who occasionally strained at the leash and tried to cover up her indiscretions, and who was too distracted to achieve her academic potential. The first boy she dated was also an outsider, with some effeminate traits.

During this period Jessie became pregnant by her father and had an illicit abortion. This brought an end to father's routine sexual exploitation of her. When the parents separated, he occasionally would force himself on her during his visits, but he used a condom. Jessie experienced her life as seen through a veil. Much was obliterated by amnesia, but at times there would be flashbacks, which she fought to suppress. The intrusion of flashbacks led to her distraction during school hours. At times, she was diverted by the conversations and voices that she heard within her head.

Ages 19-25.

Jessie attended college and had some postgraduate education. She performed with distinction, but often missed class for headaches and unexplained abdominal distress. She made three suicide attempts by ingestion, for which she was hospitalized, and was assumed to have a major depression. She was treated with antidepressants, and once, on the assumption that if electroconvulsive treatment had helped her mother it might help her, she received this modality as well. She did not admit to hearing voices, because she feared that she might be schizophrenic and that if this were discovered she would not be able to pursue a career in mental health. She married her first boyfriend, whom she liked because he was not pushy in the area of sex. On the occasion of their first intercourse, she says she "went crazy." It appears that she had flashbacks of the incest which, in the interim, she had suppressed. Thereafter, she began to ply herself with alcohol before going to bed, and found that, in this way, she could tolerate her husband's infrequent sexual advances. Soon, Jessie was medicating herself extensively with alcohol, and she became an alcoholic. Her husband proved to be a bisexual and a severe pervert. He gradually dwindled into psychosis and attempted to murder her with a hammer. Somehow she escaped him, albeit with a fractured skull. While she was recovering in the hospital, her husband committed suicide.

During this period, Jessie's alters were rather covert, and they influenced her "from behind the scenes." Their overt emergences were few. Her hospital records indicate that she was diagnosed as having depression. Although Jessie did not remember this, at least one psychiatrist learned of the voices that she heard and diagnosed her as schizophrenic.

Ages 26-32.

Jessie completed her professional education and relocated. Toward its end she met a very mild-mannered man, married him, and had a daughter. During this period her life was ostensibly conventional, but actually quite chaotic. Alone and without the constraints of others around her, Jessie's alters took over more completely and led lives of their own, for most of which Jessie was amnesic. People whom she did not know would greet her and friends would behave as if events had occurred between them of which Jessie was unaware. Most distressing, at times people would greet her by a name other than her own, and insist that they had had interactions with her which she could not recall. To her mortification, at times she would recover awareness in the middle of situations that were very much out of character for her, often of a sexual nature. Jessie continued to have headaches, and she had exploratory surgery for her unexplained abdominal pains. Nothing was found. Early in this period, she read *Sybil* (Schreiber, 1973), and found it to be unbelievable. She felt compelled to reread it, but she could not bring herself to do so. She had five copies of the book, bought at different times, but if she tried to read it, she would get a severe headache and become unable to do so. She continued to drink heavily but covertly. She made several abortive attempts at entering therapy.

During this period Jessie lived the life of a person with florid MPD. In one alter she was flagrantly promiscuous; in another she dabbled in homosexuality. She had two different circles of friends. Jessie began to suspect that something was amiss, but alters unwilling to be discovered took steps to preclude their discovery and to frustrate Jessie's efforts to learn about MPD. Furthermore, they blocked out her recollections of these efforts—hence the five copies of *Sybil*, and the amnesia for having read it once before (for a psychology course).

Despite all of this chaos, the alters stayed away from Jessie's professional activities and, if they were in control during her work hours, which was rare, they called in sick. All of the alters were scrupulous about their professional work.

Ages 33-38.

Jessie became increasingly depressed as her daughter grew beyond infancy. Her drinking increased to the point that her husband detected her problem and insisted that she reduce her use of alcohol. Her daughter resembled her as a child, and Jessie, who, by now, was amnesic for her childhood, became obsessively concerned that some harm might befall her daughter. She was so protective of this child and so afraid to do her harm that the daughter became spoiled and undisciplined. This made Jessie enraged, and she feared abusing her own daughter. One night, Jessie noted her daughter masturbating. Jessie became acutely suicidal, had visual flashbacks of abusive experiences, and heard voices in her head, including command hallucinations instructing her to destroy herself. Terrified, she drove to a hospital and admitted herself. As she drove, she heard a voice like her father's commanding her to drive her car into a concrete embankment, and felt powerful forces she could barely counter attempting to wrest the steering wheel from her control. She was admitted with the diagnosis of an acute schizophrenic episode and was placed on major tranquilizers.

The next morning she was evaluated by the psychiatrist assigned to her case. She was asymptomatic and requesting discharge. The psychiatrist declined to do so. Although Jessie volunteered a sanitized and benign history, he would not agree to a discharge until he was convinced that she was indeed stable and had been completely assessed. Jessie was on good behavior for the duration of the admission, and reluctantly agreed to outpatient follow-up. She cancelled her appointments and, when the psychiatrist telephoned her, she maintained that all was well. A few months later she was brought to the hospital after an overdose and assigned to the same psychiatrist.   She appeared to have a major depression, but again pulled together with amazing rapidity and requested discharge. Under pressure from both the psychiatrist and her husband, she agreed to follow-up sessions.   In these sessions, she gradually developed a trusting relationship with the psychiatrist. The more he saw of Jessie, the more puzzling her picture became. On some days she was bright and vivacious, on some days profoundly depressed, on some days appearing to respond to inner stimuli, and on some days she simply did not appear for sessions. More than once he called her home and was told by a female voice that Jessie was not home, or that he had reached the wrong number. Once her husband called and said he had overheard his wife tell the psychiatrist that she was not at home when, in fact, she was on the telephone.

During one session, in the eighth month of treatment, Jessie casually mentioned her first husband. The psychiatrist was astounded because Jessie had repeatedly told him that she had only been married once. Jessie seemed shaken herself, and then, in a controlled and clipped voice, said that she preferred to forget the man completely. The psychiatrist, always struck by Jessie's changeability, was impressed by this voice change, and by Jessie's shaken appearance both before and after it had occurred. Approximately 1 month later, Jessie protested that a neighbor man had blown her a kiss as she drove to the appointment, and that she could not understand why he had done so. The psychiatrist commented that there seemed to be many puzzling events in Jessie's life that she could not account for, and wondered if she had any ideas about why so many such events might be occurring. At this point Jessie looked shaken and dazed for a few seconds, and then, in a rather different and provocative voice, said, "I figure you've just about figured this out. I am Diane. He wasn't blowing a kiss to that dishrag—he was blowing that kiss to me." Before the session ended, the psychiatrist had met two other alters, had learned that there were a good many others, and had obtained an agreement for the alters to participate in the therapy. Thus began what would be a successful 5 year therapy that would identify and integrate approximately 40 alters, abreact and work through the abuses of a dismal childhood, and strengthen Jessie to avoid alcohol, confront her abuser and the mother who had, in her weakness, facilitated the abuse, and wrest admissions from them. The testimony of the family doctor, who, 30 years after the fact, remembered his futile efforts to ascertain whether Jessie had been abused, was a critical check on the veracity of her recall (at least for that incident).

During the final years of this natural history, Jessie came into treatment with the author, to whom she was assigned serendipitously years before his first publications on MPD. Prior to seeing him, she had had intermittent contact with the mental health professions for over a decade. Clearly, the precipitant of the symptoms that brought her under his care was her daughter's reaching the age at which her father had begun to violate her. Acutely aware of her daughter's vulnerability, she was reconnected to the vulnerability of her own youth and of the events that befell her then. Jessie credits the author's tenacity early in their work together with making her feel that ultimately she could reveal herself to him, but to this day she is not quite sure about why the revelation occurred in the manner that it did. It is quite true that the author had begun to suspect MPD and was searching for a way to approach the matter indirectly. Part of Jessie's history was seduction by another health care professional from whom she had sought help. This incident caused Diane to feel that all doctors could be seduced. The alter Diane, upon reflection, felt that the patient across all alters was developing an erotic transference, which she was more than willing to act out by seducing the author and eroticizing the therapy, but felt that, if she did, she and the others would never get well. Therefore, she decided to "spill the beans."

Hopefully, this extended case example will illustrate the natural history of MPD and illustrate why a patient with this disorder may prove quite difficult to diagnose accurately, and may appear to merit many other diagnoses over a period of time.

THE RECOGNITION OF MPD

A number of excellent studies discuss the diagnosis of MPD (Coons, 1980, 1984; Kluft, 1985c; 1987c; 1991a; Loewenstein, 1991; Putnam, 1989; Ross, 1989) at a given point in time, and considerations relevant to the natural history of MPD have been described (Kluft, 1985a, 1991a). This section offers some brief commentaries on the recognition of MPD in the clinical context.

To the lay person or the clinician familiar only with descriptions or videotapes of florid classic cases, the clinical realities of MPD often come as a surprise. The essence of the condition is its intrapsychic structure and its overt expression of that structure may vary quite widely. Most MPD patients are able to keep their condition disguised or dissimulated most of the time. The clearly demarcated alters that are distinctly different from one another in many major dimensions are most likely to be relaxed about the open expressions of their individuality within sessions. It is not uncommon for a person with MPD to hide this from their spouse, family, friends, and employers for long periods of time. In clinical settings, such patients may spend many years within the mental health care delivery system without their disorder being diagnosed. Simply put, the primary gains of MPD are substantial, but the secondary gains are minimal. Consequently, the patient often is motivated to maintain his or her condition without allowing it to be recognized and altered. Once "the cat is out of the bag," the manifestations may become much more florid. For example, Jessie's alter Diane had been out in the author's office several times before she declared herself. Thereafter, (a) Diane relaxed her efforts to obscure herself, and (b) the author, alerted, recognized the subtler signs of her presence.

The expectation that MPD will have a dramatic and flamboyant presentation is a major impetus toward false negative diagnoses. Elsewhere (Kluft, 1979), this author has described the SNAALS and SALES syndromes, based on remarks from colleagues who doubted his diagnosis of MPD in patients with rather drab and/or understated symptomatology. SNAALS is the acronym for "She's not at all like Sybil"; SALES stands for "She ain't like Eve, sir."

Studies of the history of large groups of MPD patients (Kluft, 1985a) demonstrate that only approximately 6% of MPD patients are significantly invested in making a public display of their disorder and playing it up for secondary gain. Also, a small cohort of adolescent females are rather overt and provocative about their MPD. In general, MPD patients are expert at a chameleon-like blending with their interpersonal background unless seen in a state of decompensation or a clinical setting. Approximately 20% of MPD patients remain classically MPD over time, and 70% of them attempt to disguise or to dissimulate it. Another 20% are very rarely overtly MPD, and the alters usually influence life by imposing their feelings and wills on a beleaguered host. The remaining 60% go through periods in which the MPD psychopathology is intrusive and symptomatic and periods in which its existence is suppressed and may be denied. Many MPD patients, then, with their secretiveness, suppression/denial, and periods with little overt dissociative activity, have only certain temporal "windows of diagnosability." At these times, the diagnosis can be made fairly readily, provided that the clinician has an index of suspicion. At others, it may be missed completely, suspected by history but unconfirmable, or possible only with intrusive inquiry.

It is well to recall that overtness is not a basic ingredient of MPD. As stated in Kluft, 1987c:

Overtness of phenomena is related to the alters' modes of interaction, manner of influencing one another, type of hierarchy, battles for control, and narcissistic investment in separateness. When alters cooperate, collude to pass as one, have inner dialogues, and establish a power distribution in which suppression is vigorous, little may emerge. If there is contention but some collaboration, alters intrude rather than dialogue, and dominance is incomplete, the patient is often polysymptomatic but shows little overt MPD. If the alters are narcissistically invested in separateness, and tend to have specialized roles, but contention is low, a smooth but overt system of alters may be evident. Such patients often value their MPD. If the same conditions prevail, but with contention, the patient may show the classic picture of major shifts of personality dominance in response to psychosocial stressors and inner battles, and emphatic differences among alters will become manifest. (p. 215)

Until quite recently, the patient who presented MPD as a chief complaint usually did not have it. This situation has changed dramatically, and may render the figures shared next rather dated. In a series collected by the author before 1980, 5% of the MPD patients presented themselves avowing the diagnosis of MPD. Another 15% dissociated openly during assessment or treatment (as did Jessie, when Diane emerged). 40% had signs that could alert a clinician with a high index of suspicion, and the remaining forty percent were discovered while field-testing specialized diagnostic protocols.

For the general mental health professional, it is well to have a high index of suspicion for MPD but to be mindful of its disguised nature. Gutheil (quoted in Kluft, 1985a) aptly described MPD as a psychopathology of hiddeness. The diagnostic assessment for MPD will most likely be initiated by the patient's showing signs that are highly suggestive of MPD. The list given here is a modification of that of Kluft (1987a), which in turn was drawn from the works of Kluft and Greaves (1980) and Putnam et al. (1984). The following signs should be scrutinized carefully:

1. A history of prior treatment failure. MPD is a great imitator. A patient who has not responded to competent and adequate treatment of the disorder that he or she is presumed to have may have a different and/or additional condition.

2. Three or more prior diagnoses. Diagnostic confusion is the rule, rather than the exception with these patients.

3. Concurrent psychiatric and somatic symptoms. The pain of

past events often persists as a somatic memory or somatic flashback, even though the cognitive recollection remains ablated. All of Jessie's symptoms proved related to past traumata and cleared after their abreaction.

4. Fluctuating symptoms and an inconsistent level of function. This reflects the interactions of the alters and their different characteristics and the compromise of global function due to their conflict.

5. Severe headaches, of any and/or all forms, often refractory even to narcotics unless the patient is simply "knocked out" with sedation. In Jessie's case, the headaches reflected the alters' conflicts or the incipient irruption of traumatic material.

6. A history of time distortion or time lapses (i.e., amnesia or less clear-cut dissociative disorders of memory).

7. The patient's having been told by others of behaviors that he or she had forgotten.

8. The patient's having been told by others of observable changes in his or her facial, voice, and behavioral style. Paradoxically, in the author's experience, MPD patients are more often described as moody than borderlines, and severe borderlines are more often described as being like two different people than most MPD patients.

9. The patient's discovery in his or her domicile, vehicle, or place of work of productions, possessions, or strange handwriting that he or she can neither account for nor recognize.

10. Auditory hallucinations, especially, but not exclusively, those that are experienced as emanating from within the head.

11. Any of the first rank symptoms of schizophrenia except delusional percept, because these have been found to be more characteristic of MPD than schizophrenia (Kluft, 1987b).

12. The use of "we" in a collective sense. This is included because it occurs on these lists with regularity, but its presence clearly implies co-consciousness. In fact, this is more characteristic of the speech of MPD patients after they have been diagnosed and treatment begun, though it is occasionally found in a "raw" case.

13. A history of child abuse.

14. The eliciting of what appear to be separate personalities with hypnosis or amytal. This suggests but does not confirm the presence of MPD, because analogous phenomena can be elicited by these means. In fact, a school of therapy has been based on this possibility (Watkins & Watkins, 1979).

15. A high score on the DES (Dissociative Experiences Scale of Bernstein & Putnam, 1986). This highly useful instrument has now been studied in many settings and is a generally reliable screening device.

The skillful inquiry about any of the signs in the preceding list will often reveal further data to suggest the presence of MPD. In some circumstances, clinical considerations dictate the consideration of more intrusive inquiries (hypnosis or amytal), despite the misgivings that many clinicians continue to hold about such measures. Recently, an excellent mental status examination for the assessment of dissociative disorders has been published by Loewenstein (1991a), and structured interviews have been developed by Ross (Ross, 1989; Ross, Miller, Reagor, Bjornson, Fraser, & Anderson, 1990) and by Steinberg (Steinberg, Rounsaville, & Cicchetti, 1990).

THE THERAPEUTIC RESOLUTION OF MPD

The treatment of MPD is a highly complex topic. It is important to realize that MPD is found in an otherwise highly diverse group of patients with a wide range of additional Axis I and Axis II diagnoses, psychodynamics, ego strengths, and life circumstances. Treatment must be individualized. The majority of successful treatments to date have been accomplished via intense and active but supportive psychodynamic psychotherapies facilitated by hypnotherapeutic interventions, and carried out by experienced therapists who were also quite experienced with MPD. The initial optimism with regard to treatment that followed Kluft's articles on his own series (1982, 1984a, 1986b) has been followed by a dawning realization that similar results cannot be expected by clinicians without comparable experience and training. Nor is Coons' (1986) follow-up of 20 patients, 19 of whom were being treated by therapists (several of whom were trainees) encountering their first case of MPD, an accurate gauge. A realistic statement of the likelihood of a given result from the interaction of the modal MPD patient with the modal therapist cannot yet be given. Likewise, it is difficult to be sure if any particular skill is essential, although the track records of those clinicians who are prepared to use hypnosis are, with some exceptions, better than those who are not. Notice that the statement is "those who are prepared to use hypnosis," not "those who use hypnosis." Hypnosis is not modality per se, but a facilitator. Many treatments can be carried out without such facilitation, but some will founder. The clinician who is prepared to use hypnosis may never have to do so, but is in a superior strategic and tactical position to the therapist who cannot use hypnosis in this group of highly hypnotizable patients, who certainly will bring their own autohypnotic talents to the treatment, and may enlist them in the service of resistance (Kluft, 1982).

The following discussion follows closely the considerations expressed in Kluft's attempt to summarize the treatment of MPD (1987a; 1991b), and invariably leans heavily on Braun's (1986) *Treatment of Multiple Personality Disorder*. The tasks of therapy are the same as those in any intense, change-oriented approach, but are pursued with a patient whose personality is not unified. Therefore, one cannot assume the presence of an ongoing and available observing ego, and may encounter the disruption of usually autonomous ego functions, such as memory. The alters may have different perceptions, recollections, priorities, goals, and degrees of commitment to the therapy, the therapist, and to one another. A successful therapy will require that the alters gradually arrive at a unity of purpose and common motivation; much of what is unique about the treatment of MPD involves efforts to facilitate and achieve such cooperation.

Integration is clearly desirable , but pragmatism must prevail. Many patients are not motivated to pursue it or cannot obtain treatment of optimal intensity and duration. In general, the terms fusion, integration, and unification are used as synonyms. As stated in Kluft (1985d) they . . .

. . . *connote the spontaneous or facilitated coming together after adequate therapy has helped the patient to see, abreact, and work through the reasons for being of each separate alter. Consequently, the therapy serves to erode the barriers between the alters, and allow mutual acceptance, empathy, and identification. It does not indicate the dominance of one alter, the creation of a new "healthy" alter, or a premature compression or suppression of alters into the appearance of a resolution. (p. 3).*

In recent years, the term integration has been used to describe an ongoing intrapsychic process of undoing all aspects of dissociative dividedness that begins long before there is any reduction in the number of the personalities, that persists throughout the treatment of the divided individual, and that continues at a deeper level even when the separate personalities have blended into one. Fusion has come to mean:

Three stable months of (1) continuity of contemporary memory, (2) absence of overt behavioral signs of multiplicity, (3) subjective sense of unity, (4) absence of alter personalities on hypnotic re-exploration (hypnotherapy cases only), (5) modification of the transference phenomena consistent with the bringing together of the personalities, and (6) clinical evidence that the unified patient's self-representation included acknowledgement of attitudes and awarenesses which were previously segregated in separate personalities. (Kluft, 1982, pp. 233-234).

Such a stable period usually occurs after the collapse of several apparent fusions that occurred prematurely, before all necessary therapeutic work had been achieved (Kluft, 1987a).

An evenhanded attitude toward the personalities and the cultivation of a therapeutic alliance both globally and with each is crucial; they are treated equally, with respect and empathy. As they gradually empathize and identify with one another, their inner battles and claims on irresponsible autonomy diminish. This advice in no way diminishes the importance of the therapist's being a firm advocate of reality and unflagging in his emphasis on responsibility—it indicates instead that these goals are best achieved in the manner outlined earlier. The therapist takes a stance with respect to actual and/or anticipated behavior, but not against an alter per se.

Braun (1986) outlined a treatment approach that is sufficiently universal as to encompass most therapeutic approaches. The steps of his outline are presented as if in sequence, but in fact are usually overlapping and ongoing:

Treatment begins with the creation of an atmosphere of safety and trust (step 1). Operationally this means enough trust to carry on the work of a difficult therapy. The diagnosis must be made and shared with the accessible personalities (step 2), soon after the patient is comfortable with the therapist and enough data are available to place the issue before the patient in a tactful and circumspect way. Only when the patient appreciates his situation can the true treatment of multiple personality disorder begin. Next, one must establish communication with the accessible personalities (step 3). In patients whose personalities rarely emerge spontaneously and cannot switch voluntarily, the use of hypnosis may be helpful. Thereafter, it is important to assess the personalities' pressures toward harming self, others, or the body they share and to contract against such activities (step 4). Failing such an agreement, aspects of the treatment may require a hospital setting. Then, the therapist must learn the origin, functions, and problems of each alter and the manner in which they relate to one another (step 5).

Subsequently work is done to address the personalities' issues and problems (step 6). Difficult times are likely, because most personalties were developed in connection with traumatic events and distressing relationships. In connection with this, it becomes possible to comprehend the structure of the system of personalities (step 7), a process that often involves special procedures such as art therapy, movement therapy, or hypnosis. Building on the above foundation, therapy increasingly focuses on enhancing communications among the personalities (step 8), either directly via inner dialog or through the therapist. Hypnosis has proven extremely valuable in such interventions. On occasion the personalities are helped to interact in an "inner group therapy" (Caul, 1984).

With communications established, therapy works toward achieving a resolution of the personalities' conflicts and their integration (step 9). Hypnosis is often a useful facilitator of these processes. Once integrated, the patient must develop new defenses and coping skills (step 10) to obviate the pressure to reconstitute dissociative mechanisms. He must learn more appropriate interpersonal behaviors, including how to optimize available social supports (step 11). Thereafter, a considerable amount of working-through and ongoing support is necessary to solidify gains (step 12), and long-term follow-up is essential (step 13). (Kluft, 1987a. p. 371).

Other therapeutic modalities may play an invaluable ancillary role to individual psychotherapy, but are not sufficient treatments. The literature is without references to the successful treatment of MPD without individual psychotherapy. The core symptoms of MPD are not responsive to pharmacotherapy, but many of the accompanying symptoms or concomitant disorders may be thereby alleviated(Kluft, 1984c; Barkin, Braun, & Kluft, 1986; Loewenstein, 1991b). It is useful to be aware that the different alters may respond differently to the same dose of a medication.

Follow-up studies of patients treated in accord with the principles outlined above indicate that when highly motivated patients enter treatment with a therapist who is experienced in the treatment of MPD, the vast majority do well. Recently, Kluft

(1986b) reported on 52 MPD patients reassessed after appearing to satisfy fusion criteria for a minimum of 27 months. For 94.2%, there was clear evidence of improved function and progress in life; the same percentage had not relapsed into behaviorally manifest MPD, and 78.8% had not suffered residual or recurrent dissociative difficulties of any form. One patient had feigned fusion; including her three had distinct personalities and could be diagnosed MPD. Less well-formed entities were found in several others, involving the return of prior alters, the formation of new ones, and the discovery of other layers of alters. All but 2 of the 11 patients with relapse events accepted further therapy immediately. As of this writing, 49 of the 52 remain completely integrated and without dissociative residua at a minimum of 5 years' follow-up (with less stringent measures). The three that were in relapse included the two who refused further therapy and the patient who had feigned fusion. One who had refused further therapy later returned to therapy and reintegrated, the other did not. The patient who had feigned fusion apparently reintegrated, but this proved to be a second deception. She ultimately suicided.

This follow-up data continues to offer an optimistic prognosis for MPD patients treated under near-optimal circumstances.

CLOSING REMARKS

Multiple personality disorder is reentering the mainstream after a long and unfortunate absence. Notwithstanding the preliminary stage of our knowledge about MPD, and the controversy that surrounds it, a review of the etiology, natural history, recognition, and treatment of this disorder demonstrates that its study and treatment is one of the most optimistic areas of work within the mental health professions.

REFERENCES

Allison, R. B. (1974). A new treatment approach for multiple personalties. *American Journal of Clinical Hypnosis, 17,* 15-32.

Allison, R. B. (1978). A rational psychotherapy plan for multiplicity. *Svensk Tidskrift Hypnos, 3-4,* 9-16.

American Psychiatric Association. (1980). *Diagnostic and statistical manual of mental disorders* (3rd ed.). Washington, DC: Author.

American Psychiatric Association. (1987). *Diagnostic and statistical manual of mental disorders* (3rd ed., rev.). Washington, DC: Author.

Barkin, R., Braun, B. G., & Kluft, R. P. (1986). The dilemma of drug therapy for multiple personality disorder. In B. G. Braun (Ed.), *Treatment of multiple personality disorder,* (pp. 107-132). Washington, DC: American Psychiatric Press.

Bernstein, E. M., & Putnam, F. W. (1986). Development, reliability, and validity of a dissociation scale. *Journal of Nervous and Mental Disease, 174,* 727-735.

Bliss, E. L. (1986). *Multiple personality, allied disorders, and hypnosis.* New York: Oxford.

Braun, B. G. (1984). Toward a theory of multiple personality and other dissociative phenomena. *Psychiatric Clinics of North America, 7,* 171-193.

Braun, B. G. (Ed.). (1986). *Treatment of multiple personality disorder.* Washington, DC: American Psychiatric Press.

Braun, B. G., & Sachs, R. G. (1985). The development of multiple personality disorder: Predisposing, precipitating, and perpetuating factors. In R. P. Kluft (Ed.), *Childhood antecedents of multiple personality* (pp. 37-64). Washington, DC: American Psychiatric Press.

Caul, D. (1984) Group and videotape techniques for multiple personality disorder. *Psychiatric Annals, 14,* 43-50.

Carlson, E. B., & Putnam, F. W. (1990). Integrating research on dissociation and hypnotizability. Are there two pathways to hypnotizability? *Dissociation, 2,* 32-38.

Coons, P. M. (1980). Multiple personality: Diagnostic considerations. *Journal of Clinical Psychiatry, 41,* 330-336.

Coons, P. M. (1984). The differential diagnosis of multiple personality. *Psychiatric Clinics of North America, 7,* 51-67.

Coons, P. M. (1986). Treatment progress in 20 patients with multiple personality disorder. *Journal of Nervous and Mental Disease, 174,* 715-721.

Coons, P. M., Bowman, E. S., Kluft, R. P., & Milstein, V. (1991). The cross-cultural occurrence of MPD: Additional cases from a recent survey. *Dissociation, 4,* 124-128.

Coons, P. M., Bowman, E. S., & Milstein, V. (1988). Multiple personality disorder: A clinical investigation of 50 cases. *Journal of Nervous and Mental Disease, 176,* 519-527.

Coons, P. M., & Milstein, V. (1986). Psychosexual disturbances in multiple personality: Characteristics, etiology, and treatment. *Journal of Clinical Psychiatry, 47,* 106-110.

Edelson, M. (1983). Is testing psychoanalytic hypotheses in the psychoanalytic situation really possible? *Psychoanalytic Study of the Child, 38,* 61-109.

Ellenberger, H. F. (1970). *The discovery of the unconscious.* New York: Basic Books.

Emde, R. N., Gaensbaure, T. J., & Harmon, R. J. (1976). Emotional expression in infancy: A biobehavioral study. *Psychological Issues, 10,* (Monograph 37). New York: International Universities Press.

Fine, C. G. (1988). The work of Antoine Despine: The first scientific report on the diagnosis of a child with multiple personality disorder. *American Journal of Clinical Hypnosis, 31,* 33-39.

Fink, D. L. (1988). The core self: A developmental perspective on the dissociative disorders. *Dissociation, 1,* 43-47.

Freud, S. (1961). The ego and the id. In J. Strachey (Ed. and Trans.), *Standard edition of the complete psychological works of Sigmund Freud* (Vol. 19, pp. 3-66). London: Hogarth Press. (Original work published 1923)

Greaves, G. B. (1980). Multiple personality: 165 years after Mary Reynolds. *Journal of Nervous and Mental Disease, 168,* 577-596.

Henderson, D. (1975). Incest. In A. Freedman, H. Kaplan, & B. Sadock (Eds.), *Comprehensive textbook of psychiatry* (2nd ed. pp. 1530-1539). Baltimore: Williams & Wilkins.

Herman, J. L., & Schatzow, E. (1987). Recovery and verification of memories of childhood sexual trauma. *Psychoanalytic Psychology, 4,* 1-14.

Hilgard, E. R. (1977). *Multiple controls in human thought and action.* New York: Wiley.

Kluft, R. P. (1979, May). Casefinding for MPD. Paper presented at a course at the Annual Meeting of the American Psychiatric Association, Chicago.

Kluft, R. P. (1982). Varieties of hypnotic interventions in the treatment of multiple personality. *American Journal of Clinical Hypnosis, 24,* 230-240.

Kluft, R. P. (1984a). Treatment of multiple personality disorder. *Psychiatric Clinics of North America, 7,* 9-29.

Kluft, R. P. (1984b). Multiple personality in childhood. *Psychiatric Clinics of North America, 7,* 121-134.

Kluft, R. P. (1984c). Aspects of the treatment of multiple personality disorder. *Psychiatric Annals, 14,* 51-55.

Kluft, R. P. (1985a). The natural history of multiple personality disorder. In R. P. Kluft (Ed.), *Childhood antecedents of multiple personality,* (pp. 197-238).

Washington, DC: American Psychiatric Press.

Kluft, R. P. (1985b). Making the diagnosis of multiple personality disorder (MPD). In F. F. Flach (Ed.), *Directions in psychiatry* (Vol. 5, lesson 23, pp. 1-11). New York: Hatherleigh.

Kluft, R.P. (1985c). Childhood multiple personality disorder: Predictors, clinical findings, and treatment results. In R. P. Kluft (Ed.), *Childhood antecedents of multiple personality* (pp. 167-196). Washington, DC: American Psychiatric Press.

Kluft, R. P. (1985d). The treatment of multiple personality disorder (MPD): Current concepts. In F. F. Flach (Ed.), *Directions in psychiatry* (Vol.5, lesson 24, pp. 1-11). New York, Hatherleigh.

Kluft, R. P. (1986a). Treating children who have multiple personality disorder. In B. G. Braun (Ed.), *Treatment of multiple personality disorder* (pp.79-105). Washington, DC: American Psychiatric Press.

Kluft, R. P. (1986b). Personality unification in multiple personality disorder: A follow-up study. In B. G. Braun (Ed.), *Treatment of multiple personality disorder* (pp. 29-60). Washington, DC: American Psychiatric Press.

Kluft, R. P. (1987a). An update on multiple personality disorder. *Hospital & Community Psychiatry, 38,* 363-373.

Kluft, R. P. (1987b). First rank symptoms as a diagnostic clue to multiple personality disorder. *American Journal of Psychiatry, 144,* 293-298.

Kluft, R. P. (1987c). Making the diagnosis of multiple personality disorder. In F. F. Flach (Ed.), *Diagnostics and psychopathology* (pp. 207-225). New York: Norton.

Kluft, R. P. (1988). On treating the older patient with multiple personality disorder: 'Race against time' or 'make haste slowly?' *American Journal of Clinical Hypnosis, 30,* 257-266.

Kluft, R. P. (1991a). Clinical presentations of multiple personality disorder. *Psychiatric Clinics of North America, 14,* 605-630.

Kluft, R. P. (1991b). Multiple personality disorder. In A. Tasman & S. Goldfinger (Eds.), *The American psychiatric press annual review of psychiatry* (Vol. 10, pp. 161-188). Washington, D.C.: American Psychiatric Press.

Kluft, R. P. (in press). The four-factor theory of multiple personality disorder. In B. G. Braun & R. P. Kluft (Eds.), *Multiple personality and dissociation.*

Kluft, R. P., & Fine, C. G. (1993). *Clinical perspectives on multiple personality disorder.* Washington, DC: American Psychiatric Press.

Loewenstein, R. J. (1991a). An office mental status examination for complex chronic dissociative symptoms and multiple personality disorder. *Psychiatric Clinics of North America, 12,* 567-604.

Loewenstein, R. J. (1991b). Rational psychopharmacology in the treatment of multiple personality disorder. *Psychiatric Clinics of North America, 12,* 721-740.

Loewenstein, R. J. & Putnam, F. W. (1988). A comparison study dissociative symptoms in patients with partial complex seizures, multiple personality disorder, and posttraumatic stress disorder. *Dissociation, 1* (4), 17-23.

Ludwig, A. M., Brandsma, J. M., Wilbur, C. B., Bendfeldt, F., & Jameson, D.H. (1972). The objective study of a multiple personality, or, are four heads better than one? *Archives of General Psychiatry, 26,* 298-310.

Nemiah, J. C. (1981). Dissociative disorders. In H. Kaplan, A. Freedman, & B. Sadock (Eds.), *Comprehensive textbook of psychiatry* (3rd ed, pp. 1544-1561). Baltimore: Williams & Wilkins.

Pines, M. (1978). Invisible playmates. *Psychology Today, 12,* 28-38.

Putnam, F. W. (1984). The psychophysiologic investigation of multiple personality disorder. *Psychiatric Clinics of North America, 7,* 31-39.

Putnam, F. W. (1985). Dissociation as a response to extreme trauma. In R. P. Kluft (Ed.), *Childhood antecedents of multiple personality* (pp. 65-98). Washington, DC: American Psychiatric Press.

Putnam, F. W. (1988). The switch process in multiple personality disorder. *Dissociation, 1* (1), 24-32.

Putnam, F. W. (1989). *Diagnosis and treatment of multiple personality disorder.* New York: Guilford.

Putnam, F. W. (1991a). Dissociative phenomena. In A. Tasman & S. Goldfinger (Eds.), *The American psychiatric press annual review of psychiatry* (Vol. 10, pp. 145-160). Washington, DC: American Psychiatric Press.

Putnam, F. W. (1991b). Recent research on multiple personality disorder. *Psychiatric Clinics of North America, 12,* 489-502.

Putnam, F. W. (in press). Models of dissociation. In B. G. Braun & R. P. Kluft (Eds.), *Multiple personality and dissociation.*

Putnam, F. W., Guroff, J. J., Silberman, E. K., Barban, L., & Post, R. M. (1986). The clinical phenomenology of multiple personality disorder: Review of 100 recent cases. *Journal of Clinical Psychiatry, 47,* 285-293.

Putnam, F. W., Loewenstein, R. J., Silberman, E. J., & Post, R. M. (1984). Multiple personality disorder in a hospital setting. *Journal of Clinical Psychiatry, 45,* 172-175.

Ross, C. A. (1989). *Multiple personality disorder: Diagnosis, clinical features, and treatment.* New York: Wiley.

Ross, C. A., Miller, S. D., Reagor, P., Bjornson, L., Fraser, G. A., & Anderson, G. (1990). Structured interview data on 103 cases of multiple personality disorder from four centres. *American Journal of Psychiatry, 147,* 596-601.

Ross, C. A., Norton, G. R., & Wozney, K. (1989). Multiple personality disorder: An analysis of 236 cases. *Canadian Journal of Psychiatry, 34,* 413-418.

Russell, D. E. H. (1986). *The secret trauma: Incest in the lives of girls and women.* New York: Basic Books.

Schreiber, F. R. (1973). *Sybil.* New York: Henry Regnery.

Schultz, R., Braun, B. G., & Kluft, R. P. (1985). Creativity and the imaginary companion phenomenon: Prevalence and phenomenology in MPD. In B. G. Braun (Ed.), *Dissociative disorders: 1985—Proceedings of the Second International Conference on Multiple Personality/dissociative States* (pp. 163). Chicago: Rush.

Schultz, R., Braun, B. G., & Kluft, R. P. (1989). Multiple personality disorder: Phenomology of selected variables in comparison to major depression. *Dissociation, 2,* 45-51.

Spiegel, D. (1984). Multiple personality as a post-traumatic stress disorder. *Psychiatric Clinics of North America, 7,* 101-110.

Spiegel, D. (1986a). Dissociation, double binds, and posttraumatic stress in multiple personality disorder. In B. G. Braun (Ed.), *Treatment of multiple personality disorder* (pp. 61-77). Washington, DC: American Psychiatric Press.

Spiegel, D. (1986b). Dissociating damage. American *Journal of Clinical Hypnosis, 29,* 123-131.

Spiegel, D. (1991). Dissociation and trauma. In A. Tasman & S. Goldfinger (Eds.), *The American psychiatric press annual review of psychiatry* (Vol. 10, pp. 361-267). Washington, D.C.: American Psychiatric Press.

Steinberg, M., Rounsaville, B., & Cicchetti, D. (1990). The structured clinical interview for DSM-III-R dissociative disorders: Preliminary report on a new diagnostic instrument. *American Journal of Psychiatry, 147,* 76-82.

Stengel, E. (1943). Further studies on pathological wandering (fugues with the impulse to wander). *Journal of Mental Science, 89,* 224-241.

Stern, C. R. (1984). The etiology of multiple personalities. *Psychiatric Clinics of North America, 7,* 149-159.

Stern, D. N. (1985). *The interpersonal world of the infant: A view from psychoanalysis and developmental psychology.* New York: Basic Books.

Thigpen, C. H., & Cleckley, H.M. (1957). *The three faces of Eve.* New York: McGraw-Hill.

Thigpen, C. H., & Cleckley, H. M. (1984). On the incidence of multiple personality disorder: A brief communication. *International Journal of Clinical and Experimental Hypnosis, 32,* 63-66.

Tolkien, J. R. R. (1965a). *The Fellowship of the Ring.* New York: Ballantine.

Tolkien, J. R. R. (1965b). *The Two Towers.* New York: Ballantine.

Tolkien, J. R. R. (1965c). *The Return of the King.* New York: Ballantine.

Watkins, J. G., & Watkins, H. H. (1982). Ego-state therapy. In B. Corsini (Ed.), *Handbook of Innovative Therapies* (pp. 252-270). New York: Wiley

2
Etiological and Maintaining Factors in Multiple Personality Disorder: A Critical Review

Brian D. Doan
Sunnybrook Health Science Centre

Susan E. Bryson
York University

The DSM-III-R (American Psychiatric Association, 1987) defines multiple personality disorder (MPD) as "the existence within the individual of two or more distinct personalities or personality states (each with its own relatively enduring pattern of perceiving, relating to, and thinking about the environment and self), [each of which] recurrently takes full control of the individual's behavior" (p.269). The DSM-III-R also acknowledges "variants of MPD, such as cases in which there is more than one entity capable of assuming executive control of the individual, but not more than one entity is sufficiently complex and integrated to meet the full criteria for MPD, or cases in which a second personality never assumes complete executive control" (p.277). These diagnostic criteria for MPD are more flexible than those that originally appeared in DSM-III (American Psychiatric Association, 1980; cf., Kluft, 1987). They were drafted in recognition of recent clinical findings that suggest, among other things, that the average person with multiple personality disorder will develop between 8 and 14 alters of variable distinctiveness, complexity, and dominance (Bliss, 1980; Braun, 1990; Kluft, 1984c, 1985, 1987; Putnam et al., 1986).

Like the other dissociative disorders (psychogenic amnesia, psychogenic fugue, depersonalization disorder), MPD is most often diagnosed in individuals between their late teens and mid-30s. However, several features of MPD distinguish it from the others. First, although childhood antecedents such as disturbed parent-child relationships have been implicated to some extent in all of the dissociative disorders, only multiple personality disorder is known to have its origins in childhood, with the initial "splitting" or dissociative episodes typically reported as occurring prior to age 12, frequently by 6 or 8, and as early as age 2 (Kluft, 1987; Putnam, Guroff, Silberman, Barban & Post, 1986).

Second, although dissociative disorders in general have been regarded as relatively rare, there has been a rapid increase during the past decade in the frequency with which MPD in particular has been diagnosed. And, although considerable skepticism exists in the literature about why this has occurred, the fact remains that by 1985, over 1,000 contemporary cases of MPD had been identified in North America (Putnam, 1985).

Third, available statistics suggest that the prevalence of psychogenic amnesia, fugue, and depersonalization disorder is roughly equal for women and men (i.e., with female to male ratios typically ranging from 0.2:1 to 4:1; Putnam, 1985). In the case of MPD, however, the larger studies typically report female to male ratios between 7:1 and 14:1, suggesting that MPD may be a predominantly female disorder (Bliss, 1980; Kluft, 1984c; Putnam, 1985; Putnam et al., 1986; Ross & Norton, 1989). It has been argued that males may be underrepresented in psychiatric samples, because the violent behavior associated with MPD may result in more men being dealt with in the criminal justice system (Putnam, 1985). The extent of such sampling bias in the literature on MPD remains to be determined. In the general population, sexual abuse in childhood is typically reported as being inflicted on at least five times more females than males; but again, sexually abused females may be overrepresented because of sampling and reporting biases. Nevertheless, the overwhelming evidence that childhood abuse—in particular, sexual abuse—is instrumental in the development of MPD does suggest a greater likelihood that the victim will be female (see the report of the Committee on Sexual Offenses Against Children and Youths, 1984, for data indicating that females are at higher risk for sexual abuse).

A fourth characteristic of MPD that distinguishes it from other dissociative disorders is its chronicity. While the other dissociative reactions tend to be relatively brief in duration, all that is now known about MPD suggests that it is a persistent, ongoing disorder that begins in the first decade of life in response to overwhelming sexual, physical, and psychological trauma, and is rarely diagnosed or treated until the third or fourth decade (Putnam et al., 1986). In the interim, the person will have experienced repeated alternations between his or her separate identities, recurrent episodes of memory distortion and frank amnesia, hallucinations, passive-influence, and other ego-alien experiences; as well as a plethora of other symptoms, including phobias, self-destructive compulsions, anxiety, depression, somatoform disorders such as severe refractory headaches and irritable bowel syndrome, and frequent disturbance of social, interpersonal, educational, and occupational functions (Kluft, 1987; Putnam et al., 1986; Ross, Norton & Wozney, 1989).

All of these distinguishing features of MPD—its early onset, its uncertain prevalence, its association with traumatic abuse, the apparent preponderance of female victims of the disorder, and the chronic, persistent nature of its symptoms—point to an urgent need for careful theorizing and research into the various factors that predispose, precipitate, and maintain this complex and mystifying disorder. In what follows, we critically review some of the leading theoretical formulations of MPD, point to some intriguing research findings relevant to dissociative phenomena, and try to help clear the way for further investigation of dissociation and multiplicity.

THEORETICAL FORMULATIONS

The oldest, and still the leading theory of dissociative psychopathology such as MPD is that it is a form of trance state or autohypnotic phenomenon (e.g., Bliss, 1983, 1984; Braun, 1984, 1985; Gruenwald, 1984; E.R. Hilgard, 1977; Kluft, 1984c, 1985, 1987; Putnam, 1991a; Putnam et al., 1986). In 1809, Puysegur first observed hypnotically induced somnambulism and spontaneous post-hypnotic amnesia in a young patient with "febrile inflammation of the lungs" (Nemiah, 1978). It was not until the late 1800s, however, that Jean Charcot and one of his most famous students, Pierre Janet (1889), articulated the concept of dissociation in the context of hypnoid states to explain the nature of hysterical symptoms, including the development of multiplicity in hysterical patients. Janet's model was taken up and elaborated by Morton Prince (1890, 1906), as well as by Breuer and Freud (1895).

In contrast to modern conceptions of hypnotizability as a special talent (cf. Hilgard, 1970; Spiegel, 1977), the earlier explanations of dissociative reactions considered hypnotic susceptibility to be a hereditary pathological trait. According to Janet (1903, 1907), the normal person is born with a quantum of nervous energy sufficient to bind together all neural processes and their associated mental functions into a unified whole, dominated by conscious awareness and by the experience of oneself as an integrated personality. Normal people, Janet believed, were not hypnotizable. In others, however, a hereditary deficiency of nervous energy was thought to account for a loosening of the normal synthesis of the personality and a "falling away," or dissociation, of memories and mental functions from conscious awareness and control. Hypnotic susceptibility was thus taken as evidence of a weakly integrated personality, secondary to an inadequate quantum of binding nervous energy.

Although Freud initially concurred with this formulation, the Charcot School's passive, static model of "hypnoid hysteria" was soon subordinated in Freud's theory by a dynamic view of the mind, in which the ego actively forces frightening, disgusting, or otherwise unpalatable ideas, emotions, and desires beyond awareness and voluntary recall and holds them in an unconscious, dissociated state. In Freud's model, dissociation came to be viewed as the result of active mental processes, such as repression, when one part of the mind came into conflict with another. Although Freud acknowledged the role of constitutional predisposition in the determination of a person's neurotic symptoms, he disagreed with the view that neurotic disorders invariably result from a hereditary deficiency, and he proposed that neurotic symptoms could occur in people with a sound hereditary endowment when confronted with a sufficiently painful trauma. Indeed, in the earlier phase of his work, Freud maintained that the major cause of all hysterical neuroses was a sexual assault suffered in childhood.

Recent theorizing about MPD has retained many elements of the arly conceptualizations of Janet, Prince, Breuer, and Freud. The assumption that dissociative symptomatology is a form of hypnotic phenomenon is certainly evident in the thinking of skeptics who dismiss MPD as an iatrogenic artifact of hypnosis (e.g., Harriman, 1942, 1943; Kampman, 1976; Leavitt, 1947; Spanos, Weekes, & Bertrand, 1985). Proponents of the reality of MPD acknowledge that phenomena similar to that occurring in MPD can be induced in hypnosis, but they argue that there is no evidence that MPD can be produced *de novo* by hypnosis, that MPD is frequently observed in persons with no previous exposure to formal hypnosis, and that, at any rate, the dissociative phenomena elicited in hypnosis only superficially resemble those observed in MPD (Braun, 1984; Frischholz, 1985; Gruenwald, 1984; Kluft, 1987. See also Dell,

1988; and Commentaries by Bliss, 1988, and Hilgard, 1988).

We note in passing that we are among those people whom Taylor and Martin (1944) described as either "very naive, [or who] . . . have worked with actual or near cases" of MPD: that is, we accept multiple personality disorder as real. This said, the case against iatrogenesis nevertheless leaves much to be desired. At best, it merely begs the question as to the nature of the relationship between multiplicity and hypnotic phenomena. Given that many proponents of the reality of MPD consider autohypnosis to be a major etiological factor in the development of multiplicity, much more work is needed to specify how hypnotically induced dissociative phenomena are like, and unlike, dissociative phenomena observed in MPD.

Recent experimental work on hypnosis seems to offer much that is useful in enhancing our understanding of dissociative disorders. In particular, E. Hilgard's (1977) "neodissociation theory" of hypnotic phenomena has attracted considerable attention. In our view, one of the most important features of Hilgard's perspective is that hypnotic phenomena are to be understood as instances of dissociation, rather than the other way around. Our reading of the contemporary literature on MPD suggests that the significance of this perspective on the relationship between dissociation and hypnosis has not been fully appreciated; a matter to which we return later.

Of the several recent formulations of MPD, Kluft's (1984c, 1987) "Four Factor Theory of Etiology" seems to provide the most comprehensive and representative model to date. Let us consider his factors in order. Briefly stated, the individual who develops MPD is thought to have Factor 1, the potential to dissociate. This dissociative capacity becomes enlisted as a drastic defense in the face of Factor 2, experiences that traumatically overwhelm the adaptive capacities of the child's ego. Given these predisposing and precipitating conditions, the actual form taken by the dissociative defenses and the way in which the child's personality will be organized are determined by Factor 3, which Kluft broadly defined as "shaping influences and substrates." They include various inherent cognitive and psychodynamic processes, as well as extrinsic influences such as the number of caretakers the child has and the degree of inconsistency or contradiction in reinforcement systems within the family. Finally, Factor 4 determines whether multiplicity will persist and refers to "inadequate stimulus barriers and restorative experiences, or an excess of double-binding messages that inhibit the child's capacity to process [and integrate] experience" (Kluft, 1987, p. 366).

PREDISPOSING FACTORS

Dissociation and Hypnotizability

Dissociative ability, Factor 1 in Kluft's model, is now widely assumed to be the major predisposing factor for MPD. This assumption, which dates back to the original conceptualizations of Janet and Prince, links dissociative potential in some way to hypnotic susceptibility, and considers each to be a genetic or biologically determined predisposition (see, e.g., Braun & Sachs, 1985; Frischholz, 1985). Note that Kluft (1987) defined Factor 1 as "the biologic, but not the compliance or suggestibility component of hypnotizability," making clear that he is not referring to a predisposition to please, or to be vulnerable to iatrogenic manipulation. Beyond that distinction, however, the literature on MPD has not yet attempted to clarify the relationship between dissociative ability and hypnotizability.

We believe that E. Hilgard's (1977) interpretation of the relationship between dissociative ability and hypnotizability is the correct one: namely, that the capacity to dissociate is primary, that it is a major component of hypnotic susceptibility, and is implicated in virtually all hypnotic phenomena that involve alterations in awareness (such as hypnotic analgesia, hypnotically induced deafness, post-hypnotic amnesia, and the phenomenon of the "hidden observer"); as well as alterations in the voluntary control of behavior (e.g., postural sway, limb levitation and rigidity, involuntary eye closure, and so on; see Frischholz, 1985, and Bowers, 1991, for related points).

Hilgard's discovery of the "hidden observer" in studies of hypnotically induced deafness and analgesia has been cited by many as an important experimental demonstration of a phenomenon similar to that which typically occurs in MPD (e.g., Braun, 1984; Frischholz, 1985; Kluft, 1987; Spiegel, 1987). Approximately half of those subjects who are highly susceptible to hypnosis will exhibit the "hidden observer" effect. Deafness or analgesia is induced in a hypnotized subject. The subject exhibits a lack of responsiveness to conversation, noise, or painful stimuli, and is then asked whether "some other part" of him or her is aware of what is happening. In those cases in which a "hidden observer" is found, the subject will deny hearing or feeling pain, while at the same time the "hidden observer" can give an accurate account of what he or she heard, or will report pain at a level comparable to when the subject was not hypnotized.

As Hebb (1980) pointed out, Hilgard's discovery calls into question a number of well-established notions about what is conscious and what is not. We tend to think of any mental process that is outside of our awareness or that cannot be recalled as being subconscious or unconscious. But the "hidden observer" phenomenon demonstrates that what is outside of our immediate awareness may be dissociated, but nevertheless conscious. It is this very aspect of the phenomenon that is thought to parallel what occurs in MPD. Consistent with Hilgard's findings for highly hypnotizable subjects, two separate studies (Frischholz, Lipman, & Braun, 1984; Kluft, 1984c) found that approximately one half of MPD patients will exhibit the "hidden observer" phenomenon under hypnosis.

At first glance, these data appear to pose a serious problem for our understanding of both MPD and the "hidden observer." If the "hidden observer" is a dissociative phenomenon, and MPD a dissociative disorder, why don't *all* MPD sufferers readily produce a "hidden observer" under hypnosis? In fact, Frischholz (1985) reported a further curious aspect to the findings from these studies: The occurrence of the "hidden observer" in the MPD patients was related to the duration of their treatment. All MPD patients who had just begun treatment produced a "hidden observer" in hypnosis, whereas those who had been in treatment for several years did not. Frischholz (1985) suggested that this finding may have to do with the patients' level of adaptive functioning: that patients well along in treatment showed no evidence of a "hidden observer" because they were on their way toward integration.

If this were true, it might mean that successful integration of the MPD patient's alternate personalities somehow reduces the capacity to dissociate. But that cannot be true, because all of these patients remain highly responsive to hypnosis, and many remain at risk for further dissociative episodes, even after "successful" treatment (Kluft, 1984a, 1987). A more appropriate interpretation of these data might be inferred from the findings of Perry and his colleagues in their studies of the "hidden observer" phenomenon in hypnotic age-regression (e.g., Perry & Walsh, 1978). Laurence and Perry (1981) found that when hypnotized subjects were regressed to age 5, roughly 60% showed no evidence of a "hidden observer." They presented as fully regressed 5-year-olds. As Laurence and Perry put it, "their imaginings appeared to be more 'believed in' (Sarbin & Coe, 1972), and they seemed more 'deluded' (Sutcliffe, 1961) in the sense that their awareness of reality was considerably diminished" (p. 343). In contrast, those who exhibited a "hidden observer" maintained their adult identities and their contact with reality, while vividly experiencing childhood either simultaneously or in alternation.

Laurence and Perry's findings suggest the possibility that the spontaneous duality experienced by some highly hypnotizable subjects may be related to a need to maintain contact with reality while under hypnosis. If correct, the greater prevalence of a "hidden observer" among MPD patients who had just begun treatment may have more to do with discomfort and inability to trust the hypnotist than with their level of adaptive functioning. E. Hilgard (1977) argued that the capacity for hypnosis—whether by self-induction or with the assistance of a hypnotist—seems to presuppose the ability to dissociate various aspects of one's executive control and monitoring functions. Although a detailed elaboration is beyond the scope of this chapter, we also suspect that dissociative ability is implicated in the various skills that have been described by others as essential to hypnosis: for example, the ability for focused concentration (Spiegel & Spiegel, 1978), for goal-directed imagining (Spanos & Barber, 1974), or for role enactment (Sarbin & Coe, 1972).

One source of indirect support for the claim that dissociative ability is the core phenomenon underlying hypnotic susceptibility comes from a comparison of research findings on the development of hypnotizability with what is known of the development of MPD. According to a number of studies, hypnotic susceptibility in the general population rises between the ages of 6 to 9, peaks around age 10 to 12, and then declines thereafter (cf. Barber & Calverley, 1963; London, 1965; Morgan, 1969; Stukat, 1958). Although it has been argued (e.g., Diamond, 1977; J. Hilgard, 1970) that younger children may prove to be responsive to hypnosis under the right conditions, the evidence to date suggests that children below age 7 are much less responsive than they are between ages 9 and 12 (see Fig. 2.1).

In contrast, clinical reports indicate that many MPD patients experience their first dissociative episodes prior to age 6 or 8 and as early as age 2. Another relatively common phenomenon of childhood associated with this preschool period is the imaginary companion. The presence in childhood of imaginary companions is a predictor of hypnotic susceptibility in adults (J. Hilgard, 1970), and has also been implicated in the development of MPD (e.g., Kluft, 1987; Lovinger, 1983). Hilgard reported that imaginary companionship begins shortly after the age of 2, and that in two out of three cases, imaginary companions will have made their appearance by age 3, 4, or 5. As shown in Fig. 2.1, the peak period for the presence of imaginary companions in Hilgard's highly hypnotizable adults seems to occur earlier than the age of maximum hypnotic susceptibility

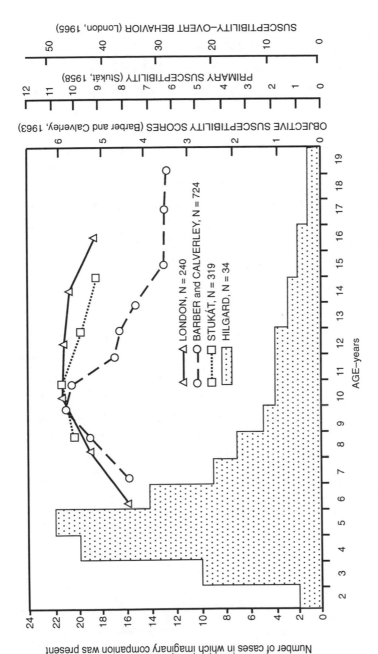

Fig.2.1. Hypnotic susceptibility in childhood (line graphs indexed to scales on the right); and ages in which an imaginary companion was reported in Hilgard's (1970) studies (histogram indexed to scale on the left). Adapted from Hilgard, 1970.

found in other developmental studies.

The co-occurrence in development of imaginary companions and the initial maladaptive splitting in MPD patients lends some credence to reports that in a number of MPD cases an imaginary companion appears to have been integrated into the system of alternate personalities. That both phenomena are likely to occur prior to the age of maximum hypnotic susceptibility also suggests that dissociative ability may be a developmental precursor of hypnotizability. If correct, a relationship between a diagnosis in adulthood of MPD and high hypnotic susceptibility may not imply any causal connection between the two, but rather that both are attributable to a propensity to dissociate (see Lynn, Rhue, & Green, 1988; Young, 1988, for related points).

Heredity

Some indirect, clinical support for the assumption that dissociative ability is biologically determined comes from reports on the transgenerational incidence of dissociative psychopathology (Braun, 1985; Coons, 1985; Kluft, 1984b). Only one of these (Coons, 1985) was a controlled study and, overall, the data attest more to a higher incidence of psychiatric disturbance in general among the parents, siblings, and offspring of MPD patients than to an inherited predisposition to dissociate.

Slightly stronger support for the hypothesis that certain individuals are predisposed to dissociate is provided in the literature on hypnosis. The advent in the mid-1960s of reliable measures of hypnotic susceptibility has indeed established the existence of stable individual differences in hypnotizability (E. Hilgard, 1965; J. Hilgard, 1970; Spiegel & Spiegel, 1978). At least three studies of hypnotizability among twins raised in the same household have shown consistently higher correlations between the degrees of responsiveness to hypnosis for monozygotic (r's ranging from 0.51 to 0.67) than for dizygotic twins (r's ranging from 0.18 to 0.24; cf.

Morgan, 1973; Rawlings, 1972). Moreover, at least two recent studies have demonstrated that, as a group, MPD patients are significantly more hypnotizable than clinical and normal controls (Bliss, 1984; Frischholz et al., 1984). Finally, some writers have also pursued the possibility that there may be biological markers of hypnotic susceptibility, such as visual field preference (Bakan, 1969; Gur & Gur, 1974), body type (Edmunston, 1977), and eye-roll capacity (Spiegel, 1974). Various questions remain, however, about the reliability of all three putative markers.

Bakan (1969), as well as Gur and Gur (1974), for example, have noted that hypnotizability scores tend to be higher among persons who show a preference for leftward eye movements when engaged in mental problem solving tasks while facing the examiner. This sinister preference suggests activation of the nondominant cerebral hemisphere. However, E. Hilgard (1977) has cautioned that the association between hypnotic susceptibility and preferred direction of gaze may not be related to brain organization per se, but rather to strategic variables such as a preference for using visual imagery in problem solving. In addition, Edmunston (1977) has reported a relationship in males between hypnotizability and "somatotype" or body build. Specifically, he found that both male Ectomorphs (tall and thin) and Endomorphs (heavier, rounder) tend to be more hypnotizable than Mesomorphs (the muscular type). Why this should be the case remains unclear, although as we discuss later, J. Hilgard (1970) found that involvement in competitive athletics may be antithetical to the development of hypnotizability. Finally, one of the more widely known, purported biomarkers of hypnotic susceptibility is "eye roll capacity" (Spiegel, 1974). Spiegel's original data yielded a significant relationship between responses to the items of his hypnotic induction profile and the degree to which subjects in his selected sample were able to roll their eyes upwards. Subsequent studies using larger, unselected samples were unable to replicate the relationship (Eliseo, 1974; Switras, 1974; Spiegel, Aronson, Fleiss, & Haber, 1976; Wheeler, Reiss, Wolff, Grupsmith, & Mordkoff,

1974). Nevertheless, a positive eye roll sign is still widely believed to be a reliable indicator of hypnotic potential. It is interesting to note that in 1890 Janet and his colleagues viewed hypnotizability as a hereditary vulnerability for psychopathology, whereas Spiegel's (1977) explanation for the *failure* to find a relationship between eye roll capacity and hypnotic responsivity in unselected samples was that a proportion of the subjects with a strong eye roll probably suffered from psychiatric disorders that reduced their hypnotizability. Contrary to what was believed in the last century, the contemporary evidence does favor the view that most highly hypnotizable people are psychologically healthy (e.g., E. Hilgard, 1965; J. Hilgard, 1970; Spiegel & Spiegel, 1978). Unlike their predecessors, the burden today for proponents of the view that dissociative ability is inborn— especially in light of the prevalence in our society of child abuse—is to explain why more highly hypnotizable people do not develop dissociative disorders such as MPD (cf. Braun & Sachs, 1985; Frischholz, 1985).

The evidence so far suggests that some individuals, including persons suffering from MPD, may be more susceptible to dissociations of the sort that are typically observed in hypnosis. Moreover, it appears that dissociative ability may be a developmental precursor of high hypnotic susceptibility. Although some evidence suggests that dissociative ability is at least in part biologically determined, there is unfortunately nothing yet in the literature that could pass for a testable model of the biological mechanisms that might be involved (but see Braun, 1984, for a speculative attempt).

We are sympathetic to the view that individual differences in the capacity to dissociate are probably attributable in part to genetic influences; however, we have difficulty with the simplicity of the contemporary formulation that an individual with such a biological predisposition develops MPD when exposed to traumatic events. Hebb (1949, 1980) always maintained that the manifestation of any *phenotypic* trait invariably results from an interaction between the genotype for that trait and environmental conditions. Similarly, we prefer the view that a genetic vulnerability to dissociation will manifest itself as a *predisposition* in an individual only under particular conditions. Note that we are not referring here to the actual occurrence of dissociative experiences in connection with exposure to traumatic events, but strictly to the development of a *predisposition* to dissociate.

It is conceivable, for example, that many individuals with a genotypic vulnerability to dissociation are raised in environments that do not promote the development of a predisposition for dissociative experiences. In the absence of the relevant learning conditions, these individuals would not dissociate, even when exposed to trauma. As adults, such persons would also be found to be relatively unresponsive to hypnosis, despite their relevant genotype. By the same token, individuals with a genotypic vulnerability to dissociation, who are also exposed to conditions that are favorable to the development of a capacity to dissociate, might never experience a single maladaptive dissociative episode in their lifetime. They would be the people raised in comparatively benevolent environments who, as adults, would be both well-adjusted and highly susceptible to hypnosis.

With this in mind, let us now consider some of the environmental conditions that seem to favour the development of a predisposition to dissociation.

Environment

In an interesting book titled *Personality and Hypnosis*, Josephine Hilgard (1970) reported an extensive investigation of personality and childhood background factors related to hypnotic susceptibility in over 800 young men and women assessed between 1957 and 1964. Very briefly, J. Hilgard (1970) found that specific aspects of the childhood histories and present personalities of her subjects were significantly correlated with hypnotic susceptibility. The relevant characteristics were: a capacity for imaginative absorption or involvement, subjects' ratings of the severity of punishment in childhood, their temperamental similarity to the opposite-sexed parent, and three related factors reflecting a generally welladjusted and outgoing personality. These factors include their judged ease of communication during the interview, their motivation for hypnosis, and the interviewer's global rating of the subject's psychological adjustment.

Not all intense involvements in childhood are related to hypnotizability in adulthood. Involvement in competitive athletics, a deep interest in or commitment to science, and certain hobbies or recreational activities, such as woodworking or botany, were found to be antithetical to hypnotic susceptibility. J. Hilgard (1970) suggested that what such involvements have in common that mitigates against the development of hypnotizability is that they typically require reality orientation, a critical attitude, alertness to detail, and the pursuit of a standard of excellence. In contrast, absorbed involvements that seem to promote the development of hypnotic responsivity typically involve imagery and imagination, the suspension of reality orientation, and the enjoyment or savoring of affective and sensory experience for its own sake. Absorption in reading, in making or listening to music, personal involvement in religion and religious experience, and participation in or appreciation of the dramatic arts are all examples of domains in which imaginative absorption seems to be related to later responsiveness to hypnosis.

J. Hilgard's (1970) data also led her to emphasize the importance of modeling and identification with parents in the development of a capacity for imaginative absorption and for hypnosis. One unexpected finding was that higher hypnotizability is associated with identification with the parent of the opposite sex. Hilgard suggested two possible interpretations of this result. One is that the opposite-sexed parent is selected as a model because his or her attractiveness to the child is based on the very qualities— imaginativeness, the valuing of sensory experience, and so on—that also happen to make the parent, and ultimately the child, susceptible to hypnosis. Alternatively, cross-sexed identification may promote the kinds of dissociative experiences upon which hypnosis is based, because it may require selective inattention to relevant gender-identity information. We consider, shortly, how the latter interpretation might also explain the greater prevalence of MPD among females.

Another unexpected finding in J. Hilgard's (1970) study, and one that provides clear support for a developmental contribution to hypnotic susceptibility, is that hypnotizability in adulthood is related to the perceived severity of punishment experienced in childhood. Earlier, in a prospective study of children, Nowlis (1968) noted a relationship between strict discipline with respect to table manners and later hypnotizability. More recently, Nash, Lynn, and Givens (1984) have reported significantly higher hypnotic susceptibility in 16 subjects who had suffered physical abuse in childhood, compared to 300 nonabused subjects.[1]

This joint association between hypnotizability, abuse, and strong identification with the opposite-sexed parent may explain why more females appear to develop MPD. Because there presumably are more males sexually abusing female children, strong ambivalence is more likely to be a factor in the relationships of daughters and fathers than in those of mothers and sons. We return to the importance of ambivalence as a factor in MPD later.

J. Hilgard's (1970) findings may have implications for our

---

[1] In view of the high incidence of childhood abuse in the histories of MPD patients, it is important to note several qualifications in J. Hilgard's (1970) analysis of the role of punishment in the development of hypnotizability. It appears that it is not simply the severity or the quantity of punishment that is important, for strict discipline involving reasoning was not related to hypnotizability. Second, inconsistency or unpredictability of punishment was not a relevant variable, but *perceived arbitrariness* was. That is, hypnotic susceptibility was found to be related to the kind of strict discipline that required the child to conform to an adult code of conduct simply because the parent insisted on it, even though the child may not have understood why. Finally, the more highly punished and highly hypnotizable subjects in J. Hilgard's (1970) samples were those who also often rated parental warmth as high, and whose discipline had evidently been successful in achieving relative conformity and respect for authority.

understanding of the development of dissociative ability which in some individuals will eventuate in MPD. At a minimum, they suggest a number of variables in a child's upbringing besides his or her genetic endowment that together may predispose the child for dissociation. J. Hilgard (1970), for example, speculated that strict discipline, including punishment involving isolation or confinement, may contribute to a propensity for dissociation and later hypnotizability in two ways: first, by establishing a tendency for vigilance and for prompt conformity to the demands of authority, however arbitrary those demands may seem, and second, by providing some kind of temporary escape from continuous, alert self-control, during which time the child may become absorbed in reading, music, or fantasy.

It might be argued that much of what J. Hilgard (1970) has classified as early environmental factors are actually inherited traits. A capacity for imaginative absorption, for example, may easily be seen as biologically determined. Similarly, cross-sex identification might reflect little more than inherited temperamental similarities between fathers and daughters and mothers and sons. Although we recognize that heredity may well be at play in the emergence of these personality characteristics, just as it presumably is important in the emergence of dissociative ability, several other considerations favor the view that environment plays a critical role.

The first consideration is that the simpler (inherited predisposition + trauma) hypothesis leads one to predict a far greater prevalence of MPD than in fact occurs, even allowing for underrepresentation in clinical samples. In contrast, the more subtle hypothesis (heredity + predisposing environment + trauma) provides a possible account of why the majority of traumatized children do not develop MPD, as well as why a minority of children who develop MPD do so in the absence of severe trauma. The second consideration is that a genetic hypothesis regarding temperamental similarity between parent and child does not explain why cross-sexed similarity should be more strongly associated with hypnotic susceptibility than similarity to the same-sexed parent. In this instance, the relative importance of hereditary and environmental variables can be examined empirically. Given the incidence in our society of blended families, the reliability of J. Hilgard's (1970) finding of a relationship between hypnotic susceptibility and cross-sexed identification could be tested with natural and adoptive parent-child relationships.

Note that some of the factors that J. Hilgard (1970) identified as contributing to hypnotic susceptibility are positive, such as the encouragement by parents of imaginative involvements and the appreciation of sensory experience for its own sake. Her studies of well-adjusted individuals serve as a reminder that there is inevitably much more involved in the childhood histories of persons with multiple personality disorder than the occurrence of traumatic abuse and overwhelming anxiety. We are reminded, for example, of Schreiber's (1973) description of the more sensitive aspects of the mothering that "Sybil" received:

The same mother who embarrassed, shamed and tortured her daughter would cut bright colored pictures from magazines and paste them on the lower part of the cupboard door so they would be at Sybil's eye level. At breakfast this same mother would often manage to have a "surprise" in the bottom of the daughter's cereal bowl: like prunes, figs, dates, all of which the child especially liked. (p. 222)

Lovinger (1983) emphasized that although they are juxtaposed with periods of terror and unbearable anxiety, these periods of caring, calm, and relaxation nevertheless promote a strong attachment between parent and child.

A number of writers (e.g., Allison, 1974, 1977; Greaves, 1980) have viewed the dilemma faced by the child who develops MPD as one of *ambivalence,* or polarized affect. Emotional polarization in a child is said to occur, for example, when, as in the case of "Sybil," the same "stimulus object"—usually a parent—produces both intensely painful and intensely pleasurable states in the child. Another example of conditions that produce emotional polarization is when the child's behavior is consistently punished or rejected by parents favoring other behavior. In this instance, the child becomes alienated from self as he or she strives to identify with the highly idealized view communicated by the parent—a process that may be at play, for example, in MPD patients who create alternate personalities to deal with conflicts over sexual and religious issues.

Most of the variables we have considered so far have been presented as possible predisposing factors in the development of MPD. We have seen that there is some evidence for a biological predisposition for dissociative experiences. We also considered a number of environmental factors that may contribute to a predisposition for dissociative experiences, such as parental encouragement of imaginative involvements, cross-sexed parental identification, and strict discipline or severe punishment which promotes alert conformity to parental demands. All of these factors have been implicated in the persistence of hypnotic susceptibility into adulthood, but obviously are not sufficient in and of themselves to provoke the development of MPD. Let us turn, then, to another important class of variables that appear to be crucial in the etiology of MPD, namely, childhood trauma.

PRECIPITATING FACTORS

Trauma

Childhood trauma has been cited by many authors as the major predisposing or precipitating factor in the development of MPD (e.g., Allison, 1974; Bliss, 1980; Boor, 1982; Braun, 1990; Braun & Sachs, 1985; Coons & Milstein, 1984; Greaves, 1980; Horevitz & Braun, 1984; Kluft, 1984, 1985b,c, 1987; Putnam, 1985; Stern, 1984; Wilbur, 1984). Putnam et al. (1986), in their report on 100 MPD patients seen by a variety of mental health professionals, presented findings that are remarkably consistent with those of previous, more circumscribed studies. We can therefore regard them as representative. In Putnam et al.'s sample, childhood trauma was a part of the histories of 97% of the cases, with the average number of different kinds of trauma reported being 3.2, and ranging from one to six different kinds. Sexual abuse was the most common form of trauma, occurring in 83% of the cases. Of these, over 80% were cases of incest. Repeated physical abuse was also reported in 75% of the cases, and of these, over 90% were *both* physically and sexually abused. Extreme neglect was reported as present in the histories of approximately 65% of the sample, and 45% had reportedly witnessed a violent death during their childhood. As well, other, unspecified abuses and extreme poverty were cited, respectively, in roughly 40% and 20% of the cases.

In essence, the onset of MPD is currently thought to be precipitated when a child enlists dissociation as a drastic defense in the face of an overwhelming event that cannot be managed in any other way (see Kluft, 1984b,c, 1987). In a distressing number of the cases reported in which abuse and even outright torture occurred, it seems clear that the inability to dissociate under the circumstances might well have compromised the child's ability to survive. As Greaves (1980) put it, "In the face of events like these, it is likely that any young child would find retreat in whatever merciful strategies of survival the mind has at its disposal" (p. 589).

Based on their respective clinical experiences, Sachs, Goodwin, and Braun (cited in Braun & Sachs, 1985) speculated on some of the possible differences between child abuse victims who have and have not developed MPD. They suggested that, on the one hand, individual differences in dissociative ability is a major moderating variable. On the other hand, the nature of the abuse itself may be a factor. Specifically, they speculated that child abuse victims who do not develop MPD may be more frequently subject to reactive aggression by a parent, whereas MPD victims may be those who are subject also to sadistic and bizarre, ritualistic abuse driven by the abuser's own motivations.

Sachs et al. also contended, as do most authors, that the abuse must be frequent, unpredictable, and inconsistent, and that the child must concurrently be exposed to some loving. The reasoning here is that infrequent abusive experiences may be repressed, or may lead to sporadic dissociative episodes that do not take on a life history of their own. Abuse that is chronic and repetitive is thought to be necessary to provoke repeated dissociations that become linked over time by a shared affective state, and develop into a personality with its own unique identity and behavioral repertoire. With regard to inconsistency, Braun and Sachs (1985) noted that the abuses to which MPD patients are exposed will often be inconsistent with the parental behavior that immediately preceded the aggression, as when a child is told "I love you," and then is burned with a cigarette. Based on our reading of the literature, we would add a few additional variables, such as the excessive use of confinement as a form of punishment, extended isolation from playmates, and punishment of a child's reactions to parental aggression, thereby leaving the child with little option but to dissociate them. Note as well that inconsistency of abuse need not be the rule, provided it is perceived by the child as arbitrary.

Traumatic events other than abuse have been reported as precipitants of dissociative episodes in some MPD cases, including the death of a parent, sibling or friend, family chaos, accidents and near-death experiences, the discovery by a child that one of his or her parents is having extramarital affairs, the birth of a sibling, separation from family, and the destruction of a cherished object such as a doll (cf. Greaves, 1980; Kluft, 1987; Lovinger, 1983; Putnam et al., 1986). It is important to emphasize here that trauma is fundamentally a psychological concept. The essence of trauma is its capacity to produce psychic injury (cf. Furst, 1967). Such injury is thought to occur when the mind is presented with stimuli too great to be dealt with or assimilated. The traumatic potential of an event is thus, in large part, a function of the age and stage of development of the person who experiences it. The childhood experiences of many MPD sufferers are quite easily regarded as unqualified trauma, even by adult standards. But in all cases, including the ones that to the adult mind seem to involve little "objective" trauma, we must remember that what matters most is how intense the relevant events were, and what they meant, to the *3-, 4-, or 5-year-old mind* that experienced them.

MAINTAINING FACTORS

For all that has been presented so far regarding the development of MPD, a difficult problem remains. Many more children than most of us are comfortable thinking about suffer psychic injuries that have lasting effects. But only a proportion of them appear to suffer enduring, organized dissociation, and personality reorganization of the sort encountered in MPD. It is comparatively easy to imagine a child dissociating into an alternate self, projecting his or her experience, say, on an imaginary companion, to escape the terror, helplessness, and rage associated with an assault. But how are we to comprehend the persistence of that dissociation?

Dissociation can be regarded as effective as an *emergency* escape in the context of an overwhelming event. However, in the broader context it must be seen as patently maladaptive. Dissociation does not provide any real escape from an abusive situation; it does not change the victim's circumstances; in the long run the disorder exacts a high price of pain, discontinuity, and misery, of waking up in strange places, of finding oneself in predicaments without knowing how one got there, and of fearing what one might have done during periods that one cannot recall (cf. Greaves, 1980; Lovinger, 1983).

The problem of adequately explaining the persistence of MPD is further complicated by the heterogeneity of the disorder (Kluft, 1987). Because every alternate personality apparently is formed defensively to serve a specific function, each case has its own unique developmental course. Despite these problems, some general accounts of the factors that maintain MPD have been proposed. Kluft's (1984b, 1987) Factors 3 and 4, for example—various "shaping influences" and the absence of "restorative experiences"— include a number of variables that are likely to foster the persistence of dissociative episodes and the further development of the alternate personalities.

Greaves' (1980) conception of the developmental course of MPD involves three levels of defensive organization, which we find useful in considering various issues relevant to the perpetuation of the disorder. In Greaves' terms, the *primary level* of defense refers to the initial use of dissociation as a defense against trauma. The subsequent strategy of coping with environmental stresses by alternating among the more dominant selves constitutes the *secondary level* of defense. The *tertiary level* of defense refers to the MPD sufferer's contrivances to hide the disorder from self and avoid detection by others.

Certainly, all of the factors that we have discussed as possibly predisposing a child to dissociate in the first place, such as the encouragement of absorption, strict discipline, pathological family dynamics, emotional polarization, and repetitive abuse, must also be considered as influential in maintaining the disorder at the secondary defensive level. Indeed, it is not only the repetition of trauma per se that may perpetuate the use of dissociative defenses, but memories of those events as well. For example, the memory of a sexual molestation in early childhood, if recalled in early adolescence, may have acquired new and sufficiently distressing significance beyond the impact of the original event to ensure that it remains dissociated.

According to several writers, one of the major maintaining factors in MPD is dissociative ability itself (see, e.g., Braun, 1984; Braun & Sachs, 1985; Kluft, 1987). Their reasoning is as follows: Once dissociation is established as a defense that rapidly and efficiently leads to temporary relief from distress, it will tend to recur as a way of dealing with subsequent overwhelming experiences. Dissociation will then eventually be enlisted in the face of more mundane pressures and stresses. Frequently, an appeal is made to the reinforcing properties of the dissociative process (e.g., Braun & Sachs, 1985).

Moreover, it appears that there are a number of respects in which dissociations, once established, may be *self-perpetuating*—not simply because of their instrumental value, but because they are mediated by contextual, attitudinal, mood, and other state-dependent variables. Such variables may determine the critical moments when "switching" occurs, and may also interfere with the person's subsequent ability to recall and integrate experience when he or she is in a different attitudinal and affective state. Bower (1981) described a series of experiments with normal subjects in which hypnotically induced, positive or negative mood states resulted in a variety of state-dependent effects, including subjects' mood-congruent recall of word lists and of recent and childhood experiences, as well as mood-congruent free associations, imaginative fantasies, social perceptions, and snap judgments of others' personalities.

To account for these findings, Bower (1981) proposed an associative network theory in which the dominant mood at a given point in time serves as a memory unit that can enter into association with other events. The activation of a given mood state is thought to facilitate recall of events associated with it, and to prime mood-specific themes in free association, fantasy, and perceptual categorization. The mood-state dependency entailed in Bower's network theory may help to explain such divergent phenomena as the forgetting of dreams, poor recall of events experienced under the influence of mood-altering drugs, the perpetuation of depression, and the amnesic episodes observed in persons suffering from MPD. The probable significance of state-dependent effects in maintaining MPD is underscored by Putnam et al.'s (1986) finding that in a majority of MPD cases, the incidence of substance abuse and affective disorders (such as depression or hypomania) is specific to one or another of the patient's alternate personalities.

Finally, Greaves' (1980) tertiary level of defense—the MPD

sufferer's efforts to conceal the disorder—constitutes yet another important factor in perpetuating the disorder. Putnam et al. (1986) found that an average of 6.8 years elapses between the time that a person with MPD is first assessed by a mental health professional and the time he or she receives an accurate diagnosis. Although such long delays likely reflect a degree of diagnostic confusion or resistance to diagnose the disorder on the part of many clinicians, Kluft (1987) has reported that approximately 94% of MPD patients try to hide, deny, or dissimulate their condition. Memory lapses can be filled in with confabulations or attributed to preoccupation. Various excuses may be given for failures to show up for work or appointments. Alternate personalities will pass themselves off as the primary personality, or will indirectly influence the person's actions (Kluft, 1985). A well-developed tertiary level of defense will help ensure that the MPD sufferer is not detected for a long time.

SUMMARY AND CONCLUSIONS

Multiple personality disorder is distinguished among the dissociative disorders by its origins in childhood, by its maladaptive persistence into adulthood and, given its relationship to sexual as well as physical abuse, by a greater likelihood that its victims will be female. While an impressive amount of clinical data gathered during the past decade has helped to clarify the parameters of the disorder, current conceptions of MPD have not changed much over the past century. Therein lies the greatest deficiency in contemporary theorizing and research on MPD. The power of an explanatory model depends on its range, specificity, and systematicity (see Macnamara, Govitrikar, & Doan, 1988). All are lacking in the accounts of MPD that have been offered to date. In particular, we note that aside from the appeal to a dissociative predisposition in certain individuals, there is little in current etiological models that specifies why a child would develop, and continue to suffer from, MPD as opposed to any number of other psychopathological disorders.

In this chapter, we critically reviewed some of the current thinking about the various factors that may cause and maintain MPD. We attempted to address the relationship between dissociative ability and hypnotic phenomena, and have come out in favor of E. Hilgard's (1965, 1977) view that hypnosis presupposes dissociative ability. Although it remains to be empirically tested, we hypothesized that dissociative ability may be a developmental precursor of hypnotic susceptibility. Our reasoning leaves open the possibility that dissociative episodes may frequently occur in the absence of an autohypnotic state. It also suggests that a broader and considerably more detailed specification is needed of both the situational and intrapsychic conditions under which dissociations and "switching" between alternate personalities may occur.

In examining the widely held belief that dissociative ability is inherited, we concluded that far too little attention has been paid to the environmental conditions that would be necessary for the actualization of a biologically determined predisposition to dissociate. None of the studies of MPD so far has addressed the question of what learning experiences may be necessary for the development of dissociative ability. We therefore considered some of the childhood variables that appear to be related to high hypnotic susceptibility among adults. Factors such as a capacity for imaginative absorption, cross-sexed parental identification, strict discipline and/or severe punishment, and emotional polarization were considered as possible environmental contributors to the development of dissociative ability in children. We hope that our review will stimulate investigators to consider the role of these and related variables in the etiology of MPD—especially in prospective studies of both normal children and those identified as being at risk for MPD.

There seems to be little doubt about the role of childhood abuse and other traumata in precipitating the onset of MPD. We reviewed some recently reported clinical impressions that there may be differences in the kinds of abuse suffered by children who develop MPD and those who do not, and we suggested a few additional variables that need to be considered. To date, much of the emphasis has been on how inconsistent or unpredictable the abuse was, how bizarre, and how repetitive it was. There is a need for systematic and controlled empirical investigations of a number of aspects of childhood abuse, as well as of the various contexts in which abuse occurs. In particular, we suggested that the perceived arbitrariness of punishment warrants attention. We are confident that such research will find that the determinants of MPD related to traumatization are far more subtle and complex than previously thought.

By far the most challenging set of problems faced by investigators, however, is to clarify the nature of the processes and mechanisms by which multiple personality disorder is maintained over time. Our reading of the available literature suggests that both instrumental and noninstrumental factors are probably involved. The immediate effectiveness of dissociation as a defense no doubt contributes to its perpetuation. Moreover, it appears that the nature of dissociation itself may result in its self-perpetuation. The continuation of recent experimental work on hypnotically induced dissociations, and on the effects of mood, attitude, and context on learning and memory seems to hold some promise for explaining, at least in part, why MPD persists for so long and at such great cost to the person's adaptive functioning and well-being.

Here again, a note of caution is in order. Investigations of dissociative phenomena that can be produced in the laboratory with normal subjects is drawing attention from proponents and detractors of MPD alike, who see in the "hidden observer," and in state-dependent learning and recall, an opportunity either to legitimize the phenomena observed in MPD or to explain them away. It seems unlikely, however, that phenomena, to which virtually anyone is subject, will ever play a decisive role in the explanation of MPD unless their descriptions are imbedded in a model of cognitive functioning that also clearly specifies the processes and mechanisms that distinguish persons with and without the disorder.

Dissociation and, in particular, multiple personality disorder are phenomena that, in their own right, warrant the most careful scrutiny of scientists and clinicians. Although the focus of this chapter has been on the clinical aspects of dissociation and MPD, we hope that we have also conveyed a little of what Donald Hebb recognized in these phenomena that fueled his enthusiasm for their investigation: namely, an opportunity to better understand the human mind and brain and their organization.

REFERENCES

Allison, R. B. (1974). A new treatment approach for multiple personalities. *American Journal of Clinical Hypnosis, 17*, 15-32.

Allison, R. B. (1977). When the psychic glue dissolves. *Hypnos-nytt, 6*, 25-27.

American Psychiatric Association. (1980). *Diagnostic and statistical manual of mental disorders*, (3rd ed.). Washington, DC: Author.

American Psychiatric Association. (1987). *Diagnostic and statistical manual of mental disorders*, (3rd ed. Rev.). Washington, DC: Author.

Bakan, J. (1969). Hypnotizability, laterality of eye-movements and functional brain asymmetry. *Perceptual and Motor Skills, 28*, 927-932.

Barber, T. X., & Calverley, D. S. (1963). "Hypnotic-like" suggestibility in children and adults. *Journal of Abnormal and Social Psychology, 66*, 589-597.

Bliss, E. L. (1980). Multiple personalities. *Archives of General Psychiatry, 37*, 1388-1397.

Bliss, E. L. (1983). Multiple personalities, related disorders, and hypnosis. *American Journal of Clinical Hypnosis, 26*, 114-123.

Bliss, E. L. (1984). Spontaneous self-hypnosis in multiple personality disorder. *Psychiatric Clinics of North America, 7*, 135-148.

Bliss, E. L. (1988). "Professional skepticism about multiple personality:" Commentary. *Journal of Nervous and Mental Disease, 176*(9), 533-534.

Boor, M. (1982). The multiple personality epidemic: Additional cases and inferences regarding diagnosis, etiology, dynamics and treatment. *Journal of Nervous and Mental Diseases, 170*, 302-304.

Bower, G. H. (1980). Mood and memory. *American Psychologist, 36*, 129-148.

Bowers, K. S. (1991) Dissociation in hypnosis and multiple personality disorder. *International Journal of Clinical and Experimental Hypnosis, 39*(3), 155-176.

Braun, B. G. (1984). Towards a theory of multiple personality and other dissociative phenomena. *Psychiatric Clinics of North America, 7*, 171-193.

Braun, B. G. (1985). The transgenerational incidence of dissociation and multiple personality disorder: A preliminary report. In R. P. Kluft (Ed.), *Childhood antecedents of multiple personality* (pp. 128-150). Washington, DC: American Psychiatric Press.

Braun, B. G. (1990). Multiple personality disorder: An overview. *American Journal of Occupational Therapy, 44*(1), 971-976.

Braun, B. G., & Sachs, R. G. (1985). The development of multiple personality disorder: Predisposing, precipitating and perpetuating factors. In R. P. Kluft (Ed.), *Childhood antecedents of multiple personality* (pp. 37-64). Washington, DC: American Psychiatric Press.

Breuer, J., & Freud, S. (1895). Studies on hysteria. In J. Strachey (Ed.), *Standard edition* (Vol. 2, 1-335). London: Hogarth Press.

Committee on Sexual Offenses Against Children and Youths. (1984). *Sexual offenses against children in Canada* (Vol. 1 and 2). Ottawa: Suppy and Services Canada.

Coons, P. M. (1985). Children of parents with multiple personality disorder. In R. P. Kluft (Ed.), *Childhood antecedents of multiple personality* (pp. 152-165). Washington, DC: American Psychiatric Press.

Coons, P. M., & Milstein, V. (1984). Rape and post-traumatic stress in multiple personality. *Psychological Reports, 55*, 839-845.

Dell, P. F. (1988). Professional skepticism about multiple personality. *Journal of Nervous and Mental Disease, 176*(9), 528-53.

Diamond, M. J. (1977). Issues and methods for modifying responsivity to hypnosis. *Annals of the New York Academy of Sciences, 296*, 119-128.

Edmunston, W. E. (1977). Body morphology and the capacity for hypnosis. *Annals of the New York Academy of Sciences, 296*, 105-118.

Eliseo, T. S. (1974). The hypnotic induction profile and hypnotic susceptibility. *International Journal of Clinical and Experimental Hypnosis, 22*, 320-326.

Frischholz, E. J. (1985). The relationship among dissociation, hypnosis, and child abuse in the development of multiple personality disorder. In R. P. Kluft (Ed.), *Childhood antecedents of multiple personality* (pp. 100-125). Washington, DC: American Psychiatric Press.

Frischholz, E. J., Lipman, L. S., & Braun, B. G. (1984, September). *Hypnotizability and multiple personality disorders.* Paper presented at the First International Conference on Multiple Personality/Dissociative States, Chicago, IL.

Furst, S. S. (1967). Psychic trauma: A survey. In S. S. Furst (Ed.), *Psychic trauma.* (pp. 3-50). New York: Basic Books.

Greaves, G. B. (1980). Multiple personality: 165 years after Mary Reynolds. *Journal of Nervous and Mental Disease, 168*, 577-596.

Gruenwald, D. (1984). On the nature of multiple personality: Comparisons with hypnosis. *International Journal of Clinical and Experimental Hypnosis, 32,* 170-190.

Gur, R. C., & Gur, R. E. (1974). Handedness, sex and eyedness as moderating variables in the relation between hypnotic susceptibility and functional brain asymmetry. *Journal of Abnormal Psychology, 83,* 635-643.

Harriman, P. (1942). The experimental production of some phenomena of multiple personality. *Journal of Abnormal and Social Psychology, 37,* 244-255.

Harriman, P. (1943). A new approach to multiple personality. *American Journal of Orthopsychiatry, 13,* 638-643.

Hebb, D. O. (1949). *Organization of behavior.* New York: Wiley.

Hebb, D. O. (1980). *Essay on mind.* Hillsdale, NJ: Lawrence Erlbaum Associates.

Hilgard, E. R. (1965). *Hypnotic susceptibility.* New York: Harcourt, Brace, Jovanovich.

Hilgard, E. R. (1977). *Divided consciousness: Multiple controls in human thought and action.* New York: Wiley.

Hilgard, E. R. (1988). "Professional skepticism about multiple personality:" Commentary. *Journal of Nervous and Mental Disease, 176*(9), 532.

Hilgard, J. (1970). *Personality and hypnosis.* Chicago: University of Chicago Press.

Horevitz, R. P., & Braun, B. G. (1984). Are multiple personalities borderline? *Psychiatric Clinics of North America, 7,* 69-88.

Janet, P. (1889). *Automatisme psychologique.* [Psychological Automatism]. Paris: Bailliere.

Janet, P. (1903). *Les obsessions et la psychasthenie* [Obsessions and Psychasthenia] (Vols. 1 and 2). Paris: Felix Alcan.

Janet, P. (1907). *Major symptoms of hysteria.* New York: Macmillan.

Kampman, R. (1976). Hypnotically induced multiple personality. *International Journal of Clinical and Experimental Hypnosis, 24,* 215-227.

Kluft, R. P. (1987). An update on multiple personality disorder. *Hospital and Community Psychiatry, 38,* 363-373.

Kluft, R. P. (1984c). Treatment of multiple personality disorder: A study of 33 cases. *Psychiatric Clinics of North America, 7,* 9-29.

Kluft, R. P. (1984a, October). Age regression in multiple personality patients before and after integration. Paper presented at the annual meeting of the Society for Clinical and Experimental Hypnosis, San Antonio, TX.

Kluft, R. P. (1984b). Multiple personality in childhood. *Psychiatric Clinics of North America, 7,* 121-134.

Kluft, R. P. (1985). The natural history of multiple personality disorder. In R. P. Kluft (Ed.), *Childhood antecedents of multiple personality* (pp. 198-238). Washington, DC: American Psychiatric Press.

Laurence, J. -R. & Perry, C. (1981). The "hidden observer" phenomenon in hypnosis: Some additional findings. *Journal of Abnormal Psychology, 90,* 334-344.

Leavitt, H. (1947). A case of hypnotically produced secondary and tertiary personalities. *Psychoanalytic Review, 34,* 274-295.

London, P. (1965). Developmental experiments in hypnosis. *Journal of Projective Techniques and Personality Assessment, 29,* 189-199.

Lovinger, S. L. (1983). Multiple personality: A theoretical view. *Psychotherapy: Theory, Research and Practice, 20,* 425-434.

Lynn, S. J., Rhue, J. W., & Green, J. P. (1988). Multiple personality and fantasy proneness: Is there an association or disassociation? *British Journal of Experimental and Clinical Hypnosis, 5*(3), 138-142.

Macnamara, J., Govitrikar, V. P., & Doan, B. (1988). Actions, laws, and scientific psychology. *Cognition, 29,* 1-27.

Morgan, A. H. (1969). Decline of hypnotizability with age. Cited in J. Hilgard (1970) *Personality and hypnosis.* Chicago: University of Chicago Press.

Morgan, A. H. (1973). The heritability of hypnotic susceptibility in twins. *Journal of Abnormal Psychology, 82,* 55-61.

Nash, M. R., Lynn, S. J., & Givens, D. L. (1984). Adult hypnotic susceptibility, childhood punishment, and child abuse: A brief communication. *International Journal of Clinical and Experimental Hypnosis, 32,* 6-11.

Nemiah, J. C. (1978). The dynamic bases of psychopathology. In A. M. Nicholi, Jr. (Ed.). *Harvard guide to modern psychiatry* (pp. 147-172). Cambridge, MA: Belknap/Harvard University Press.

Nowlis, D. P. (1968). The child-rearing antecedents of hypnotic susceptibility and of naturally occurring hypnotic-like experience. *International Journal of Clinical and Experimental Hypnosis, 17,* 109-120.

Perry, C., & Walsh, B. (1978). Inconsistencies and anomalies of response as a defining character of hypnosis. *Journal of Abnormal Psychology, 87,* 547-577.

Prince, M. (1890). Some of the revelations of hypnotism. *Boston Medical and Surgical Journal, 122,* 463-467.

Prince, M. (1906). *Dissociation of a personality.* New York: Longmans, Green.

Putnam, F. W. (1985). Dissociation as a response to extreme trauma. In R. P. Kluft, (Ed.), *Childhood antecedents of multiple personality* (pp. 66-97). Washington, DC: American Psychiatric Press.

Putnam, F. W. (1991). Dissociative disorders in children and adolescents: A developmental perspective. *Psychiatric Clinics of North America, 14*(3), 519-531.

Putnam, F. W. (1991). Recent research on multiple personality disorder. *Psychiartric Clinics of North America, 14*(3), 489-502.

Putnam, F. W., Guroff, J. J., Silberman, E. K., Barban, L., & Post, R. M. (1986). The clinical phenomenology of multiple personality disorder: Review of 100 recent cases. *Journal of Clinical Psychiatry, 47,* 285-293.

Rawlings, R. M. (1972). The inheritance of hypnotic amnesia. Paper presented at the meeting of the Australian and New Zealand Society for the Advancement of Science. University of New South Wales, Sydney, Australia.

Ross, C. A., & Norton, G. R. (1989). Differences between men and women with multiple personality disorder. *Hosptial and Community Psychiatry, 40*(2), 186-188.

Ross, C. A., Norton, G. R., & Wozney, K. (1989). Multiple personality disorder: An analysis of 236 cases. *Canadian Journal of Psychiatry, 34*(5), 413-418.

Sarbin, T. R., & Coe, W. C. (1972). *Hypnosis: A social psychological analysis of influence communication.* New York: Holt, Rinehart & Winston.

Schreiber, F. (1973). *Sybil.* Chicago: Henry Regnery.

Spanos, N. P., & Barber, T. X. (1974). Toward a congruence in hypnosis research. *American Psychologist, 29,* 500-511.

Spanos, N. P., Weekes, J. R., & Bertrand, L. D. (1985). Multiple personality: A social psychological perspective. *Journal of Abnormal Psychology, 94,* 362-376.

Spiegel, H. (1974). *Manual for the hypnotic induction profile.* New York: Soni Medica.

Spiegel, H. (1977). The hypnotic induction profile (HIP): A review of its development. *Annals of the New York Academy of Sciences, 296,* 129-142.

Spiegel, H., Aronson, M., Fleiss, L., & Haber, J. (1976). A psychometric analysis of the Hypnotic Induction Profile. *International Journal of Clinical and Experimental Hypnosis, 24,* 300-315.

Spiegel, H., & Spiegel, D. (1978). *Trance and treatment: Clinical uses of hypnosis.* New York: Basic Books.

Stern, C. R. (1984). The etiology of multiple personalities. *Psychiatric Clinics of North America, 7,* 149-160.

Stukat, K. G. (1958). *Suggestibility: A factorial and experimental analysis.* Stockholm: Almqvist and Wiksell.

Sutcliffe, J. P. (1961). "Credulous" and "skeptical" views of hypnotic phenomena: Experiments on esthesia, hallucination, and delusion. *Journal of Abnormal and Social Psychology, 62,* 189-200.

Switras, J. E. (1974). A comparison of the eye roll test for hypnotizability and the Stanford Hypnotic Susceptibility Scale: Form A. *Journal of Clinical Hypnosis, 17,* 54-55.

Taylor, W., & Martin, M. (1944). Multiple personality. *Journal of Abnormal and Social Psychology, 39,* 281-300.

Wheeler, W., Reiss, H. T., Wolff, E., Grupsmith, E., & Mordkoff, A. M. (1974). Eye-roll and hypnotic susceptibility. *International Journal of Clinical and*

Experimental Hypnosis, 22, 327-334.

Wilbur, C. B. (1984). Multiple personality and child abuse. *Psychiatric Clinics of North America, 7,* 3-8.

Young, W. C. (1988). Observations on fantasy in the formation of multiple personality disorder. *Dissociation: Progress in the Dissociative Disorders, 1*(3), 13-20.

3
Morton Prince and B. C. A.: A Historical Footnote on the Confrontation Between Dissociation Theory and Freudian Psychology in a Case of Multiple Personality

John Barresi
Dalhousie University

When Sigmund Freud made his triumphant debut in North America with his Clark University lectures of September, 1909, the state of abnormal psychology in America was dominated by the French school of psychopathology. The leader of this school, Pierre Janet, had already visited America on several occasions and had recently completed a course of lectures at Harvard University. Janet's concepts of "dissociation," "subconscious," and "fixed ideas" pervaded American thought. The French masters—Ribot, Binet, and Janet—had a number of their works already published in English when the first sampling of Freud's papers, mostly on hysteria, were translated by Brill in 1909 (Freud, 1909). His most important work, *The Interpretation of Dreams*, was not to be published in English until

1913. Yet, because Freud's lectures "On the Origin and Development of Psychoanalysis" had been translated into English and published in the *American Journal of Psychology* early in 1910 (Freud, 1910), and because several of his most important English-speaking students, including Ernest Jones and A. A. Brill, were now in North America, Freud's psychoanalysis began to spread. After a period of intense conflict, it soon dominated abnormal psychology in America. Janet and the French school became no more than a footnote in the prehistory of the psychoanalytic movement.

History has a way of rewriting (or righting) itself however, particularly when concepts, such as those developed by the French school, capture a reality that their replacements are not able to handle. Hence, after several generations dominated by the psychoanalytic perspective, we must try to reconstruct a psychology of dissociative disorders when the original source material of this alternative psychology has been "repressed" in our culture's memory and when its substitute finds it difficult even to recognize the original phenomena of such disorders—for instance, hypnotic dissociative states and multiple personality. Therefore, a historical introduction to some of the work of a leader of this opponent view to Freud's, that of Morton Prince, the leading representative of French psychopathology in America, and of his early encounter with the onslaught of psychoanalysis, might help us to see the nature of the original conflict that still needs to be resolved between these two great approaches to abnormal psychology.

As often happens in historical quirks of fate, while Freud, Jung and Ferenczi were in Worcester, Massachusetts, describing the wonders of the "unconscious" and of "psychoanalysis," Morton Prince was still in Europe after giving a talk at the Sixth International Congress of Psychology in Geneva, where the major theme was the subconscious and where Janet, the originator of this concept, had given the keynote address. At the congress, Janet explained the "subconscious" as an empirical, clinical concept and distinguished it from the "unconscious," which he viewed as a philosophical concept.

Dr. Morton Prince, who was then a Professor of Nervous Diseases at Tufts Medical School, spoke on his new concept—the "co-conscious." In a published symposium on the subconscious, Prince (1907) had introduced the concept "co-conscious" to replace "subconscious" for conscious mental activities, outside of the consciousness of what was then termed the "personal consciousness," and which we would now, after Freud, probably call the "ego." That such co-conscious mental activities were indeed a reality was evidenced by the existence of a variety of mental states accessible through hypnosis, automatic writing, crystal gazing, and other dissociative methodological techniques. Probably not the least important factor leading Prince to make his distinction between co-conscious mental events and other "physiological" versions of subconscious or unconscious mentation was that he had an acquaintance with a personality, "Sally Beauchamp," who claimed to be co-conscious while another personality of the Beauchamp "family" was in charge of the "personal consciousness". Prince had written up this multiple personality case several times already, but it was his 1906 book, *The Dissociation of a Personality*, that had immortalized this personality disorder by bringing it in a popular form to the general public, while at the same time introducing the wonders of psychotherapeutics in the form of hypnotic suggestion and the resynthesis of this fissioned personality.

In the same year, 1906, Prince founded the *Journal of Abnormal Psychology*, which played an important role in the diffusion of psychoanalysis to the English-speaking world and was the main center for the confrontation of Freud's theories with his French competitors' theories. In its first issue, a paper by J. J. Putnam, a professor of neurology at Harvard and eventually one of the leading converts to the Freudian fold, appeared in the *Journal* (Putnam, 1906), describing psychoanalysis and giving it a tentative negative evaluation. That paper was written as a substitute for one by Freud himself, who refused Prince's offer to publish an article by him. Some of Jung's work on associations also appeared in the first volume and, not surprisingly, the lead article of the *Journal* was written by Pierre Janet. This journal became a forum for discussion of psychoanalysis and carried in single issues amazingly brutal statements in articles, replies to articles, conference proceedings, and so forth, from both sides of the controversy. The *Journal* makes a living reality of the conflict for anyone who reads it from its inception to 1921 when Ernest Jones resigned his post as assistant editor, which he held from 1910, and the Journal became the *Journal of Abnormal and Social Psychology.* Shortly thereafter the *Journal* was given by Prince to the American Psychological Association to become one of its main organs.

There are a number of fascinating stories that might be told from the *Journal's* pages about the early years of the rise of psychoanalysis and the decline of dissociation theory, and of Prince's role in these developments. However, in this chapter, I focus our attention on a single patient of Prince's during this important period of his confrontation with psychoanalysis. B. C. A. is the second case of multiple personality that he treated. From a scientific point of view, Prince felt that this case was more important than the earlier Beauchamp case, and I quite agree with him. He studied B. C. A. more closely, performing experiments and generating detailed case material. The patient herself, who developed a strong interest in abnormal psychology, contributed enormously to this work, including two remarkable autobiographies written by two of her personalities and published in the *Journal of Abnormal Psychology* (B. C. A, 1908, 1908/1909). These have yet to be matched by anything in the literature on multiple personality. Furthermore, as I have discovered by studying the Prince papers at the Francis A. Countway Library at Harvard, the patient, whose name is Nellie Parsons Bean, became deeply involved in Prince's research, probably in part as a transference phenomenon. (Kenny, 1986, in his interesting study of multiple personality as a sociocultural phenomenon, seems to have been the first to reveal B. C. A.'s identity.) She learned shorthand and typed out session notes and Prince's manuscripts, as well as commenting on them. She also wrote out her own dreams and interpreted them. It seems that she planned to write a book that would include her autobiographies, as well as other material, in particular her dreams. Apparently nothing came of it, except indirectly in Prince's work. Prince formally thanked Mrs. William G. Bean in the preface of his 1914 book, *The Unconscious,* for her "great assistance . . . in many ways." In addition to thanking her for her practical assistance, he also stated that her "unusually extensive acquaintance with the phenomena has been of great value" (p. xii). When Prince finally published the psychogenesis of her case in 1919, he had inspected her autobiographies and letters and other case material and "found that when the pieces of evidence were pieced together they allowed of only one conclusion, namely, that which the subject herself in the main reached independently as the facts were laid bare and brought into the field of her consciousness . . ." (Prince, 1914/1921, p.553). As we shall see shortly, Nellie Bean, in her several personalities—but especially as the co-conscious, B—worked out a theory of the ontogenesis of her dissociation of personality, based on an analysis of those memories of past events available to introspective analysis. Morton Prince merely organized this material, and provided a more detailed articulation of it, in his own psychogenesis of the case.

Since my visit to Boston to study the Prince collection with a particular focus on the B. C. A. material, I have collated t ie pieces of evidence that remained in this collection and have been able to look over the shoulder of Prince in his treatment of and research with Nellie Bean. In the main, I agree with Prince's statement that she contributed enormously to his understanding of her case. However, both Mrs. Bean and Prince contributed to our misunderstanding of this case as well, because, by suppressing sexual content, they left her case description less than fully disclosed. Had this censorship occurred at another time and place, it might not have mattered as much, but it was at this very time that Freud's sexual theories were causing the greatest difficulties in assimilating psychoanalytic thought. Hence, Prince's reserve in publishing this material more fully, even though based on Mrs. Bean's desires, or insistence (see,

his letter to J. J. Putnam, Oct. 21, 1910 [Hale, 1971, pp. 321-322]),
did little to demonstrate that he could evaluate fairly Freud's sexual
hypotheses when they seemed to apply to his own cases. Indeed, as
can be seen later in this chapter (pp. 29 ff.), Prince's quasi-
experimental study of B. C. A.'s dreams published in 1910, shortly
after Freud's visit, raised havoc in the Freudian camp, eliciting
critiques by both Jones and Jung. Prince's response to his assistant
editor's critique in the *Journal* was one of the earliest claims that
psychoanalysis appeared less as a scientific theory than as a messianic
movement.

However, this public confrontation between Prince and
psychoanalysis is not the major focus of the present chapter. My
intention is to look closely at the published and unpublished material
involving the B. C. A. case during this critical period, when the scope
and importance of Freudian psychology was just becoming
recognized. In this one case, we can see how a dissociation theorist
and his patient responded to this new psychology. In addition, the
case itself provides great insight into the relationship between
repression and dissociation in the psychogenesis of a multiple
personality. In the next section, I present Nellie Bean's dissociation
of personality as much as possible in her own words as she developed
insight into it from one or another of her personalities; thus, I
concentrate on the original letters rather than on the conclusions
presented in the autobiographies. This presentation is followed by
a theoretical account of the case that draws heavily on other
unpublished documents in the Prince collection, as well as on the
published material. In the following section, I present a historical
description of the research that Nellie Bean and Morton Prince
pursued, with a particular focus on the dream research that produced
the major confrontation between Prince and the Freudians. This
period also provides insight into Nellie Bean's further development
after the synthesis of her several personalities. I conclude with some
general observations on the history of the conflict between these two
schools of abnormal psychology in an attempt to rectify some of the

errors caused by Freud's almost demonic influence on its development to the exclusion of non-Freudians of the stature of Janet and Prince.

NELLIE PARSONS BEAN (A.K.A. B. C. A.)

When Nellie Parsons Bean came to Morton Prince for help in December 1906, she was in a very bad state. As Prince described it: "[She] presented the ordinary picture of so-called neurasthenia, characterized by persistent fatigue and the usual somatic symptoms, and by moral doubts and scruples" (B. C. A., 1908, p. 204). She was the widow of a railroad executive, William G. Bean, who had died on June 29, 1905, 4 years after his first cerebral hemorrhage. For almost a year after his death, she was depressed but courageous; she worked hard on her business affairs and acted responsibly toward her teenage son, Robert, as well as toward her mother and two unmarried sisters. However, because nervous exhaustion developed, her doctor sent her to a sanatorium, Nashua, for a rest cure. The rest did not succeed; instead, her situation worsened. At first she seemed to get better, though she exhibited an almost manic recovery from her earlier state. But then something happened that changed her—it made her into an entirely new personality, who Prince later called B. She was no longer the widow who constantly wore black, but a gay young 18- or 19-year-old unmarried woman who no longer cared about any of the responsibilities that wore down Mrs. Bean. This personality, which first appeared after a young drug addict, Mr. Hopkins, kissed Mrs. Bean on July 26, 1906, disappeared and was replaced by a second personality, named A, a month later when a second shock involving Mr. Hopkins and money affairs occurred. This second personality was an exaggerated version of the responsible, but seriously ill, Mrs. Bean. During the fall of 1906, the two personalities alternated a number of times, but because they shared memories to a great extent, neither personality was clear about her status as a shattered piece of the original Mrs. Bean who went to Nashua.

Apparently, however, Dr. Cummings, her general practitioner, realized that something strange had happened, for he suggested in October of 1906 that she see Dr. Prince, and she finally did, as A, in December.

Not long after she came under Prince's care, an amnestic barrier was created between the two personalities. Prince, who was using hypnosis on A to relieve her of some of her symptoms, found her switched to the personality B while A was in a hypnotic state. He realized then that she was a multiple personality. After this encounter, all subsequent switches between the two personalities involved amnesia for A of B's alternating activities, though she retained memory for most of B's activities prior to this time. For B, her status as a co-conscious, as well as alternating personality became clearer at this time. As Prince described it:

Complex A had no memory for complex B, but the latter not only had full knowledge of A, but persisted co-consciously when A was present. B was therefore both an alternating and a co-conscious state. Besides differences in memory, A and B manifested distinct and marked different characteristics, which included moods, tastes, points of view, habits of thought, and controlling ideas. In place, for instance, of depression, fatigue, and moral doubts and scruples of A, B manifested rather a condition of exaltation, and complete freedom from neurasthenia and its accompanying obsessional ideas. With the appearance of B it was recognized that both states were phases of a dissociated personality, and neither represented the normal complete personality. After prolonged study, this latter normal state was obtained in hypnosis, and, on being waked up, a personality was found which possessed the combined memories of A and B and was free from the pathological stigmata which respectively characterized each. This normal person is spoken of as C. The normal C had, therefore, split into two systems of complexes or personalities, A and B (B. C. A., 1908, pp. 240-241).

Actually, the fusion of A and B into C was much more difficult than Prince indicated. Although he expanded on this point in his introduction to the second autobiography, he never made clear the troubles he had in finally obtaining a fusion that would persist for more than a few days or weeks. It seems to me that progress was made in forming stronger fusions only as Nellie herself, in all of her personalities, came to appreciate the direction in which fusion lay—in other words, what kind of balance of A and B characteristics would be most adaptive to her current and future life.

Because the role that hypnosis plays in forming multiple personalities is still very much an issue that concerns us, it is important to be clear about the status of the A and B complexes of Nellie before Prince's hypnosis created an amnestic barrier. Were A and B already different personalities before this dissociation of memories, or not? If episodic memory of one's past life is used as the diagnostic criterion, then Nellie might not be considered a multiple personality until Prince hypnotized her and B appeared. Although, because she did have amnesia for a short period following the traumatic incident that seems to have divided the original personality into A and B, even using this criterion sensitively, she might be classified as a multiple personality. If multiple personality is defined in terms of mutually incompatible and distinctive mood and motivational complexes that appear and disappear suddenly, each occurring for an extended period of time and alternating with the other, then Nellie was a multiple personality before the amnestic barrier appeared. But even here it is possible to question the diagnosis and difficult to separate it in the present case from manic-depressive disorder until more is known about the details of the case.

I next present the details that support the diagnosis of multiple personality through letters written by the patient herself, in her several personalities, to Prince after she came under his care in December 1906. It may help the reader to refer to the chronology in the appendix to this chapter in order to keep track of the incidents in the case. By viewing the case through the points of view of Nellie's several personalities, it is hoped that the reader will gain greater insight into multiple personality disorder (MPD) than if I merely described the case in my own words.

In a letter that Nellie wrote on August 9, 1907 in her A state, but didn't mail, and that later formed part of the basis of C's autobiography, she wrote what she was like the previous summer when the B complex and personality first appeared:

As B I was very happy, lively and light-hearted; ready to do anything for pleasure—ride on the electrics, walk in the woods, or a long walk anywhere, canoeing—I was ready for anything; and enthusiastic. I felt perfectly well, more vigorous than ever in my life before. I had no headache, never felt tired. I think it would express it to say I was filled with the "joy of life." The whole world looked different to me. I seemed more alive. I realized the beauty of the world keenly—the blue of the sky, the clouds, the green of the woods, the sound of the wind in the pines all filled me with a sort of ecstasy. It was so beautiful to me—life seemed so good. As far as that went it was all right and much as I used to be before Mr. Bean was ill and before I had so much trouble, but there were other things which were not all right and not like me. I seemed to lose all sense of responsibility; to my son [Robert], to my mother and sisters, to my business affairs. I became absolutely indifferent. . . . It seems to me that I was like B all that time though I place her coming at a certain moment later than the time I am describing. I certainly was not myself. I certainly was not A. I was not yet what we call B. What was I? I was dominated by what came to be a "fixed idea"—I must help Mr. H. I could save him and I must. Nothing else influenced me or carried any weight . . ..

Then came the time when I was wholly B [July, 26, 1906]. Everything but my own pleasure was cast to the winds. I felt and acted like a girl of eighteen and I know that I looked years younger than I do now.

But all this time I was conscious of an undercurrent of disapproval—as I look at it now I was living a double mental life—B ruling my life—A subconscious to her. I think there were two trains of thought much of the time and I seemed to myself to be two persons. I can remember of saying so many times—but that had seemed so for a year or two—more than that, three or four years . . . .

When in Sept. [1906] I became wholly A—B dropped out of sight entirely and I was like a person who wakes from a dream or delirium. I don't mean that it seemed unreal to me or that, at first, I regretted it but I was numbed with the shock of my discovery and suddenly realized that I had know[n] it would be so all the time. I could not believe I had been so wholly mistaken and deceived—or would not—that is nearer right— and I also realized how strangely I had acted—and what my friends would say if they knew etc etc. I don't think I can describe the time from the middle of Sept to the middle of Dec. [1906] very clearly. I was submerged in a sea of . . ., humiliation, regret. I realized more and more clearly how strange I had been—how unlike myself . . . . I burn with humiliated pride now when I think of the things I did, I shall never understand why and it seems very wrong and cruel that such a thing should happen to me . . . . (letter, Aug.9, 1907, Bean, 1907-1913)

A claimed that it was she who behaved oddly and was confused in the fall of 1906 before Prince started treating her in December. In an undated note, B gave a somewhat different interpretation:

C disappears at time of shock [the kiss by Mr. Hopkins on July 26, 1906] leaving A and B. A being subconscious. B stays till Sept, but B has her moods—grave as well as gay. B came to Boston and stayed that time—it was B in this mood all through Sept. A did not come till Oct. Then A and B's grave mood alternated till sometime in Nov. A began to come then but A has so many moods—the A who went to Dr. P. in Dec. was not as she is now. B happy./BI sad [or B/A if B1 sad = A]. (undated note, Bean, 1907-1913)

What one sees in the divergence of these two descriptions is that when there are no clear amnestic boundaries to separate personality states, the subject, herself in either of her alternative ego-states, is unsure how to evaluate changes of mood from changes of ego-state.

And it may be that the personality states themselves slide gradually from one to the other. Indeed, for final fusion it seems that the mutual approach of the ego-states might be a necessity.

Although there is some confusion between moods and ego-states when global amnesia is not involved, I believe that Prince was right to assume that alternating personalities occurred in this case before the amnestic boundary between them was formed. Furthermore, it was a particular incident, the kiss of Mr. Hopkins, that was the precipitating cause of the first appearance of B as a separate personality and later after another shock also involving Mr. Hopkins, that A appeared. A referred to these events in one of her earliest letters:

I place the date of this change in me as July 26 [1906] I could tell you almost the minute it came. I understand some things about this better than you think, perhaps, but have not reached the place where I can discuss it from a scientific point of view. It is too intensely personal . . . Just a line more. It seems to me, as I think over what you said to me yesterday, that the shock of finding what Mr. H_ really is changed me again [in Sept. 1906]—made me as I was when you first saw me, and as I am now. Perhaps I am not really myself now any more than during the time I forget. Is that possible? These two selves seem extreme and neither one is as I used to be. There must be a straight thread through this tangle—if we can only find it (letter, June 8, 1907, Bean, 1907-1913)

It was not long after this letter that Prince was able to synthesize the first C in hypnosis (on June 13 or 14, 1907). To return to the incident on July 17, 1907, A wrote in another letter: "I wish you would ask C if she knows exactly what happened about eight o'clock in the evening on the twenty sixth of last July. It seems to me that is the time all this came about." A apparently had amnesia for this event or at least for what happened shortly thereafter (cf. Prince, 1914/1921, p. 509). B wrote on October 10, 1907, "You have no idea how that word (kiss) makes A writhe—and she doesn't know anything of all that followed." Three days later, A wrote:

You have asked me if I know what changes me to B. I don't know, always, but often I lose myself from experiencing a certain emotion. I lose myself many times when I do not have this emotion but always when I do. Now this emotion I never experienced until last year and a half—in fact, it came when B came; so I have always thought that she was governed by it and that is why I am so afraid of her; but she disclaims any knowledge of it; says she knows nothing about it and indeed she says my thoughts on that subject are like a foreign language to her—she does not know what they mean. It is very queer. B has been writing to me; using my hand to answer my thoughts. It is very curious and I can't help being interested in spite of the fact that it rather frightens me. Does this explanation make things any clearer and easier? (letter, Oct.13, 1907, Bean, 1907-1913)

It was at about this time that she was seeing another man and thinking about marrying him. He was rather a "stick-in-the-mud," as Prince apparently called him. B wrote on November 7, 1907:

Send for A. [She is] thinking of getting married—ridiculous. She doesn't really care anything about him. [She plans to] tell him about Mr. Hopkins silly thing! as if that made any difference.—Is she the only woman who ever kissed any man except her husband and is kissing a crime? and she didn't do it anyway—I did it—myself and it never hurt me a bit—I am glad of it—and she didn't have a husband anyway . . .. (letter, Nov.7, 1907, Bean, 1907-1913)

Another undated letter by B and probably written during the fall of 1907 is also of interest in this context:

Something is happening to me Dr. Prince. I don't know what it is, but I am frightened. I am afraid I am going to be a woman just like A and C. I don't want to, Dr. Prince, I can't. I want to be just what I always have been—just "B", free as the wind, no body, no soul, no heart. I don't want to love people for if one loves one must suffer—that is what it means to be a woman—to love and suffer. I never felt so strangely, I hardly know what it is—it is what C calls the "heartache" I guess—and I can't have it, I won't. Please help me not to feel anything . . .. B (letter, undated, Bean, 1907-1913).

A did not end up marrying this man. Later in November, Prince and Mrs. Bean went to New York to do an experiment with Peterson using psychogalvanic techniques to demonstrate the physiological effects of co-conscious knowledge (Prince & Peterson, 1908). During this trip a new C synthesis was formed—more complete than the earlier C—though also not long lasting—she fell back to the earlier C and alternated still with B. Apparently the difference in the two C's dealt with the kissing incident, which the new C had more detailed memory of; she also remembered better her letters to Mr. Hopkins written in the B personality (letter, November 27, 1907). A seemed to drop out of the picture at this point, only making reappearances at times of deep depression or anxiety. But it was not until May of 1908, when another Mrs. Bean spontaneously appeared as B was thinking about the kissing incident at Nashua, that the final synthesis was formed. This new Mrs. Bean remembered nothing after the kissing incident, when the shock of this experience presumably formed B as an alternating personality with the subsequent A phase. This Mrs. Bean of Nashua was the original personality which had ceased to exist after the shock of the kiss, and whose return signaled the restoration of Nellie Bean to a fusible state once memory for the missing time was made available to her. From the time of her disappearance on July 26, 1906, to the time of her return on May 21, 1908, Nellie Bean alternated among a variety of incomplete, fissioned, and partially fused personalities, predominantly those of A and B.

It should be apparent that it is a sexual emotion that A talks about in her preceding letter, that B knows nothing about—yet fears she will in her letter—and that Nellie Bean first experienced at the time of the kiss. But the kissing incident probably also generated anger, fear, guilt, disgust, remorse, and so forth. These conflicting emotions burst her apart, and in a moment she was B who thought the kiss a "lark," only later to switch to A in September, 1906, when Mr. Hopkins provided another shock by disappointing her in money affairs. Prince's psychogenesis describes these psychic traumas rather extensively, as does B's published autobiography, though it leaves out the particulars related to the so-called "X affect"—or in other words the sexual emotion (Prince, 1914/1921, pp. 545-633; B.C.A., 1908, 1908-1909).

I turn now to Nellie Bean's theorizing about the prehistory of the A and B personalities, which to me is the most fascinating and instructive part of this case history, particularly in regard to the relationship between repression and dissociation. The very first theory relates directly to this issue. It was put forward by A a few days after the first C was synthesized. On June 20, 1907, or so A wrote:

Is there not danger in waking up another one: C—Have you any theory as to how B came into Existence. Could B be a part of myself which has long been suppressed? She seems a good deal as I used to be before Mr. Bean was ill, before I had any trouble. After that time I was never happy—never had any but anxious apprehensive thoughts, but rebelled bitterly, internally against the inevitable. I could not bear to think that life was over for me, and that I must give up all that made it sweet, and I did not want to do but I made myself do then because I had sworn myself never to fail Mr. Bean in any way again [sic]. I felt that perhaps I had and that I might be somewhat to blame for his illness, so I did my best but I suffered a great deal and life was extremely hard for me and all the time it was a battle with myself. This was about 6 years ago. Then when everything was over and I was physically better could it be possible that this long suppressed part of me—the part that longed so to be gay and happy and light hearted—came to life, so to speak, and dominated me? It seems something like that to me. Then the same old battle went on only the strength was on the other side. Would those years of suppression allow for B's seeming younger? (letter, June 20, 1907, Bean, 1907-1913).

A year later, when her son, Robert, had failed from Andover, Nellie was so distressed that she went to bed wishing to forget her own name—Bean—and literally did (see, Prince, 1914/1921, pp. 74ff, 512ff, who described this event). On May 17, 1908, only a week or so before her final synthesis, C wrote about this event:

I have a theory of my own about all this and am going to write it out for you (sometime). You know I do not read German so I can't read Freud, but from what I have been able to learn of his theory of suppressed ideas it is exactly the same as the explanation which I have applied to me [sic] own case. I have here a paper which "B" wrote a long time ago, before I had ever heard of Freud , in which she advances the same theory in explanation of her existence. It is rather queer, is it not? (letter, May 17, 1908, Bean, 1907-1913)

I will get to the letter by B that I think is referred to in the preceding one shortly, but first an earlier theory by B written in an August 4th letter is worth considering:

As you are on the hunt for a "real person" and I can't seem to persuade you that I am that individual let me give you a new theory. I think I am the real one only somewhat changed. In my mind it is like this: go back 6 years, before Mr. Bean's illness, for that was when the foundation for all this trouble was laid, say that the original personality had 2 parts, A and B—not the A and B you know, but the two elements in her character—and that B was the stronger, more natural element. She was naturally very lighthearted and happy, buoyant. The day Mr. Bean was taken ill she received a terrible shock. He had a cerebral hemorrhage. Then she began to change, very slowly—you know something of the four years that followed. She rebelled bitterly, she could not have it so and it was so, no one knew what his illness was and she bent every energy to

*conceal his true condition. She blamed herself for it and after a time she
began to have that sense of being double. More than anything else she
wanted to be happy. She saw all happiness going and she could not let it
go—it must not—she would be happy and couldn't. It was a fight with
herself all the time. We were A and B then just as much as we are now—
A doing all that a devoted conscientious wife could do, determined that
her husband should never miss anything of love or care, and B rebelling
against it all, not willing to give up her youth—longing for pleasure, and
above all for happiness. To be happy—that was always the cry—and it
was not possible.*

 *Then after Mr. Bean's death B—the original B you know—sank
completely out of sight and she was all A,—not this A—but the original
A—. I am afraid I don't make this very clear. This old A [pencil note
by Prince—"i.e. C"] was different from A now for though she was sad,
and worn and ill, she still had plenty of courage. She did not want to
die, she expected to live on in just the same way, and she worked herself
nearly to death over business affairs and got so ill she was sent away to
that sanitarium. Then after a little she began to get better and she became
something I will call C—not your C, I don't know anything about her—
but sort of a combination of the A and B I am talking about. I think
she was natural enough at that time only shaken from the long nervous
strain, the self-reproach, the grief etc.—But there came a time when
something happened to her [the kiss and its consequences]—you know—
and she did change completely and you can never get that old original
B, for she does not exist. I came, but I am not exactly like the old B—I
have lost something—and this A is not exactly like the old A—we are
both quite different though we represent the same elements. But beside
all this there is a new element which is, I think, a part of the real
personality. This new element don't mix with either of us—I don't know
what it is—and A can't bear it—it changes her to me. We are all shaken
apart like the pieces of glass in a kaleidoscope can you ever get the pieces
back in the original pattern? You see I know all that A thinks but I do
not feel her emotions. . . . (letter, Aug. 4, 1907, Bean, 1907-1913)*

The new element that B speaks of here is, of course, the sexual element, which being aroused in Mrs. Bean of Nashua, led to her fissioning into two personalities, one for whom sexuality did not exist at all (i.e., B), and one for whom it was abhorrent (i.e., A). B's further investigation into this new sexual element led to a deeper understanding of her origins. In a letter that was probably written in October 1907, and referred to by C earlier, B discussed this theory:

Time division marriage. shock. unhappy. will call that one X [as the original personality] to avoid confusion.

After marriage we began to pull different ways. I can't make it very clear—the division was nebulous but I think I am now made up of all the impulses which began to come then. I was not an I then you know but to understand what I write you will have to call me so. I remember them now as my thoughts but at that time had never thought of myself as a "self".

You know, Dr. P_ I don't understand some things very well. I know the condition; I know, in a way, what the words mean, but the thoughts which fill A with such horror and break her up so—and they break C [an early incomplete synthesis] up too—I do not really understand.

I know such things are not spoken of tho I can hardly see why— but anyway A or X, shrank from the relation of marriage. Perhaps I ought not to tell you this—it may make lots of trouble when A and C find it out but I do think that the whole trouble came from that.

I don't know why she felt so—it was nothing about Mr. B. don't think that. He was a man out of a thousand—a man any woman might be proud of—and X was very proud of him—of his success in his business, . . . but she did not really what is called—love—him. And someway that shrinking became part of the system of thought we are calling 'me'(B).

After Robert came she was happier in him but very frail in health. I have already written you something of that time. Then we came to W[inchester] about 12 years ago. She was much happier for a while and in better health, and I don't think there was much division—only that same shrinking from the obligations of marriage and accusing herself because of it.

Then came Mr. B's illness more than six years ago; and with that all this undercurrent seemed to become synthesized and a true division took place: not that I was an I even then but there was a double train of thought—she, X or A, is conscious of that, you know. All that shrinking became intensified—she suffered very much—and this internal rebellion increased more and more, and also the intensity of her self-reproach. As Mr. B's mind became slightly affected it was worse and . . . she used to long to die.

I think the rebellion was myself Dr. P. but A [she means X] knew. Then after his death she thought she had killed him you know.

I think all this division springs from that one cause—first because she had no feeling of that kind and now because she has. So you see, it seems to me that I was there, as a seperate [sic] train of thought, from the time of her marriage—pulling a different way all the time from the way she had to go and not wanting to live the life she had to live, but I really came as a self at Nashua. I ruled A for weeks before I came [there was a period before the kiss when the moods and behaviors later associated with B dominated Mrs. Bean, but not as a separate personality]— she can't understand about that time, she was so well and strong and happy—but it was I. She has told you about that [cf. the August 9 letter and C's autobiography, 1908-1909], and these thoughts and impulses and acts were mine not hers.

A good deal of it is so mixed up I can't make it out myself. A [Mrs. Bean at Nashua], as herself, began to feel differently about that time and so she thinks I feel that way, but I don't feel anything, you know—and because I like to talk to the men I know better than to the women, she thinks that is the reason. I like the men better because they talk about more interesting things. A likes to talk to them best too. Why should she think I mustn't? But that is one reason she worries so about the time I am here.

It is awfully mixed up—the shock that brought me as a personality woke that feeling in A [Mrs. Bean of Nashua now converted to A], and so she [A] thinks that feeling belongs to me, but it doesn't, I don't know anything about it except what she thinks . . ..

I did like Mr. H_ Dr. Prince, better than I ever liked any man but I never wanted to marry him. I wouldn't marry anyone for the world.
  As ever, B
(letter, undated, Bean, 1907-1913)

This critical letter seems not to have been mailed to Prince—he obtained it at a later date; however, I believe that A's letter of October 13th, mentioned earlier, indirectly refers to it. On November 13th, B had begun to write her autobiography, which was published a year later and which she didn't finish until just about the time of the final C synthesis in the spring. But B's insight into the case went even further, for in one more theoretical letter, on Nov. 28th, she foresaw the final synthesis:

I am here once more—I hope you don't mind. Poor A has been here too and I followed her. The C you got this time was not quite right—as she wrote you. I call her the magic lantern C because her memories are like pictures. She has emotions also and A came. A longed to speak to you—she cried when she thought of you—but she is sure you are tired of trying to make her well. She felt pretty bad, of course, and after a while I came.

  Now I have a theory about all this: I suppose you will laugh at it but it seems sensible to me.

  I think the real one, the one you are hunting after, is that lost creature whom I once saw here and who came once at your office [Mrs. Bean of Nashua]. I don't know how you can get her or what you can do to restore her memories - perhaps she can never have them—but I think she is the one, and that she is like the C you got in New York, only the New York C is too much mixed up with me to stay. I think the real one won't know anything about me, and C does you know.

  My theory is this. I think that long ago—twenty years, you know, at the time of that shock [i.e., the sexual act with her husband]—I became "split off" from the main personality (is that right?) and that I dropped into the subconscious region—wherever that is—I disappeared; and I was

*nineteen years old. Then a shock of something the same nature brought
me back and, as I had had no independent life—now don't laugh—I
was still nineteen. That is why that affair with Mr. H. seemed all right
and why I was so well and gay and happy—as a girl of nineteen would
be. Do you see how I reason it?*

*Now I am quite different from what I was a year ago. You see that,
do you not? My point of view is different—I am much older.*

*Now all those twenty years A, (or whoever she was) knew nothing
about me and when you get the real one she will know nothing about
me. Do I make my idea clear?*

*But whoever you get, I shall be there just the same, Dr. Prince,
always and forever. As a subconsciousness I shall always exist (Oh, dear.
It's so hard for me to write this(?)) and even if you get the real personality,
well and strong, I know I shall always be able to communicate with you.
I know it, and if I can prove it we can have some interesting experiments,
can't we? Perhaps everyone has a subconsciousness if we only knew about
it. I am going to try and go away now and get C back because I think
you would rather have her here, but I don't believe I can get her. This
an awfully long letter. I hope it won't bother you.   As ever   B"*
(letter, Nov.28, 1907, Bean 1907-1913)

As usual, B was right, for the final synthesis was based on the
Mrs. Bean of Nashua who knew nothing about her. Furthermore,
even after the final synthesis, B's existence didn't terminate, for she
was still accessible during hypnosis and, as late as 1912, there are
session notes with experiments on the subconscious involving *b*, the
hypnotic version of B.

One of these session notes is particularly interesting. In July,
1911, when Prince was apparently working on his psychogenesis of
the case, he interrogated the hypnotic state *b* about the critically
important undated letter described earlier, trying to trace back *b*'s
knowledge of sexual experiences and of her origin, even further than
before marriage. Her responses were made in automatic writing—
the most intriguing of which has a figure of overlapping circles with

words in them. Unfortunately, I cannot make much sense of what she wrote, and it is not clear whether Prince got much out of it either, other than her verification of what was said in the letter. But what is important here is that Prince did try to trace B's origin to possible earlier causes of the repression of sexual motives and to the original inciting cause of this dissociation. It may be that Prince's dissociative techniques were too crude to solve this puzzle. When repression is very strong, it may be that the inhibition of episodic memories makes them inaccessible to dissociative techniques and that only long term free-associative interviews (or psychoanalysis) would finally uncover the material. I am unsure about this issue, but do think it is an empirical one worth investigating. However, it also appears that some material is easier to access through dissociative techniques than through free-association, and it is suggested by Kluft (this volume) that treatment of MPD using traditional psychoanalytic therapy is less effective than therapy using the dissociative hypnotic method. It may be that the relative effectiveness of the two methods is the surest sign of the real differences between amnesia due to traumatic dissociation and amnesia due to ego defense and repression. At any rate, the dream material that I discuss shortly hereafter is at least suggestive of the limits of dissociative interview techniques in interpreting dreams.

Prince's own theoretical interpretation of the case (Prince, 1919, 1914/1921) relied heavily on Nellie Bean's two autobiographies and on the letters presented herein. As a result, his interpretation begins with Nellie's marriage and ends with the personality synthesis of Mrs. Bean of Nashua in May, 1908, and is fundamentally a restatement of Nellie Bean's own interpretation. In the next two sections, I present an account that extends beyond these self-conscious narratives of the patient. I consider earlier events in a theoretical account of the dissociation of personality in the next section. In the following section I give a historical account that describes the period subsequent to Nellie's synthesis in 1908.

A THEORETICAL ANALYSIS OF THE MULTIPLE PERSONALITY DISSOCIATION OF NELLIE PARSONS BEAN

Both Nellie Bean, in her several personalities, and Morton Prince agreed in assigning the occurrent cause of her dissociation of personality as the kiss by Mr. Hopkins on July 26, 1906. I agree with this determination. Before that event, Nellie at Nashua seemed to express two opponent complexes of personality traits—the grieving widow, and the playful unattached girl—but they had appeared concurrently as a dual consciousness or as temporary mood states of a single personality. It seems that she became attached to Mr. Hopkins because he satisfied the two conflicting urges that became prominent in her marriage to Mr. Bean. On the one hand, Mr. Hopkins satisfied her need to be a devoted, helping person committed to caring for another who was in need of her care. Previously, the person had been her dying husband, now he was this young drug addict. However, his youth cultivated the second, relatively unexpressed part of her personality as well, the playful teenager desirous of fun and freedom, which had been suppressed and partially repressed since marriage. The two aspects of her personality had been under great stress since her husband became sick, when their mutual demands on her gave her the feeling that she was a dual consciousness, or two persons in one. Each seemed to demand of her a coherent mode of living, the first as the devoted, conscientious wife, and the second as the carefree, funloving young woman. The first, of course, won out, but the second was carried along as a separate, partly dissociated stream of thought that she could not entirely repress; she was aware of the suppression of it, though she constantly worked to push it entirely out of her consciousness. After her husband's death, this second stream of thought seemed to disappear for a while as she became the grieving widow, but it returned at Nashua, in that relaxed, apparently country environment, which reminded her of the woods she seemed to have loved in her youth, and grew to dislike in later life. Here she met Mr. Hopkins, who became a substitute object for Mr. Bean, but with the difference of arousing in her youthful feelings, and perhaps even passions, which she had not felt freely for many years.

However, when Mr. Hopkins kissed her she burst apart because of the conflicting set of emotions and motivations that she felt in that crucial traumatic moment, and it was not until 2 years later that she was able to bear as a unified personality the conflicts aroused by that kiss. Until then, her several personalities bore stigmata that indicated their incompleteness. The courageous widow turned into A, the carrier of pain and the pursuer of duty at any cost, an individual who seemed to prefer death over life and who was apparently prevented from committing suicide several times by alter-ego B. A's reaction to the kiss was a feeling of revulsion and anger at Mr. Hopkins. While this part of the original Mrs. Bean became submerged at the time of the kiss she reappeared when Mr. Hopkins in September showed his darker side. Yet she did not immediately terminate her relationship with him. Rather, her sense of duty and commitment continued to tie her to him; she had "promised," and would not go back on her word. As far as the kissing event and its consequences, A had amnesia for the immediate consequences, but apparently had little amnesia for B's other activities, until the amnestic barrier between A and B occurred after Prince began to use hypnosis. Along with Prince and Nellie, I believe that A existed as a separable alternating personality from the time of the kiss, and that the amnestic barrier that developed between A and B merely clarified for both of them the existent differences between their personalities.

The second personality to appear as a result of the kiss was B, an even more restricted personality than A, though in many ways the more interesting of the two. For her the kiss had no serious meaning, it was a "lark." B was anesthetic to sexual arousal as well as to pain; she could only feel pleasure. Whereas A thrived on pain and unhappiness, B thrived on play and happiness. A was an old woman and B was a young girl. Although A seems at least a continuous, if exaggerated, form of the widow, Mrs. Bean, B seems to have arisen from nowhere. Yet this is not quite true, for we do have the story of her development from her own letters and autobiography. She was the playful part of the original Nellie Parsons that became suppressed in marriage. Apparently, Nellie found the sexual encounter with her husband traumatic and repulsive and never grew to enjoy sex in her marriage. Yet she saw it as a duty to engage in sex with her husband and so she became the conscientious, yet rebellious, wife depicted in her letters and B's autobiography. The playful, happy young girl became the mature woman and wife but with the young girl still existing in a suppressed part of her personality. This playful girl, who denied the reality of sex and was thus anesthetic to it and to the pain and suffering engendered by it, and who could not commit herself to this and other duties of marriage, became the subconscious seed out of which B emerged. It is not clear whether Nellie's response to sex with her husband involved repression of her own sexual arousal or merely an abhorrence of the act itself. It seems likely that both emotions were involved, but neither Nellie nor Prince ever fully clarified exactly what happened when Nellie got married.

Prince's (1919) analysis of the case seems to suggest that both emotions were involved, but he did not pursue the "X affect" very far, and, as we have seen, his interview of B in July, 1911 did not produce much—at least in his notes. In Prince's (1923) last empirical article based on the case (though not identifying the patient as B.C.A.), he talked of a "life-long repression of the sexual instinct" and gave a wonderful account of how the repression of this instinct results in a general anesthesia to all sensation as an associative response, with the exception of the auditory modality. He applied this explanation to Mrs. Bean of Nashua—I believe—in a hypnotic state, and regretted that he did not investigate it further at the time. (His session notes of May 1908 first refer to this phenomenon with reference to Mrs. Bean of Nashua, though B reports the same state as a co-

conscious personality in her autobiography.)

It seems apparent that the emergence of B was the result of this anesthetic response to the conflicting emotions aroused by Mr. Hopkins' kiss. It was a re-enactment of the traumatic event at the time of her marriage, only this time the rebellious, playful, anesthetic response had grown into a personality all its own, rather than remain as a subconscious self. Over the years it had accumulated strength in its conflict with the dominant personality characteristics exhibited in Mrs. Bean's marriage, and the stress of her husband's illness had solidified this complex into a self-consciousness that could emerge as a separate mode of being after his death. With Mr. Hopkins' kiss, the whole mass of this complex emerged as a discontinuous, separate, incomplete personality in the form of B. This personality was 19, had the dominant characteristics of the young Nellie Parsons, and completely denied her marriage to Mr. Bean as her own, also denied that Robert was her son, and had no sexual sensitivity at all, for sexuality and all its problems had no existence for her.

Whereas, before the kiss, the dual elements of Nellie Parsons Bean's personality were joined in an unstable compromise with Mr. Hopkins as its focal point, the kiss destroyed this unity and resulted in two complementary but incomplete personalities and left the shocked Mrs. Bean of Nashua behind. B and A then played out their respective roles until first A and then B disappeared and various forms of a fused personality including these two personalities appeared, when finally Mrs. Bean, as a whole being, was ready to face again the kiss at Nashua and the conflicts that it raised. Only then did the original personality reappear ready to be synthesized with the dominant stream of consciousness of the missing 2 years of her life.

On May 22, 1908, Dr. Prince had the hypnotized Mrs. Bean of Nashua recall the evening of July 26, 1906. She remembered: "I walk up a hill to a pine grove. Mr. H. is with me. I smell the pines . . . It is very dark. I see Mr. Hopkins. I can't think what he says or does[?] that part eludes me—sudden (shrinks-shudders etc etc [Prince's notes]) Oh I remember Oh Oh Oh no I remember Dr.

Prince I can't bear it . . . (session note, May 24, 1908, Prince, 1907-1912)." But she did bear it this time, and as a result was able to be synthesized with the subsequent events and the strange personality transformations that she experienced during the 2 years that followed this traumatizing kiss.

Thus far, I have only considered the period from Nellie's marriage to her re-fused state in May 1908, the period that is the focus of the autobiographies and Prince's psychogenesis of the case. My account has not differed substantially from theirs. Perhaps the major difference is that Prince believed that he fused the personalities by using deep hypnosis to find the core personality and waking her. By contrast, I believe that this hypnotic technique could only succeed when Nellie was ready to face the traumatic kiss as a unified person.

I want to deal now with the period before Nellie's marriage as part of the present theoretical account of her dissociation of personality. The critical question in any causal account of Nellie Bean's life history viewed as a case of multiple personality, must be *why* she became a multiple personality. I have argued so far, along with Prince and Nellie herself, that she became a multiple personality with the kiss by Mr. Hopkins. Furthermore, we have traced the causal antecedents of that event as far back as the initial shock of sexual activity with her husband and the conflicting motivations that were the consequence of that event. What we still need to explain is why Nellie had such a strong reaction to sexual activity in her marriage and why dissociation, and not some other normal or abnormal reaction, was the ultimate consequence of her apparent aversion to sexual activity. Based on the positive evidence available in the case, I believe that these two questions can be given independent answers (though later I suggest a possible deeper connection, p. 121). As to why her sexual relations with her husband created the conflict that eventually resulted in the dissociation of personality with Mr. Hopkins' kiss, I believe that Prince's theory of a lifelong repression of sexual motivation is essentially right. There is abundant evidence in the case that Nellie Bean was a prude. Probably the most important evidence for our present purpose is some of the associations that Nellie presented to the "Jewess" dream reported by Prince in his study of her dreams (Prince, 1910). Among these (unpublished) associations she stated: "I think of a time years ago when I was about sixteen and a boy tried to kiss me. I was awfully angry; told my mother and cried. (Laughs). (That is probably why I hate kissing [a later editorial comment]). My sister was quite a flirt; lots of fellows round; I did not approve of it, I was eight years younger and prudish . . ." (session notes, Dec. 4, 1909, Prince, 1907-1912).

That her prudery is tied—at least in her own consciousness— to class differences is also apparent in her associations to the dream. She thinks that people, such as Prince and herself, of a higher class than the Jewess she is helping "are never tempted," and the whole context of the dream and its analysis at the time focuses on temptation, particularly sexual temptation. So it seems fairly evident that Nellie had a highly restricting Victorian moral code and, probably long before her marriage, had repressed all sexual motivation.

However, even if we credit Nellie with a well-developed Victorian sexually repressive character, her reaction to sex in marriage and her later dissociation of personality still need an additional causal factor. Why did she go beyond hysteria and neurasthenia and become a multiple personality? The dual consciousness of her married life and her later dissociation of personality requires another ingredient. What is necessary is some factor that will make Nellie prone to use dissociation as a coping mechanism for dealing with conflict rather than other ego-defense mechanisms that result in other symptomatic expressions of sexual repression.

I believe that there is evidence of a causal factor of the appropriate kind in the present case. When Nellie was a child of 5 or 6 she was left alone in a room with a white cat that had an epileptic seizure while she was playing with it, and she was unable to get help. This apparently terrifying experience gave her a permanent phobia of cats—especially white ones—though she could not remember the original cause of this phobia. Prince unearthed it using automatic writing, involving another dissociative state labelled "alpha and omega." This dissociative state has much in common with what we call the "hidden observer" after Hilgard (1977). The state claims not to be a person at all, but is, in a sense, the collection of the thoughts of all the personalities. I believe the cat trauma planted the seed out of which the later dissociations grew. This psychic trauma occurred during that critical period when the ego is being formed, and was of a sufficient intensity to overwhelm it and probably to put young Nellie into her first dissociative state. Once she experienced dissociation, the seed was planted for later dissociations to occur as a method for coping with internal conflict as well as externally generated trauma.

It is interesting to note that childhood traumas occurred in the Beauchamp case as well. Rosenzweig (1987), in a very interesting article that tracks down a number of the traumas that entered into the Beauchamp case, has suggested that an early traumatic experience involving the death of a baby brother was the primary incident causing Sally's emergence as a co-consciousness. If these hypotheses based on two of Prince's patients are correct, then perhaps we should think less that childhood sexual trauma or abuse is the main instigator of dissociation, as is often held, and instead try to determine what kinds of situations, are likely to prove traumatic enough to overwhelm the growing ego, predisposing it to use dissociation as a coping mechanism to later, perhaps less traumatic, experiences. In the present case, I have found no positive evidence in favor of either sexual or physical abuse, and because there is positive evidence that the cat incident caused dissociative amnesia for the event as well as the phobia, I see no reason for us to speculate that these other factors might have been involved. Nor is there any reason to suppose that she had a hypnotic sensitivity that predisposed her to her first dissociation. Such speculation should be reserved for cases where evidence tends to support the hypothesis, or where no other alternative hypothesis can account for the data in an adequate manner. This is not so in the present case, where the cat incident combined with Victorian prudery might very well have been sufficient antecedent causes to lay the groundwork for later developments in the case.

PRINCE AND B. C. A. VERSUS FREUD ON DREAMS

Before concluding this chapter, I turn to one last topic involving Nellie Bean, that is the research that she and Prince engaged in for several years, and particularly, the research on dreams. Early in his treatment of Mrs. Bean, Prince suggested that she might be able to help him. This is first mentioned in a July, 1907, note from B to A:

I can tell you why you don't hear from Dr. Prince—it is because he is tired of you and no wonder. . . .. you say you want to die—well die then— just stay away—I can manage things all right and am glad to—I want to live . . . you are a trusting little fool and believe everything you are told. Dr. Prince only got us to study short-hand to interest us in something and you believe you are going to help him in some vague way.—I guess it will be vague. He means nothing you are only a 'case' to him can't you see that? (note, July 1907, Bean, 1907-1913)

But Prince seems to have been quite serious, perhaps not realizing the "transference" possibilities of maintaining such a relationship with a patient. At any rate, Prince and Nellie Bean did engage in research, and all of the personalities, including B, came to depend heavily on this meaningful activity. Nellie read Prince's first book at this time (Letter from C, July 13, 1907, Bean, 1907-1913) and started an extensive reading program in abnormal psychology. By the fall of that year, Nellie's several personalities were engaged in research with Prince that was to lead to two important empirical articles on co-conscious mentation (Prince, 1908; Prince & Peterson,

1908), and at least B had begun to write her autobiography. By May 21, 1908, B, in her very last letter, written the day before Mrs. Bean of Nashua appeared, stated:

C [is] only peaceful when she is working over your book [The Uncon-scious Lectures]—busy happy and hopeful but as soon as finished [she is] restless nervous and unhappy. Is this perhaps because when she is studying and working I am interested also and there is less pulling in different ways? That is why I always say she will never get well unless she is happy. If she could be happy we would come nearer to being one, don't you see? I am studying her all the time now. I want to help, I don't want to live like this, and I know I shall always be co-conscious anyway—I can never be blotted out—you can always get me when you want me—but I want to finish what I am writing for you first [her autobiography], can't I do it now? (letter, May 21, 1908, Bean, 1907-1913)

B concluded the letter by describing C's reading, which included Janet, Binet, James, Sidis, Munsterberger, Hyslop, Prince and the *Journal,* and she wrote that C was "planning next winter to go to some lectures . . . and she wants very much to do some experimental work with you. I wonder if you put that into her head in hypnosis." I assume that Prince did not, but the role that he began to play in her life was so large that it could hardly have differed if he had mesmerized her into working with him.

By February of 1909, after the autobiographies were published, Nellie Bean, Morton Prince, and his assistant, Dr. George Waterman had begun a series of sessions that would terminate in the 1910 publication of two articles in the *Journal* on B. C. A.'s dreams (Prince, 1910; Waterman, 1910). Little did they realize what dangerous waters they had stepped into. In the dreams that they reported, as opposed to those they decided against using, there is little overt reference to erotic motives, and the little that remained is discreetly left out of one dream by imposing a gap. But as anyone in the least bit acquainted with Freud's theory should have known, the "manifest content" is not all one must concern oneself with if one wishes to be discreet; furthermore, discretion and science often don't mix very well. As Jung (1911/1974) put it in his critical review of Prince's article:

> *The gap in the dream is a praiseworthy piece of discretion and will certainly please the prudish reader, but it is not science. Science admits no such considerations of decency. Here it is simply a question of whether Freud's maligned theory of dreams is right or not, and not whether dream-texts sound nice to immature ears . . . .. "The analysis of this scene would carry us too far into the intimacy of her life to justify our entering upon it" [Prince, 1910, p. 164]. Does the author really believe that in these circumstances he has any scientific right to speak about the psychoanalytic dream-theory, when he withholds essential material from the reader for reasons of discretion? By the very fact of reporting his patient's dream to the world he has violated discretion as thoroughly as possible, for every analyst will see its meaning at once: what the dreamer instinctively hides most deeply cries out loudest from the unconscious. For anyone who knows how to read dream-symbols all precautions are in vain, the truth will out. We would therefore request the author, if he doesn't want to strip his patient bare the next time, to choose a case about which he can say everything (p. 79).*

Jung then went on to find sexual wishes in this dream as he found them in all of the other dreams that Prince presented. The article was written 2 years before Jung rejected Freud's sexual "reduction" of all mental life, when he was still heir-apparent to Freud's throne and under the sway of Freud's thought. Jung went too far in finding sexual content in every dream symbol—for instance, he interpreted a dream that ended with Nellie fearfully walking through a sea of cats as a dream involving a repressed sexual desire because in a previous patient of his own, cats symbolized the sexual act. Although he constantly jumped to such conclusions in his interpretation of Nellie's dreams, I think he was often close to the truth—especially in his transference interpretations, where he suggested that she was unconsciously in love with Prince and wanted to give herself to him. Several of the unpublished dreams in the Prince collection support this interpretation. Moreover, Nellie also fell in love at a later date with Dr. Waterman, for in 1912 she had a vision, reported in *The Unconscious* (Prince, 1914/1921, p. 204 ff), involving a man and woman kissing that resulted in a poem ending with the line "And my rent soul." The date of this vision was about the time that Dr. Waterman must have announced his forthcoming marriage to the woman we know as Miss Beauchamp, who also seems to have fallen in love with the debonair Morton Prince, and transferred instead to his assistant (Kenny, 1986). However, Nellie was to have neither doctor and was to remain an unremarried widow until she died at 85 in 1950 (Kenny, 1986).

Let us return now to Prince's dream article and to the Jones-Prince debate over it (Jones, 1911; Prince, 1911). Unlike Jung's paper, which analyzed the dreams, Jones' critique—which appeared in the *Journal*—was much more reserved and focused on the main issue, that Prince's research was an inadequate test of Freud's theory because he didn't fully adopt the psychoanalytic method. At the time of his research, Prince did not, in fact, know Freud's theory of dreams very well. In December of 1908, Prince had invited Jones to visit Boston from Toronto to talk about psychoanalysis to the Boston psychopathologists, and at that time asked him to become an assistant editor for the *Journal*. Early in May of 1909, as Prince's dream research was in the process of development, Jones had lectured again at the psychotherapeutics conference on psychoanalysis, where Prince also gave a paper (Jones, 1909; Prince, 1909). But it was not until December 1909, at the American Psychological Association meeting, that Jones gave an extensive lecture on Freud's dream theory that was published in 1910 in the *American Journal of Psychology* in the same volume that contained Freud's Clark lectures (Jones, 1910). It was at this same meeting that Prince first presented his study on B. C. A.'s dreams. Moreover, as Jones reported in several letters to Putnam,

Prince told him that he had not read (or at least finished) Freud's book on dreams when he wrote his own article, and Prince seemed indirectly to confirm this in a letter to Putnam (Hale, 1971b).

It is not surprising, therefore, that Prince misrepresented the Freudian method and theory in his article, just as Putnam had done several years earlier. But this misunderstanding caused him to miss the valid side of Jones' critique of his article. Instead, he noticed that "attitude of mind" insufficiently critical of their own concepts that made Freudianism appear more like a religious cult than an empirical science. So he wrote an antagonistic reply to Jones' paper. At this point Jones, who had been hopeful of converting Prince—as he had Putnam—to psychoanalysis, almost quit the *Journal* as assistant editor. But Putnam seems to have cooled both men down, and so Jones and Prince continued to play out their respective roles in keeping the psychoanalytic controversy alive in the pages of the *Journal* until much later when Jones founded the *International Journal of Psychoanalysis* in 1920 and finally left the *Journal* in 1921.

In the original article on dreams, Prince used dissociative techniques to interpret the dreams, though one of these techniques, which used free-associations, he called psychoanalysis. B. C. A. at this time could not remember her dreams, yet she often awoke with fragments of images from them and on many occasions she exhibited hysterical symptoms caused by them. Waterman's (1910) article focuses on this latter fact—that the dreams seemed to cause the hysterical symptoms of temporary blindness, nausea, headaches, aphonia, and so forth, and that these were able to be removed by suggestion. Prince also mentioned this fact, but focused more on the interpretation of the dreams. In the research for both articles, the dream was recovered by hypnotizing B. C. A. and putting her into the b-hypnotic state, in which she recalled the dream as well as the pre-dream thoughts. Prince (1910) described how B. C. A. was then asked to free-associate to the elements of the dream in three different states—the normal personality, that personality hypnotized, and, finally, in the b-hypnotic state. Then Prince reconstructed the meaning of the dream based on these associations, in light of the pre-dream thoughts.

The procedure is interesting, and it provides an excellent account of the manifest content of the dream and, to some extent, reaches into the latent content from a Freudian perspective. But, as Jones pointed out, and as Jung demonstrated, there can be deeper layers that have not been accessed using this superficially psychoanalytic technique. In the original article, Prince claimed that he only found one incidence of repression, only occasional wish-fulfillment, and no resistance. Yet, in a later article, Prince (1917) reversed his opinion of one of the dreams—admitting that repression was involved. And there is plenty of evidence of resistance because, in the original notes and in other reports, it is noted that the b personality often could not describe the main personality's thoughts because "alpha and omega" prevented her from speaking and she would get aphonia or lose consciousness when trying to speak on certain—usually sexual—issues related to the dreams (Prince, 1914/1921, p. 471ff). In his book, *The Unconscious* (1914/1921), Prince again looked at the process of dreaming and admitted that the interpretations given in his original article were not definitive and that other, more sexual ones had been proposed as alternatives (p. 220). He also provided new evidence on dream constructive processes—a classic example of which is the "temple dream," whose source, B. C. A., is unacknowledged. This dream had, as its basis, the hypnotic suggestion: "You want to do a good piece of work and your dream tonight will be the fulfillment of the wish" (Prince, 1914/1921, p. 197ff). The poetic vision that occurred at the time of Waterman's wedding announcement, about a month before the temple dream, also contributed to Prince's understanding of the dream process. He used these sources of evidence to suggest that dream thoughts use symbolization and plot to express themselves, and that the activity of dream construction goes on in a region of the subconscious or unconscious that is inaccessible to recall using dissociative interview techniques.

What Prince failed to get at, but what seems important toward understanding B. C. A.'s dreams, is that dreams may be constructed out of apparently mutually exclusive, conflicting motives or thoughts that sometimes, through primary process thinking, result in highly condensed symbols that resolve the conflict. B. C. A's dreams, however, often failed to achieve such a resolution and instead produced hysterical symptoms that were associated with symbolic representations that were only partial resolutions to the conflict (cf. Rivers, 1923, for a very similar view of dreams). It seems to me that one can observe a slow development of dream syntheses through the years of dreams found in the Prince collection. They came closer and closer to resolving the conflicting motives represented at an earlier stage by the A and B personalities and by the missing sexual factor not found in one of these personalities and inhibited or repressed in the other.

As these dream syntheses developed, Nellie came to recognize that her life was not over just because her husband had died and that love was a real possibility still open to her. Her fears that A and B might reappear diminished in time as she fused the best—most realistic—aspects of both personalities into herself. Even her anxiety dreams involving cats diminished in intensity. In one poignant dream—the last in the collection involving cats—her love was represented by a bunch of red roses that she was carrying. They were more beautiful than the roses of other women around, yet no man seemed to want hers as they went to other women instead. The dream report continues:

Suddenly Mr B[ean]came out of the lane and went to [another woman] and she gave him her roses and they walked off past [her] and [the woman] laughed in a hateful way and said, "What do you suppose any one wants of those—those are poor man's flowers." Then [she] looked down and saw the roses had turned to nasty little white kittens and they were crawling over her and clawing her breast. Suddenly she found herself in a church at an altar looking into a coffin with Dr. P[rince]. Inside the coffin she saw herself dead but looking as she did at the age of twenty-five. She was dressed only in a nightgown. Then Dr. P[rince] said, "The rose that once has bloomed forever dies" [session notes, July 12, 1910, apparently obtained from Dr. Waterman, Prince, 1907-1912]

The dream depicts the fear that she would never be loved again so that she might as well be dead. But perhaps more interesting than this aspect of the dream is the role that the white kittens played in it—as if her love, the roses, and the white kittens were intimately connected. My own interpretation of this element is that Nellie's understanding of love—that "love means suffering" and that it "lured" but "rent and tore" her in other contexts—was intimately tied to her first experience of love, her love for a white kitten. This kitten's epileptic fit gave her a "rent soul," which was never entirely healed by subsequent experiences, and hence continued to inhibit her full capacity for trust and for love.

Although none of the dreams seems to have fully resolved these conflicting motives in Nellie Bean's life history, Nellie as a conscious personality seemed sufficiently synthesized on July 29, 1911, probably after a recent interview with Prince about the role of sex in her psychogenesis, to write the following description of herself:

. . . One fact, which I am sure is true and which may have some bearing on the case of B. C. A., is that I matured very slowly . . . I enjoy things which women who are past forty do not usually care for—dancing, riding, tramping, gymnastics, etc. As far as pleasures are concerned I stopped living when I was little more than thirty, and it seems sometimes as if all the pleasure I should have felt, but did not, was pent up within me unused. If the conditions of my life were different I should be very active and gay.

Then as to love, I loved my husband truly and deeply, and I love him just the same now; he was one of the finest men I have ever known; but nevertheless, if love should come to me again, if I should meet the "right man" I could love him with a depth and passion impossible to me

at any time before in my life. It is a little as if I had not been really awake
before.

It seems almost too bad, doesn't it? that I can never experience the
fullness of life which I feel within me. I feel quite sorry for myself
sometimes. I have experienced the heights and depths of bitter suffering,
but ecstatic joy and happiness have been denied me. A certain part of
me isn't more than thirty years old—you can understand this, can you
not? Possibly the change in my health explains some of these things for I
am stronger than I have ever been before. If this is of no help in solving
the problem of B. C. A. just destroy the letter . . . (letter, July 29, 1911,
Bean, 1907-1913)

Thankfully, Prince did not destroy this letter, nor any of the
others included in the collection upon which the bulk of this chapter
is based. Although Nellie Bean apparently never did find the "right
man", I imagine, with her spirit and intelligence, that she ultimately
made a meaningful life for herself. The last act that I know that she
performed in the service of psychology is in its own way an interesting
symbolic note upon which to conclude this section. In 1914 the
Journal of Abnormal Psychology published a translation of Janet's
devastatingly bitter critique of psychoanalysis, in which he viewed it
as an unnatural extension of his own "psychological analysis" (Janet,
1914-1915; cf. Ellenberger, 1970, for a fair treatment of the
relationship between Janet and Freud). The translator of the article
was Mrs. William G. Bean.

CONCLUSION

In this chapter I have tried to draw the reader into that exciting period
at the beginning of the present century when those two major views
of mental activity outside of the "personal consciousness," that is, the
subconscious (Janet), or co-conscious (Prince), and the unconscious
(Freud) first confronted each other in a North American context.
Prince, as the leading figure of the dissociative school, tried to keep

open the doors to Freudian psychology through public confrontations between the two perspectives in the pages of the *Journal of Abnormal Psychology*. He also tried to incorporate some of Freud's new insights into his own work, beginning with his lectures on the unconscious (Prince, 1908-1909), which resulted in his 1914 book. Although in this and his later works, he continued to try to separate the wheat from the chaff in Freudian theory, he never gave up his predominantly structural dissociative perspective for Freud's dynamic approach; nor did he accept most of Freud's terminology or his wide ranging speculations. An empiricist at heart, he cared very little for what he saw as interpretations heaped on interpretations. From the point of view of the Freudians, Prince seemed not only conservative but indeed "stupid." In retrospect, at least from the perspective of psychology as a science, Prince's assessment of Freud's positive and negative contributions to psychology seems just (see, e.g., Prince, 1921). It is difficult , however, even to evaluate this question fairly because we have all been infected with the Freudian perspective, from which it is difficult to extricate ourselves. The followers of Freud became legion, and we all grew up under his influence on our culture, even if not on our science.

Prince's weakness, if anything, was that he assimilated too slowly the positive Freud and reacted too quickly to the negative Freud. Prince never accepted—at least publicly—the importance of sexuality in the B. C. A. case, though it was critical to a fair evaluation of the relevance of Freudian theory to his own work. Furthermore, to see Prince's floundering in his analyses of Nellie's dreams because he has failed to finish reading Freud's greatest single work, *The Interpretation of Dreams*, is to see a man drowning in a sea of concepts that are slippery but of great depth, who swims quickly to the safe shore of descriptive concepts of more certain but shallower meaning. Without doubt, Freud's work is seriously flawed when viewed from a scientific perspective, yet the genius of it cannot be denied. Prince was,, by far, the better empirical scientist of the two, but Freud's creative imagination and ability to synthesize ideas more than made up for his scientific weaknesses when it came to the proliferation of ideas. It is unfortunate that the controversy between Freud and his competitors turned into an either/or, a pro- or con-Freud, and that the Freudians won. If Prince and others had kept pace with the Freudians, assimilating the good while rejecting the bad, and if they had organized as well as the Freudians, perhaps today we would not be in the confused state that we are in vis-à-vis the problems of dissociative and Freudian psychology.

In my interpretation of the B. C. A. case, I have tried to combine these two perspectives to some degree. I have talked of dissociation and of repression. I have integrated both structural and dynamic descriptions of the case. Finally, I have focused on the all-important sexual component that Prince and B. C. A. tried to avoid discussing overtly. However, my use of the terminology of the two traditions has been necessarily imprecise. There is a good deal of overlap in the material that is labeled *dissociated* and *co-conscious* in one tradition and *unconscious* and *repressed* in the other. What is needed is the development of a more refined vocabulary that integrates these two traditions, but that does not buy wholly into one or the other. However, the development of such a language will take time, as we attempt to reinstate the lost dissociation psychology in a more up-to-date form. I believe that the B. C. A. case and all of Prince's work can contribute toward this development. Thus, I strongly recommend to those who want to understand how the two great traditions of abnormal psychology might be integrated that they go back and read the original works of Janet and Prince. Freud's ideas have been engraved in our brains; may Janet's and Prince's ideas be painted on top of them, and may illuminated brains result.

ACKNOWLEDGEMENTS

The chapter is based on manuscript material in the Morton Prince papers at the Francis A. Countway Library, which reserves rights to the use of material not previously released for publication. With the exception of material obtained from the Morton Prince papers, most of the unreferenced historical material in the paper derived from the following books: Ellenberger (1970), Hale (1971a, 1971b). The dates provided in the Appendix have been estimated based on several conflicting sources; hence they are only approximate. Kenny (1986) was the source for Nellie Parsons Bean's birth and death dates, and the Prince material was the source of other dates. The author wishes to thank Richard Wolfe, Curator, Rare Book and Manuscript Collection, Francis A. Countway Library, Harvard University and his staff for their generous assistance in obtaining access to and in using the Prince papers. I also wish the thank the Dalhousie research development committee for a grant to support travel to see these papers.

REFERENCES

B. C. A. (a.k.a. Nellie Parsons Bean). (1908). My life as a dissociated personality. *Journal of Abnormal Psychology, 3*, (Oct-Nov), 240-260.

B. C. A. (a.k.a. Nellie Parsons Bean). (1908-1909). An introspective analysis of co-conscious life (My life as a dissociated personality) by a personality (B) claiming to be co-conscious. *Journal of Abnormal Psychology, 3*, 311-334.

Bean, N. P. (a.k.a. B. C. A.). (1907-1913). Unpublished letters and notes to M. Prince. Prince collection, The Francis A. Countway Library, Harvard University.

Ellenberger, H. F. (1970). *The discovery of the unconscious: The history and evolution of dynamic psychiatry.* New York: Basic Books.

Freud, S. (1909). Selected Papers on hysteria and other psychoneuroses (A. A. Brill, Trans.). *Journal of Neurons and Mental Disease* (Monograph series, No. 4).

Freud, S. (1910). The origin and development of psycho-analysis. *American Journal of Psychology, 21* (April), 181-218.

Freud, S. (1913). *The interpretation of dreams* (A. D. Brill, Trans). New York: Macmillan.

Hale, N. G., Jr. (1971a). *Freud and the Americans: The beginnings of psychoanalysis in the United States, 1876/1917.* New York: Oxford University Press.

Hale, N. G., Jr. (Ed.). (1971b). *James Jackson Putnam and psychoanalysis: Letters between Putnam and Sigmund Freud, Ernest Jones, William James, Sandor Ferenczi, and Morton Prince, 1877/1917.* Cambridge, MA: Harvard University Press.

Hilgard, E. R. (1977). *Divided consciousness: Multiple controls in human thought and action.* New York: Wiley.

Janet, P. (1914-1915). Psychoanalysis. *Journal of Abnormal Psychology, 9,* 1-35, 153-187.

Jones, E. (1909). Psycho-analysis in psychotherapy. In Gerrish, F. H., Putnam, J. J., Taylor, E. W., Sidis, B., Waterman, G. A., Donley, J. E., Jones, E., Williams, T. A., and Prince, M. *Psychotherapeutics:* Boston: The Gorham Press.

Jones, E. (1910). Freud's theory of dreams. *American Journal of Psychology, 21,* 283-308.

Jones, E. (1911). Remarks on Dr. Morton Prince's article: "The mechanism and interpretation of dreams." *Journal of Abnormal Psychology, 5,* (Feb-Mar), 337-353.

Jung, C. (1974). Morton Prince, "The mechanism and interpretation of dreams": A critical review. In R. F. C. Hull (Trans.), *The psychoanalytic years.* Princeton: Princeton University Press. (original work published in 1911)

Kenny, M. G. (1986). *The passion of Ansel Bourne: Multiple personality in American culture.* Washington, DC: Smithsonian Institution Press.

Prince, M. (1906). *The dissociation of a personality: A biographical study in abnormal psychology.* New York: Longman.

Prince, M. (1907). A symposium on the subconscious. *Journal of Abnormal Psychology, 2* (June-July), 67-80.

Prince, M. (1908). Experiments to determine co-conscious (sub-conscious) ideation. *Journal of Abnormal Psychology, 3* (April-May), 33-42.

Prince, M. (1908-1909). The unconscious. *Journal of Abnormal Psychology, 3,* (Oct-Nov 1908), 261-297, (Dec 1908-Jan 1909), 335-353, (Feb-Mar 1909), 391-426; *4* (Apr-May 1909), 36-56.

Prince, M. (1910). The mechanism and interpretation of dreams. *Journal of Abnormal Psychology, 5* (Oct-Nov), 139-195.

Prince, M. (1909). The psychological principles and field of psychotherapy. In Gerrish, F. H., Putnam, J. J., Taylor, E. W., Sidis, B., Waterman, G. A., Donley, J. E., Jones, E., Williams, T. A., and Prince, M. *Psychotherapeutics.* Boston: The Gorham Press.

Prince, M. (1911). The mechanism and interpretation of dreams—A reply to Dr. Jones. *Journal of Abnormal Psychology, 5* (Feb-Mar), 337-353.

Prince, M. (1907-1912). Unpublished session notes on N. P. Bean (a.k.a. B. C. A.). Prince collection, The Francis A. Countway Library, Harvard

University.

Prince, M. (1921). *The unconscious: The fundamentals of human personality, normal and abnormal.* (2nd Ed.) New York: Macmillan (First edition published in 1914).

Prince, M. (1917). Co-conscious images. *Journal of Abnormal Psychology, 12,* 289-316.

Prince, M. (1919). The psychogenesis of multiple personality. *Journal of Abnormal Psychology, 14* (Oct) 225-280 [Also in Prince, 1914/1921].

Prince, M. (1921). A critique of psychoanalysis. *Archives of Neurology and Psychiatry, 6* (Dec), 610-633.

Prince, M. (1923). Complete loss of all sensory functions except hearing but including coenesthesis and visual images of body. *Journal of Abnormal Psychology, 18* (Oct-Dec), 238-243.

Prince, M., & Peterson, F. (1908). Experiments in psycho-galvanic reactions from co-conscious (sub-conscious) ideas in a case of multiple personality. *Journal of Abnormal Psychology, 3* (June-July), 114-131.

Putnam, J. J. (1906). Recent experiences in the study and treatment of hysteria at the Massachusetts General Hospital; with remarks on Freud's method of treatment by "psycho-analysis." *Journal of Abnormal Psychology, 1* (Apr), 26-41.

Rivers, W. H. R. (1923). *Conflict and dream.* New York: Harcourt, Brace.

Rosenzweig, S. (1987). Sally Beauchamp's career: A psychoarchaeological key to Morton Prince's classic case of multiple personality. *Genetic, Social, and General Psychology Monographs, 113,* 5-60.

Waterman, G. E. (1910). Dreams as a cause of symptoms. *Journal of Abnormal Psychology, 5* (Oct-Nov), 196-210.

APPENDIX

B. C. A. Chronology

1864 – Birth of Nellie Parsons.

1869/70 – A white cat has a fit causing first dissociation and cat phobia.

Feb. 22, 1885/6 – Marriage to William G. Bean.

1887/8 – Robert, son, born.

1900/1 – William has first cerebral hemorrhage.

June 29, 1905 – William dies.

Spring or Summer, 1906 – Nellie goes to Nashua sanatorium for rest cure and meets Mr. Hopkins.

July 26, 1906 – Mr. Hopkins kisses Nellie, she dissociates and B appears as separate personality and remains until September.

Sept., 1906 – Mr. Hopkins disappoints her on a money matter and A appears for the first time.

Sept.–Dec., 1906 – Confused period where A and B alternate but share knowledge of each other's activities and not clearly aware of the dissociation.

Dec., 1906 – Nellie, as A, sees Prince for the first time; B appears in hypnosis of A sometime after the first meeting; A alternates, B is co-conscious and alternates.

May 2, 1907 – First letter from Nellie, as A, in the Prince files, which refers to another letter by B.

June 13, 1907 – First fusion into a short-lived C occurs.

Summer, 1907 – A great deal of alternation between A and B occurs following C's permanent disappearance.

Fall, 1907 – Research on co-conscious mentation begins.

Nov. 13, 1907 – B begins working on autobiography.

Nov. 19/20, 1907 – Prince and Nellie go to New York to do psychogalvanic study with Peterson, and a new C synthesis develops.

Nov., 1907–May, 1908 – C and B alternate, with B co-conscious; A appears only briefly on a few occasions.

May 21, 1908 – Mrs. Bean of Nashua appears as B is thinking of the original kissing incident, and her autobiography is nearly complete.

May 22, 1908 – Mrs. Bean of Nashua is fused with the period from July 26, 1906 to May, 1908 at Prince's office; she remains fused after that date, though b, the hypnotic state of B, is still accessible.

Fall, 1908 – Autobiographies of the final fused "C" and B are published.

1909 – Prince and Nellie engage in research mostly on dreams.

Summer, 1909 – Prince and Nellie go to Europe to the conference on the subconscious, and miss Freud's lectures at Clark in October.

December, 1909 – Prince lectures on Nellie's dreams, published in the *Journal of Abnormal Psychology* in 1910.

1910 – Dr. Waterman takes over Nellie's case and research on dreams (Waterman, 1910), while Prince is in California.

July, 1911 – Prince interviews B about sexuality for case history.

Spring, 1912 – Waterman announces engagement and Prince helps Nellie; poetic vision and temple dream.

1950 – Nellie Bean dies at 85, having never remarried.

4
Dissociative Phenomena and Disorders: Clinical Presentations

George A. Fraser
Royal Ottawa Hospital

One of the most neglected areas in psychiatric illnesses, until recent years, has been the field of dissociative disorders. Although the roots of our current understanding are well known through the histories of such investigators as Pierre Janet, Jean Charcot and Sigmund Freud which are beautifully told in the classic book, *The Discovery of the Unconscious* (Ellenberger, 1970), it is only in recent years that books devoted to the description and treatment of dissociative disorders have entered the medical literature (Beahrs, 1982; Braun, 1986; Bliss, 1986; Kluft, 1985; Putnam 1989). Since the inaugural meeting of The International Society for the Study of Multiple Personality and Dissociation in Chicago in 1984, there has been a dramatic increase in the literature of dissociative disorders now available to mental health care professionals (Goettman, Greaves & Coons, 1991, 1992). Currently, it is being recognized that the prevalence of dissociative disorders is quite high (Ross, 1989) and it is essential for therapists to be able to recognize and treat these disorders.

This chapter is dedicated to those therapists who are beginning to work with these patients or clients. My intention is to breathe life into the DSM classification system by giving clinical examples of actual patients whom I have treated over the past decade. I also mention certain symptoms which suggest dissociative phenomena which, though not dissociative disorders by themselves, should alert the clinician to be on the watch for one of the classical dissociative disorders (psychogenic amnesia, psychogenic fugue, depersonalization, multiple personality and dissociative disorders not otherwise specified).

The dissociative phenomena are more likely present in highly hypnotizable patients (as also are the dissociative disorders), however, the presence of dissociative phenomena may only be isolated clinical findings. In addition, patients who have high hypnotic potential need not have any dissociative symptoms. The connection between hypnotic potential and dissociation has been discussed in other writing (Bliss, 1986; Horevitz, 1992). Certainly, training in hypnotherapy will be advantageous to anyone intending to work in the area of dissociation. Books dealing with clinical aspects of hypnosis will also generally contain sections on dissociative issues (Crasilneck & Hall, 1985; Spiegel & Spiegel, 1978).The American Psychiatric Association's (1987) Diagnostic and Statistical Manual of Mental Disorders (3rd ed., rev.) states that the essential feature of these disorders is a disturbance or alteration in the normally integrative functions of identity, memory, or consciousness. The disturbance or alteration may be sudden or gradual, and transient or chronic. If it occurs primarily in identity, the person's customary identity is temporarily forgotten and a new identity may be assumed (as in Multiple Personality Disorder), or the customary feeling of one's own reality is lost and is replaced by a feeling of unreality (as in Depersonalization Disorder). If the disturbance occurs primarily in memory, important personal events cannot be recalled (as in Psychogenic Amnesia and Psychogenic Fugue) (p. 231).

I begin by discussing nine symptoms or phenomena that are familiar to those using hypnotherapy and likely owe their existence to auto-hypnotic or auto-dissociative processes. While they may exist as isolated phenomena unrelated to dissociative disorders, such experiences have been present in a significant number of my patients with dissociative disorders. Now, whenever I hear any one or more of these mentioned, I always question carefully to rule out a dissociative disorder.

DISSOCIATIVE PHENOMENA

Autoscopic Phenomenon. More commonly called an "out of body experience," this dissociative-like experience has frequently been described by those who have had near-death experiences. A nineteen-year-old patient told me of having had a cardiac arrest while undergoing renal surgery. He reported that during the operation he was suddenly aware of himself "floating over the operating table". He distinctly heard the words, "We've lost him!" He recalled watching doctors doing cardiac massage "on the body on the operating table" which, in a sense, he knew was his body. Later, in the recovery room, he related the operating room conversation and the sequence of events that had transpired to his doctor. The doctor had confirmed that he indeed had suffered an arrest and that they had thought for a moment they were not going to be able to revive him. It is most likely that he did indeed dissociate at that moment.

I have had multiple personality patients describe a similar sensation of 'watching' one of their own personalities from a distance as if they were actually watching another person. An extension of this experience is one in which the patient feels not only that has he or she floated out of his or her body, but has actually floated or travelled beyond that room. This latter experience has been termed *astral travel.*

Automatic Writing. In this situation, the writing does not appear to be done voluntarily; rather, the hand picks up a pen or pencil and writes as if it had a mind of its own. The person will look at this process passively or with a puzzled feeling that some force has somehow taken over the body. One could technically question whether any such writing is *purely* non volitional, for the patient, in fact, most often has to cooperate by allowing his or her hand to do the writing. Patients have reported that some mysterious inner source seemed to be making them write. Sometimes this automatic writing is continuous, without separation between the written words. Less frequently, it may be mirror-image writing. Being a little more modern, one patient stated that while sitting at a computer she found her hands suddenly typing out a message on the computer. One might call this computer-age "automatic typing!" Likely, cases reported in the press relating to a person who enters a trance state and becomes a medium for some deceased great composer are indeed merely other variations of this dissociative process. (Somehow, mediums are only possessed by *great* composers!).

Four of my multiple personality disorders (MPD) patients had childhood traumatic events revealed to them through automatic writing. This all began prior to their clinical diagnosis of MPD and thus, was not an artifact of therapy. In all of these cases, the writing was done by an alter personality who later admitted to and explained the purpose of the writing.

Glossolalia. This is the experience of "speaking in tongues." The person generally appears to be in a trance state when speaking in this manner. A few of my patients have reported this experience. They were able to reproduce this glossolalia under hypnosis in my office. This gibberish-like speech cannot generally be related to any common language pattern, though it may have meaning of some sort to the person who utters the words. Similar reports of glossolalia experiences have been reported from charismatic prayer meetings. Although I seriously doubt such verbalizations in any way belong to a "dead language" as has been suggested, I concede that one could argue for either side of the issue, probably without ever being able to convince those of the opposite view. I had the chance to do hypnotic profiles in a couple of non-multiple personality disorder patients who have experienced glossolalia at church gatherings. They were not suffering from dissociative disorders, nor did they have any serious psychiatric illness. They did, however, turn out to be extremely high hypnotic subjects. I believe that glossolalia is a dissociative phenomenon until proven otherwise.

Color Auras. Some highly hypnotizable patients have discussed the experience of seeing color auras around other people. They describe it as a halo or colored energy field surrounding the person they are observing. This may extend about 1 inch around the body. The colors may change, and they often have special significance to the observer (i.e. yellow may represent pain, and red anger, while dark colors, especially black, could represent danger). Comparing the color meanings in about eight such patients, no common pattern was observed concerning the significance of the colors. The meaning of the color seems to be based on a personal meaning or symbolism. One patient seemed surprised to learn that all people do not see auras. It is proposed here that these patients are highly sensitive to nonverbal cues of those they are observing and convert their emotional perceptions into a colored aura around the other person. Although such auras are not a frequent finding, they were seen in enough dissociative disorders to be worth noting.

Auditory Hallucinations. This, at first glance, seems almost out of place in dissociative symptoms. Traditional teaching, until recently, has correlated auditory hallucinations (hearing voices) with schizophrenia. However, the work of such researchers as Richard Kluft and Colin Ross have shown that auditory hallucinations and other Schneiderian first-rank symptoms can be present in MPD. From my experience, these voices are, for the most part, heard within the patient's head or, more rarely, just outside the head. In a review of my last 44 cases diagnosed as dissociative disorder, 90.9% (40) on initial interview responded in the positive as having auditory hallucinations. Of the 44, 32 were MPD. 96.8% (31) MPD patients reported auditory hallucinations, as did 75% (9 of 12) with atypical dissociation (dissociative disorders not otherwise specified). I believe that this high incidence of auditory hallucinations may be explained by two factors. First, patients being referred to a clinic specializing in dissociative disorders are less likely to conceal their history of auditory hallucinations. A decade ago, there was realistically more of a fear of being diagnosed schizophrenic. Patients have reported to me that they deliberately concealed this information of hallucinations "because I knew I wasn't schizophrenic." The second factor may be the style of inquiry about such a phenomenon. Rather than first asking about the hearing of "auditory hallucinations", I phrase the initial question, "Have your ever heard your thoughts spoken aloud?" I believe this subtle change in phrasing gives the patient the chance to answer "yes," without feeling that he or she is "crazy." I then proceed to determine if a "yes" response definitely indicates an auditory hallucination.

Such voices are generally those of the alter personalities. Some alters are copies or "clones" of outside people such as a critical mother. Learning the personality of the actual mother may give us a pretty good idea of the personality of the copy. Conversation is frequently of a critical or derogatory nature by the alter personalities to the host personality. Auditory hallucinations should alert clinicians to include not only schizophrenia, but also the dissociative disorders in their differential diagnosis.

Visual Hallucinations. Highly hypnotizable subjects and those with dissociative disorders, in my experience, have also reported visual hallucinations. It is less common than auditory hallucinations, but is included here to remind the reader that occasionally a visual hallucination can be produced by a dissociative process. As an example, one patient reported that she frequently saw snakes and spiders crawl around the office. When asked why she was not alarmed, she said that she had learned that they were unlikely real because, in the past, if she tried to step on them there was nothing there, and besides, she reasoned, if they were there the therapist would have acted alarmed. However, some have been convinced that their visual hallucinations are real and are surprised that the therapist does not see them.

Of course, it is essential to rule out disorders such as schizophrenia, organic brain syndrome, and temporal lobe epilepsy when differentiating visual hallucinations.

Conversion Symptoms. Although conversion disorders are classified separately in DSM-III-R, it is important to recognize that there is a close relationship between conversion and dissociative disorders. The World Health Organization's (1987) (ICD-9-CM) still groups conversion and dissociative disorders together under "Hysteria." One could view dissociative disorders as dissociation of the central functioning of the brain (i.e., identity, conscious awareness, and memory), whereas conversion is dissociation of the perception of the *peripheral* system. In this context, peripheral system refers to the internal psychological *schema* of the sensory-motor system and special senses. An example of conversion of the schema of the motor system is hysterical paralysis of a limb; conversion of a "special sense system" would be hysterical blindness. Though conversion symptoms may occur as a separate disorder, one must be alert to the possibility of this being only one facet of a more global dissociative disorder. While working for 2 years as a family practitioner in West Africa, I noted a fair number of traditional conversion disorders, such as hysterical seizures. On return to North America, I found such classical conversion disorders to be much less common. A colleague wisely noted that the conversion process is always about a decade ahead of the medical profession. As physicians, we were alerted to the presentations of these classical conversions, but these rarely present now in the classical mode in North America. I suspect that such psychogenic stress reactions are now presenting as post-traumatic stress disorders, atypical dissociative disorders, or somatoform disorders. As an example of a traditional conversion disorder, I discuss hysterical blindness. I have treated two hysterical blindness cases. Both were young male military recruits who had been "strongly encouraged" to join the military by relatives. One of the cases was referred to psychiatry with a 2-week history of "blindness." He had been fully investigated neurologically and ophthalomologically. No pathology was found. All eye reflexes were normal, yet despite efforts to catch him in an unguarded moment, suggesting malingering, he persisted with his blindness. He had even sustained some bruising by bumping into objects. History revealed his loss of vision occurred suddenly while doing combat maneuvres on the bayonet range. Interestingly, he stated, "I just couldn't see myself killing people." He feared telling his parents that he was terrified to be in military life. After confirming the diagnosis and the cause, I told him that he would be released from the military services, but it was only with hypnosis (one session, as was the case with the other soldier) that he immediately regained his vision. Also he was able to visually describe accurately all the locations he had been to during the 2 weeks of conversion blindness.

Somnambulism. This is more commonly called "sleep walking." It is not so long ago that this was classified as a dissociative disorder. More recently, somnambulism has been moved to the sleep disorders known as *parasomnias.* This appears to be a valid change. Somnambulism, as we know today, is a sleep disorder of Phase 4 sleep (as measured by sleep EEGs), generally seen in the first third of the night. It really has nothing to do with the process of dissociation.

On the other hand, there are people who awaken in a trance state and carry out activities in the nighttime, which the patient has no recollection of in the morning. Here the nocturnal activity is more purposeful than the parasomnias. It appears that the patient awakes, but in a trance state (which is *not* a sleep state). I have had a number of patients with dissociative state disorders having had alter ego states (personalities) who would take over when the host personality went to sleep.

In one case, a young soldier complained that strange things were happening to him. He would go to bed, lay his uniform out neatly for the next morning, lock his door, and retire for the night. He would awaken in the morning only to find his clothes scattered everywhere and the room disarranged, yet the door was still locked. In addition, his car was much lower on gas than when he went to bed. In therapy, it was discovered that he had an alter personality who scorned the soldier's puritanical lifestyle and would take over as the soldier "slept." This alter frequented bars and fornicated liberally, but generally made sure he returned to the barrack room before morning. What sounded like a somnambulism on initial history was in fact a dissociative switch of personalities. Thus, one should carefully scrutinize a history of somnambulism to rule out a nighttime switching due to an altered or dissociated state.

Another example of this from my own caseload concerns a divorced, overweight female. She was referred from an eating disorders clinic. She had been gaining weight in spite of apparent strict compliance to her diet. The unusual aspects of the case, which had resulted in a referral for hypnotic investigation, was the fact that many times in the morning she would awaken and find dirty dishes in her kitchen that were not there when she had retired to bed. She was living alone, and the doors were locked. This led her eating disorders clinician to suspect that she was eating in a somnambulistic state. He referred her to me to determine if hypnosis could be used in therapy. She was a good trance subject, and during hypnotic recall of the somnambulistic periods a voice suddenly took over, much to my surprise, and introduced itself as the part that was doing the eating. It stated that when the patient was slim she had been sexually abused by her ex-husband. This dissociative part said it had thus taken on the role of "protector" and was taking control occasionally while the patient assumed she was sleeping. This part would go the kitchen and eat to keep the body fat and thus safe from sexual problems in the future. The patient had been unaware both of the nighttime bingeing and the motivations for the overeating.

Flashbacks. Sudden, unexpected, and often of brief duration, flashbacks are relatively common in those who are subsequently diagnosed as having dissociative disorders. (I exclude those suffering from flashbacks in relation to drug toxicity or withdrawal). Flashbacks are often the intrusion of past episodes of abuse that had been rendered amnestic by repression or dissociation. It may consist of a quick visual still image of a scene, or a short video-like replay of an abuse scene. The patient may have a feeling of fear or dread during the scene, which may be a brief revivification experience. Frequently, upon investigation, these scenes reveal forgotten abuse memory and may open the door to many forgotten episodes of childhood trauma. The recollection in a flashback, however, does not guarantee that the memory is 100% true.

DISSOCIATIVE DISORDERS

I proceed now to the actual dissociative disorders. DSM-III-R has divided these into five categories: Depersonalization Disorder, Psychogenic Fugue, Psychogenic Amnesia, Multiple Personality Disorder, and Dissociative Disorders Not Otherwise Specified.

Depersonalization Disorder. DSM-III-R states: "The symptom of depersonalization involves an alternation in the perception or experience of the self in which the usual sense of one's own reality is temporarily lost or changed. This is manifested by a feeling of detachment from and being an outside observer of one's mental processes or body, or feeling like an automaton or as if in a dream" (American Psychiatric Association, 1987, p. 276). This symptom is presented in DSM-III-R as follows:

300.60 Depersonalization Disorder (or Depersonalization Neurosis)
A. Persistent or recurrent experiences of depersonalization as indicated by either (1) or (2):
    (1) an experience of feeling detached from and as if one is

an outside observer of one's mental processes or body
(2) an experience of feeling like an automaton or as if in a dream
B. During the depersonalization experience, reality testing remains intact.
C. The depersonalization is sufficiently severe and persistent to cause marked distress.
D. The depersonalization experience is the predominant disturbance and is not a symptom of another disorder, such as Schizophrenia, Panic Disorder, or Agoraphobia without History of Panic Disorder, but with limited symptom attacks of depersonalization, or temporal lobe epilepsy (American Psychiatric Association, 1987, p. 277).

An associated feature is derealization, which is "a strange alteration in the perception of one's surroundings so that the sense of this reality of the external world is lost" (American Psychiatric Association, 1987, p. 276). Although I have seen depersonalization and derealization symptoms in the context of other dissociative disorders, this is a somewhat uncommon primary diagnosis in my experience. One case concerns a 29-year-old woman of German origin. She had been under stress and had returned to Germany for a holiday. On returning to Canada she complained of difficulty in sorting out events. Her memories of her time in Germany were all "dream-like". She was not sure if events had happened or if they were dreams. Everything was like a dream. Even her present experience was frightening to her. At times, she didn't know if things around her were real or unreal. She even questioned if I was really just a part of her dream. In spite of this, she was able to carry out her normal day-to-day functioning, and an observer would not have noticed that all was not right for her. Her EEG was normal. She was a good hypnotic subject, and eventually we discovered that there were concerns about her marriage. She had met an old boyfriend in Germany. The conflict of seeing what might have been her life with this man compared to what it was like in Canada with her husband caused the stress. As these conflicts were worked out, she was able to see that she had created a fantasy that became so real she had lost control. Although her depersonalization and derealization symptoms decreased with therapy, she returned after 2 years, stating that she was still having trouble with intermittent feelings of unreality. New stressors were managed and she has been out of therapy for the past four years.

Another patient, age 40, who was functioning quite well in her marriage and job, nonetheless suffered from periods of depersonalization. The problem began in adulthood when she began to experience flashback memories of incest. Her functioning was being interfered with by episodes that were ego dystonic. She wrote the following: "Very often, I feel that I can't make contact with people, as if we are existing in different dimensions. I think they hear me speaking, but are puzzled about what I'm saying and, as I talk, I feel a gap between my intentions and my voice, as if my thoughts were a high slow-moving gear and way out the top of my consciousness is a little tiny gear going at top speed, which is my voice and I can't feel the connection. Sometimes I feel like I don't overlap with people." At first reading, these statements sound rather bizarre, but the patient was not psychotic, and I believe she was desperately trying to verbalize a very uncomfortable feeling of depersonalization that can sometimes be very difficult to convey in words.

Psychogenic Fugue. According to DSM-III-R, the criteria for psychogenic fugue are:

> **300.13 Psychogenic Fugue**
> A. The predominant disturbance is sudden, unexpected travel away from home or one's customary place of work, with inability to recall one's past.
> B. Assumption of a new identity (partial or complete).
> C. The disturbance is not due to Multiple Personality Disorder to an Organic Mental Disorder (e.g., partial complex seizures in temporal lobe epilepsy. (American Psychiatric Association, 1987, p. 273).

An example of psychogenic fugue concerns a young adult male who was referred to me from the neuropsychiatric unit, where he was being investigated for possible temporal lobe epilepsy. He had had three recent outbursts of violent activity. In one case, he had suddenly become violent and, in an ensuing fight, fractured a person's jaw. In another, he became suddenly agitated and tore a room apart. In all cases, he returned to conscious awareness far away from the scenes of the violent behaviors and had total amnesia for these events. The time period lost was about 15 to 30 minutes in each event. There was no previous history of fugue or amnesia, and he was normally a mild-mannered person. Neurological exam and EEG were normal. History revealed that he was recently released from prison where he was sent for theft. He did not want to discuss the 6 months in prison, but he reluctantly admitted he had gaps in his memory for that time. Hypnosis helped him recall being gang-raped by a group of prison inmates who had singled him out because he was mild mannered and of different racial origin. He had been sexually abused by these men on numerous occasions. Apparently, attempts to tell the prison guards only resulted in laughter by the guards, who told him the prison "was not the Holiday Inn and didn't cater to room change requests." When some of the more sadistic events were being recalled, in hypnosis, a state that called itself "Empty" stated that it had taken over and accepted the severe episodes of anal intercourse. It was revealed that the three episodes of fugues being investigated were related to situations in which a male had inadvertently touched the patient. "Empty" interpreted these as homosexual advances and went into a rage, attacking everything in the environment. It was in this temporary fragmentary personality state of Empty that the patient acted out and fled. We were able to work this out with hypnosis, and the fugues have not recurred in the four years since therapy. It is pointed out here that fugue states can be of short duration, with only short distances of travel involved and the identity assumed need not be a complex personality, but could be a partial one such as "Empty" in this case. I suspect that, in short duration fugues, such ego states may not have time to take on any personal identity. Even if this state had not had an identity, as required by DSM-III-R, I would have felt comfortable with a diagnosis of "psychogenic fugue." I believe this position will also be reflected in the soon-to-be-released DSM-IV.

Psychogenic Amnesia is probably more common, and I doubt if anyone has not seen a movie or television show depicting some hero or heroine with psychogenic amnesia. Of psychogenic amnesia, DSM-III-R states:

> **300.12 Psychogenic Amnesia**
> A. The predominant disturbance is an episode of sudden inability to recall important personal information that is too excessive to be explained by ordinary forgetfulness.
> B. The disturbance is not due to Multiple Personality Disorder or to an Organic Mental Disorder (e.g., blackouts during alcohol intoxication). (American Psychiatric Association, 1987, p. 275).

An example of this is a 17-year-old female student who was referred because of two episodes of amnesia. The first had happened while she was returning home from school by bus. She was just about to get off the bus, and then the very next moment she found herself in her home. She had no idea how she got home but did not dare to tell anyone. Several nights later, as she disembarked at the same bus stop, she suddenly found herself lying in a field alone, stripped to the waist. She had no idea of the time interval lost but felt it was the same evening. She went home and reported the incident. She was investigated neurologically, and all was normal, and she was referred to psychiatry. Under hypnosis she recalled that on the first incident, there were four boys at the bus stop. As they started to make sexual advances, she bolted away and ran home. It is assumed that she did this in a dissociated state. On the second incident, the same group of boys was waiting at the bus stop. This time they grabbed her and hauled her into a nearby field. They pulled off her brassiere and appeared to be intending to do more when somehow they were frightened off. She was able to recall her memories for both amnestic periods by the use of hypnosis.

Multiple personality disorders were little diagnosed in this century until the past couple of decades because the medical profession thought it rare and, also, because it can be mistaken for such conditions as schizophrenia, severe cases of borderline personality disorder, or temporal lobe epilepsy.

DSM-III-R states, "Recent reports suggest that this disorder is not nearly so rare as it is commonly thought to be" (American Psychiatric Association, 1987, p. 271). Diagnostic criteria are:

> **300.14 Multiple Personality Disorder**
> A. The existence within the person of two or more distinct personalities or personality states (each with its own relatively enduring pattern of perceiving, relating to, and thinking about the environment and self).
> B. At least two of these personalities or personality states recurrently take full control of the person's behavior. (American Psychiatric Association, 1987, p. 272).

As clinicians, to make the diagnosis, we rely not only on the history and being alert to the mention of any dissociative phenomena, such as the ones already mentioned, but we are also especially attuned to any indication of episodes of amnesia that are frequent in patients suffering from multiple personality. More recently, we have been aided by the presence of questionnaires or interview scales (Bernstein & Putnam, 1986; Ross, Heber, Norton, Anderson, Anderson, & Barchet, 1989; Steinberg, Rounsaville, & Cicchetti, 1991). Of all dissociative disorders, multiple personality disorder (MPD) is the one that I see most frequently, though the DDNOS category is also relatively common.

A 25-year-old single female was referred by a psychiatrist who suspected the presence of MPD. Originally, he had thought drug and alcohol abuse were the reasons for her drastic personality changes and amnestic episodes. When seen, she was fearful of her own life, for there were homicidal threats written in lipstick on her walls. These were written at a time when she was in her apartment alone with the doors locked. She had a history of childhood sexual abuse and admitted to many episodes of amnesia, finding herself in locations to which she had no memory of travelling. Her boyfriend told her that, at times, she would behave and cry like a child, and, at other times, she would be violent and aggressive. Once she attacked him and fractured his jaw. Using hypnotic trance or guided imagery (Fraser 1991), she readily dissociated into different personality patterns. Besides the present personality, which was very passive and introverted, she had: a 6-year-old male; a 5-year-old female; two 20-year-old sisters; a nonhuman state called "The Animal;" and an 80-year-old grandmother.

These various personalities had "shared" her body for many years. Her knowledge of them was strictly through the reports of others, which generally corresponded to her periods of memory gaps. She admitted that she had heard inner voices of varying ages for a few years, but for the most part had tried to ignore them.

Therapy gradually revealed the following personality information: the 5-year-old female had emerged when the patient herself was 5 years old. She had been the subject of sexual fondling by the father and was aware of verbal fights between parents. The 6-year-old boy came about a year later. He would play with the girl, but would leave her when she was being abused by her father. After all, he was a boy, and men *surely* don't abuse boys (so he thought!). He would "go to another room" while she was being abused.

Two sisters were about 20. One had taken over from the 5-year-old about a year after her abuse had begun. The father had begun anal penetration, and the 5-year-old had dissociated. When the anal penetration progressed to vaginal penetration, the other sister took over. Both were tough and took over all further episodes of sexual abuse through the years and aged along with the host personality, though about 5 years younger, as one might expect. Clinically, one would have no trouble diagnosing either sister as an antisocial personality, although the host personality was passive, very pleasant and likeable.

There were certain other unexpected crises in her life that were not sexual assaults, but were nonetheless terrifying. One was a miscarriage at age 15; another related to terrifying unexpected panic attacks. Panic disorder appears to be fairly common in MPD patients (Putnam, Guroff, Silberman, Barban, & Post, 1986, Fraser & Lapierre 1986). A special state called "The Animal" handled these episodes. When this state was first encountered in therapy, it shrieked like a frightened animal and bolted out of my office running much like a terrified lizard. Gradually, in therapy this personality was "tamed," taught to speak, and "transformed" into a human personality, mainly by the other personality states between therapy sessions (much to my relief and delight!).

The 80-year-old grandmother was the loving caretaker of the preceding personalities. She was a copy of an actual grandmother who lived in another country. She was the only source of nurturing for the personalities, as both parents were abusers and negligent in normal childcare provision.

In therapy, the various dissociated traumatic memories were shared, and eventually the personalities were fused into a functional unit made up of all of the personalities. She has remained fused for the past 6 years and functions very well.

Dissociative Disorders Not Otherwise Specified. Finally, we have the diagnostic category for all the dissociative disorders that do not fit into the more classical cases that I have already mentioned. This category is called "Dissociative Disorders Not Otherwise Specified". At times this has been called an atypical dissociative disorder. Although this has not been a common diagnosis in the past, I predict that it is one that will be used with increasing frequency. Many referrals I have recently seen to determine if MPD is the proper diagnosis have not reached the full criteria required for MPD. However, they are less complete forms of dissociation similar to MPD and properly fit into the category of Dissociative Disorders Not Otherwise Specified (NOS), as described in DSM-III-R:

> **300.15 Dissociative Disorders Not Otherwise Specified**
> Disorders in which the predominant feature is a dissociative symptom (i.e., a disturbance or alteration in the normally integrative functions of identity, memory, or consciousness) that does not meet the criteria for a specific Dissociative Disorder. Examples:
> 1) Ganser's syndrome: the giving of "approximate answers" to questions commonly associated with other symptoms, such as amnesia, disorientation, perceptual disturbances, fugue, and conversion symptoms.
> 2) cases in which there is more than one personality state capable of assuming executive control of the individual, but not more than one personality state is sufficiently distinct to meet the full criteria for Multiple Personality Disorder, or cases in which a second personality never assumes complete executive control.
> 3) trance states, i.e., altered states of consciousness with markedly diminished or selectively focused responsiveness to environmental stimuli. In children this may occur following physical abuse or trauma.
> 4) derealization unaccompanied by depersonalization
> 5) dissociated states that may occur in people who have been subjected to periods of prolonged and intense coercive persuasion (e.g., brainwashing, thought reform, or indoctrination while the captive of terrorists or cultists)
> 6) cases in which sudden, unexpected travel and organized, purposeful behavior with inability to recall one's past are not accompanied by the assumption of a new identity, partial or complete. (American Psychiatric Association, 1987, p. 277)

Into this category I would also place those patients who experienced states they refer to as possession states, demon possession or the like. Some eventually turn out to actually be MPD. Those who have reported previous life experiences might be considered in this category if this belief produces current symptomatology, though, generally, these are only memories recalled under hypnosis.

A case in my practice that fits into the second example of the NOS category (the second personality never assumes complete control) was that of a 45-year-old successful married businessman. He presented for therapy complaining that there was something inside that was sabotaging his functioning in business and in his personal life. He also admitted to hearing a critical female voice in his head. He had never experienced episodes of amnesia. His father had died when the patient was a child and his mother had been very possessive and especially jealous of his wife. Using Ego-State Therapy (Watkins & Watkins, 1981), he was able to produce a dissociated ego state that believed itself to be his mother (in effect, it was a "clone" of his mother). This ego state said that "she" was very angry that he left her and got married, and she was determined to ruin his marriage and job so he would return home and look after her. This mother ego state said, "He's not very smart," and she didn't know how he ever made it in business. She never took over executive control, but she certainly believed she was separate and was a very negative force in his life. Certainly, there was a fine line between this DDNOS 'inner influence' and MPD which I believe will be better clarified in DSM-IV. In business meetings she would "make him" lose his temper, hoping if he lost his job he would come home to her. He had never understood why he had such violent outbursts of anger in meetings.

In closing, I hope these descriptions of dissociative disorders and phenomena, along with clinical excerpts taken from my clinical practice in this area, will help prepare clinicians for the types of presentations to expect when working in the field of dissociation. A familiarity with the phenomena of dissociation will insure that this will no longer be the neglected area of psychiatry it once was. In addition, such patients will no longer be condemned to years of useless therapy due to erroneous diagnoses as has been all too common in the past.

REFERENCES

American Psychiatric Association (1987). *Diagnostic and statistical manual of mental disorders* (3rd ed., rev.), Washington, DC: Author.

Beahrs, J.O. (1982). *Unity and multiplicity: Multilevel consciousness of self in hypnosis, psychiatric disorder and mental health.* New York: Brunner/Mazel.

Bernstein, E.M. & Putnam, F.W. (1986). Development, reliability, and validity of a dissociation scale. *Journal of Nervous and Mental Disease, 174,* 727-735.

Bliss, E.L. (1986). *Multiple personality, allied disorders and hypnosis.* New York: Oxford University Press.

Braun, B.G. (Ed.) (1986). *Treatment of multiple personality disorder.* Washington, DC: American Psychiatric Press.

Crasilneck, H.B. & Hall, J.A. (1985). *Clinical hypnosis: Principles and applications.* Orlando, FL: Grune & Stratton.

Ellenberger, H.F. (1970). *The discovery of the unconscious: The history and evolution of dynamic psychiatry.* New York: Basic Books.

Fraser, G.A. (1991). The dissociative table technique. A strategy for working with ego states in dissociative disorders and ego-state therapy. *Dissociation, 4,* 205-213.

Fraser, G.A. & Lapierre, Y.D. (1986). Lactate induced panic attacks in dissociative states (multiple personalities). Third International Conference on Multiple Personalities and other Dissociative States. September 1986.

Goettman, G., Greaves, G.B. & Coons, P. (1991). Multiple personality and dissociation, 1791 - 1990: A complete bibliography. Atlanta, Georgia: George B. Greaves.

Goettman, G., Greaves, G.B. & Coons, P. (1992). Multiple personality and dissociation, 1791 - 1990: A complete bibliography. 1991 Supplement. Atlanta, Georgia: George B. Greaves, Ph.D., P.C., 529 Pharr Road N.E., 30305

Horevitz, R.P. (1992). Hypnosis and multiple personality disorder: Connections and controversies. American Psychological Association, Presidential Address. Washington, DC.

Kluft, R.P. (Ed.) (1985). *Childhood antecedents of multiple personality.* Washington, DC: American Psychiatric Press.

Putnam, F.W. (1989). *Diagnosis and treatment of multiple personality disorder.* New York: Guilford.

Putnam, F.W., Guroff, J.J., Silberman, E.K., Barban, L., & Post, R.M. (1986). The clinical phenomenology of multiple personality disorder: A review of 100 recent cases. *Journal of Clinical Psychiatry, 47,* 285-293.

Ross, C.A. (1989). *Multiple personality disorder: Diagnosis, clinical features and treatment.* New York: Wiley.

Ross, C.A., Heber, S., Norton, G.R., Anderson, D., Anderson, G. & Barchet, P. (1989). The dissociative disorders interview schedule: A structured interview. *Dissociation, 2,* 169-189.

Spiegel, D. & Spiegel, H. (1978). *Trance and treatment: Clinical uses of hypnosis.* New York: Basic Books.

Steinberg, M., Rounsaville, B. & Cicchetti, D. (1991). Detection of dissociative disorders in psychiatric patients by a screening instrument and structured diagnostic interview. *American Journal of Psychiatry, 140,* 1050-1054.

Watkins, J.G. & Watkins, H.H. (1981). Ego-state therapy. In R.J. Corsini (Ed.), *Handbook of Innovative Psychotherapies* (pp. 252-70).

World Health Organization (1987). International classification of diseases, Ninth Revision, Clinical Modification (annotated). (ICD-9-CM). Ann Arbor, MI: Edwards Bros.

II
PSYCHOLOGICAL
CONCEPTS

5
Three Levels of Consciousness: Implications for Dissociation

Kenneth S. Bowers
University of Waterloo

The year 1904 was a very good year for psychology. Donald Hebb, the man to whom this book is dedicated, was born that year, on July 22. So too, and only 3 days later, was Jack Hilgard, whose work on divided consciousness and neo-dissociation Hebb so much admired. And finally, B. F. Skinner, whose work Hebb admired somewhat less, was also born in 1904. It is perhaps unclear what relevance Skinner's *radical behaviorism* has for this symposium. But I am persuaded that there is an important sense in which Skinner's work speaks to the notion of dissociation. Perhaps a few quotations from Skinner will set the stage for my subsequent remarks.

In his classic paper, "Behaviorism at Fifty," Skinner (1963) first introduced the problem of privacy and of knowing oneself, especially in light of the failures of introspection to reveal mental processes. He then stated:

The problem of privacy may be approached in a fresh direction by starting with behavior rather than with immediate experience . . . . Instead of concluding that man can know only his subjective experiences—that he is bound forever to his private world and that the external world is only a construct—a behavioral theory of knowledge suggests that it is the

private world which, if not entirely unknowable, is at least not likely to
be known well. (p. 953)

Skinner then argued that *knowing* and *being* are are really "verbal
responses which name and describe the external and internal stimuli
associated with [prior contingent] events." And, because these prior
contingent events are generally arranged by the social community,
awareness is a social product. However, "because the community
cannot reinforce self-descriptive responses consistently, a person
cannot describe or otherwise 'know' events occurring within his own
skin as subtly and precisely as he knows events in the world at large"
(Skinner, 1963, p. 953).

This inevitable imprecision regarding knowledge of one's inner
life seems especially prone to engender reliance on what Skinner
termed *mental way stations*—in effect, explanatory fictions that are
accepted and reinforced by the social community in which the person
develops. Whether these consensual accounts of first-person behavior
have anything to do with its actual determinants remains a moot
point. In other words, Skinner's behaviorism provides the basis for
a dissociation between the actual determinants of a person's behavior,
on one hand, and the conscious experience and/or explanation of it,
on the other.

Compare this Skinnerian view of self-knowledge, published 27
years ago, with the following recent article on self-deception by
Timothy Wilson (1985). Wilson argued that:

People often attempt to infer their internal states with the use of a
conscious, verbal, explanatory system. This verbal system involves
conscious attempts to estimate one's feelings, independently of cognitive
processes mediating behavior . . . . In essence the argument is that there
are two mental systems. One system mediates behavior . . . , is largely
nonconscious, and is, perhaps, the older of the two systems in evolutionary
terms. The other, perhaps newer system, is largely conscious, and attempts
to explain and communicate mental states. (p. 101)

It is hard for me to read this passage without experiencing déjà vu for an earlier era though, to be sure, it is gussied up with the interim contributions of modern cognitive psychology that Skinner would disavow even today.

FIRST ORDER CONSCIOUSNESS

The basic point that I wish to emphasize is this: Both behaviorists (circa 1960) and contemporary psychologists under the sway of the cognitive revolution argue that a stimulus must be perceived in order to reinforce and/or influence behavior; but, just as surely, they reject any claim that a perceived stimulus must be consciously represented in order to be an effective mover and shaper of behavior. Indeed, consciousness of a stimulus is viewed as only one possible consequence of perceiving it. What is more, our conscious experience of events is, according to Skinner, itself subject to the vagaries of the verbal community in which we live. In contemporary terms, accounts of our behavior are based on various cognitive heuristics, such as representativeness or availability—which are, in effect, socially endorsed versions of action that can unwittingly overlook, underestimate, or disavow important determinants of behavior (Kahneman, Slovic, & Tversky, 1982). These cognitive heuristics are presumably a function of the second, more advanced mental system that Wilson referred to in the preceding quotation.

According to a radical behaviorist view, all that is required to document perception is discriminative behavior. Such discriminative behavior can be demonstrated in worms or ants, when surely there is no serious question of awareness or consciousness ever playing a role in mediating behavior. I have earlier termed such simple discriminative behavior as reflecting perception without noticing— the implication being that the environment exercises stimulus control over the organism without the mediation of consciousness or awareness (Bowers, 1984, 1987). However, once evolution has produced sufficient grey matter for selective attention to emerge as a biological possibility, and when sufficient stimulus energy impinges on sensory receptors to foster selective attention, we have the necessary conditions for what I have referred to as *first order consciousness* (Bowers, 1984, 1987). In effect, first order consciousness implies that selective attention transforms something perceived into something noticed. Thus, we can speak of perceived information when referring to information that simply engenders discriminative responsiveness, and reserve the term *noticed information* for perceived information that is, in addition, selectively attended and therefore consciously perceived. Humans can typically verbalize noticed information, but I am perfectly willing to assume that many animals are quite capable of selective attention—and hence of first order consciousness—even though they are not capable of verbalizing its contents.

Subliminal Perception

One of the historic debates in modern psychology concerns whether or not *humans* can respond discriminatively to information they do not consciously perceive or notice. The tacit assumption of people like Charles Eriksen (1959, 1960) and, more recently, Daniel Holender (1986) seems to be that, once a species has evolved the biological substrate necessary for first order consciousness, the very possibility for unconscious—or, if you prefer, nonconscious—perception is lost. To illustrate, consider one form of unconscious perception, namely subliminal perception. Whether subliminal perception even exists has been a more or less ongoing controversy for more than 30 years (Dixon, 1971, 1981). The chief argument against it goes something like this: (a) The antecedent probability that subliminal perception exists is extremely low; (b) consequently, evidence in its favor must be extremely convincing before subliminal perception is accepted as a genuine phenomenon; (c) the evidence for subliminal perception is not extremely convincing; (d) therefore, the phenomenon of subliminal perception has no scientific status.

The force of this argument depends critically on the merits of the first proposition. My hunch is that the assessment of subliminal perception as having an extremely low antecedent likelihood has been, in part, based on an aversion to psychoanalytic concepts of the unconscious, out of which some of the early studies on subliminal perception emerged (e.g., Lazarus & McCleary, 1951). However, when disconnected from its psychoanalytic moorings and looked at in strictly evolutionary terms, unconscious perception—perception without noticing—doesn't seem so improbable. After all, how else do ants and worms perceive? What seems unlikely is that discriminative behavior *requires* consciousness of what is perceived. And indeed, more than one cognitive psychologist has waxed puzzled about the functions of consciousness, given that so much human behavior seems to occur in its absence (e.g., Tulving, 1985; Velmans, 1991). In sum, the antecedent probability that unconscious perception occurs in human beings increases considerably when it is considered in light of Darwin, rather than Freud. And, as the antecedent likelihood of unconscious perception increases, some of the research offered in support of it becomes rather compelling. (cf. Greenwald, 1992).

This is not the time or place for a critical review of the evidence for and against unconscious perception in general, or subliminal perception in particular (see Dixon, 1971; Holender, 1986). Let me mention only that my colleagues at the University of Waterloo, Jim Cheesman and Phil Merikle (1986), have recently been engaged in experimental work on subliminal perception that seems reasonably compelling to many investigators. Without going into the experimental details, these investigators have shown that there are *two* thresholds that have been conflated in past research. The first, *objective threshold*, is reached when a subject is able to respond discriminatively above chance to a stimulus without being aware of it; the second, *subjective threshold*, is reached when the stimulus is presented for a long enough duration to permit its conscious perception. According to Cheesman and Merikle, what has traditionally been referred to as subliminal perception is perception that occurs above the objective threshold but below the subjective threshold. Unfortunately, both the advocates and critics of subliminal perception have typically given the impression that subliminal perception must occur *below* the objective threshold—that is, below the threshold at which discriminative responses can be achieved.

What is crucial to Cheesman and Merikle's findings is that when the subjective threshold is crossed, the effect is quite different from perceiving the same stimulus without awareness. When a stimulus is consciously perceived, it engenders expectations and response strategies that are absent when the same information is perceived without awareness. These expectations and strategies have the very reliable effect of altering how people respond to the stimuli.

The importance of the Cheesman and Merikle studies is twofold. First, their work documents with considerable authority that "conscious perceptual processing is not merely a stronger version of unconscious processing" (Cheesman & Merikle, 1986, p. 365). In other words, there are qualitative differences that awareness contributes to the perception of information. Second, their findings indicate that, at least under carefully controlled conditions, people can respond to word meaning without awareness of the physical stimulus that conveys it. Traditionally, this kind of unconscious perception has been referred to as subliminal perception, and it represents a dissociation of perception from consciousness that deserves our continued consideration (cf. Erdelyi, 1985).

Other Forms of Unconscious Perception

Demonstrating the existence of subliminal perception is not the same thing as demonstrating its importance in everyday life. And to be perfectly honest, I have a hunch that subliminal perception is not a routine event outside the laboratory. This is not to say, however, that perception without noticing is rare. Perception without noticing requires only the absence of selective attention to the perceived stimulus. One way—but only one way—of assuring that selective attention has not occurred is to disallow it—by immediate masking of the stimulus, for example. The working assumption behind this research strategy seems to be that, unless the very possibility for selective attention is eliminated, one can never be sure of having demonstrated unconscious perception—that is, perception unmediated by the awareness of the stimulus perceived.

However, it has long been argued that selective attention to a particular stimulus can also be eliminated for reasons that don't disallow the possibility of its occurrence—for example, by diverting attention from a stimulus, either by some external distraction or by some self-initiated strategy of avoidance (e.g., Luborsky, Blinder, & Schimek, 1965). Self-initiated avoidance of selective attention to a perceived stimulus is one presumed basis for perceptual defense. The enabling assumption behind perceptual defense is that enough meaning can be extracted from a perceived but unnoticed stimulus to appreciate it as threatening; hence, the person can actively avoid selectively attending the stimulus, thereby preventing its conscious perception. Needless to say, the research on perceptual defense is no less controversial than the research on subliminal perception—with which it is often confused (e.g., Dixon, 1971, 1987).

There is another means of reducing, if not eliminating, the impact of selective attention on the information perceived—namely, the simple failure to mobilize selective attention to a stimulus that would ordinarily be quite noticeable. This technique of impairing selective attention is best illustrated by research in altered states of consciousness, including hypnosis. However, I forestall consideration of this issue until the last section of the chapter.

At this point, I would like to stress that unconscious perception—that is, perception without noticing the stimulus perceived—is only one basis for a viable notion of how humans are subject to unconscious influences in everyday life. But here I must introduce a distinction between two levels of consciousness that are typically confused in the psychological literature.

SECOND ORDER CONSCIOUSNESS

Whereas first order consciousness involves noticing something perceived, what I have termed *second order consciousness* involves beliefs, theories, and understandings about information represented in first order consciousness. Insofar as one's own action is concerned, second order consciousness involves beliefs about how one's thought, feeling, and behavior are influenced by a variety of factors accessible to observation or introspection. However, it is here that we begin to run into some formidable problems of self-knowledge that, in turn, have profound implications for the entire notion of dissociation.

It is philosophically well established that observations do not entail particular beliefs about them (e.g., Lakatos, 1970). What we see, even under highly controlled laboratory conditions, underdetermines our interpretation of the phenomenon observed (Bowers, 1984). This general limitation on induction is no less true when our own behavior is the target of observation and inquiry, rather than some impersonal event in nature.

Introspection is also a very fallible source of information about the causes and influences operating on one's thought and behavior (Lyons, 1986;Nisbett & Ross, 1980). For example, in a study reported by Nisbett and Wilson (1977), people were asked to select which of four pairs of stockings was superior. They were not told that all the stockings were in fact identical, and they had little introspective access to the fact that their (typical) selection of the rightmost pair of stockings was probably due to a position effect, rather than to considerations of quality or color, which were the features ordinarily proffered as the reason for choosing them as superior (Nisbett & Wilson, 1977).

In general, then, recent work in philosophy and psychology has argued convincingly that introspection has no special or privileged access to the causal connections linking thought and behavior to its determinants (Bowers, 1984, 1987). Instead, how we understand, in second order consciousness, our own and other's behavior is based on implicit or explicit theories, cognitive heuristics, and inferences, which are underdetermined by the available data. Whether our theories, beliefs, and understandings are in fact sensitive to and incorporate the actual determinants of behavior is not something that can simply be assumed, but is subject to doubt, examination, and verification.

In effect, self-understanding is like understanding anything else—first there is a hypothesis, and then there is some attempt to validate it. Such attempts are often limited, tiresome, and onerous, and can be circumvented simply by assuming the validity of one's conscious experience—an assumption that may or may not be warranted. Insofar as the assumption is unwarranted, I think it is fair to regard the person as ignorant and/or self-deceived. In either case, it makes sense to regard the person's thought and behavior as unconsciously determined—that is, determined by factors that are not well represented in second order consciousness, even if they are noticed in first order consciousness. In effect, this state of affairs implies a potential dissociation between what we notice—that is, consciously perceive in first order consciousness—and our self-understandings, as represented in second order consciousness. In other words, people can have first order consciousness *of* influences without having second order consciousness *that* they are influential. Perhaps an example of the dissociation between first and second order consciousness will help illustrate my point.

Dulany (1962) and others (e.g., Spielberger, 1962) argued long ago that people must be aware of the response/reinforcement contingencies in a verbal conditioning paradigm in order to show conditioning effects, and that so-called learning or conditioning without awareness did not occur. In other words, just as Eriksen (1959) and Holender (1986) argued against the possibility for unconscious perception, Dulany and others argued against the possibility for "unconscious learning."

Consider however, a pilot subject that I ran in a conditioning task several years ago (Bowers, 1975). The subject in fact showed a clear conditioning effect. Moreover, she later revealed under questioning awareness of her response, of my reinforcement, and of the response/reinforcement contingencies. However, when asked subsequently whether my reinforcement had anything to do with her responses, she replied rather emphatically in the negative. She argued that my reinforcement always came after her response, so the former couldn't possibly have influenced the latter. Clearly, the subject's working theory of interpersonal influence mistakenly assumed that trials are independent. Nonetheless, she noticed in first-order consciousness everything that Dulany (1962) insisted was important for conditioning to occur; she simply remained unaware in second-order consciousness of how influential these noticed events were. Accordingly, I think it quite legitimate to argue that this woman was, in a very important sense, unconsciously influenced by the contingent reinforcement of which she was clearly aware. In sum, it is quite possible for a person to be aware of events at one level that they remain unconscious of at another level, and conflating first and second order consciousness into a unitary concept of consciousness has worked all sorts of mischief in psychology (cf. Lundh, 1979).

Because neither observation nor introspection confer indubitable knowledge about the why's and wherefore's of thought and behavior, we are left with implicit or explicit beliefs, understandings, theories, attributions, and the like, to provide plausible accounts in this regard (cf. Kruglanski, 1980). However, theories about one's own thought and behavior are as provisional and subject to error as any other theory. Consequently, I have argued elsewhere (Bowers, 1984, 1987) that human thought and action are *necessarily* subject to unconscious influences. By way of clarifying the "logically necessary unconscious," consider that thought and behavior are unconsciously influenced until such time as a valid account of them is forthcoming. However, *thought and behavior are logically prior to valid theories about them.* Even when an action seems to flow from a theory or belief, one can still question the validity of that belief. Thus, bizarre and disturbed behavior may flow ineluctably from paranoid delusions, but this does not imply the validity of the delusions on which the psychotic behavior is based.

Practically speaking, rendering a valid account of one's action typically requires more and different kinds of information than was necessary to engender the action in the first place. For example, a person in Nisbett and Wilson's (1977) "consumer survey" of stocking preferences might have been considerably helped in identifying an important, if previously unsuspected, position effect on his or her choice by knowing that almost 80% of the participants in the study chose the rightmost pair of stockings. This knowledge would not of course prove the impact of position on choice of stocking; but, surely, such an account is far more likely to surface as plausible than it would if a person knew only that his or her own preferred pair of stockings just happened to occupy the rightmost position. In general, the better informed a theory is, the more likely it is to be valid. And, because we get a great deal of our information from observation and introspection, each of them are important links in the chain of self-knowledge. But neither observation nor introspection guarantees the validity of self-knowledge—that is, neither of them provides privileged access to the causal link between a response, on one hand, and its determinants, on the other. It is at the level of theory, conceptualization, and perspective-taking that we begin to provide a meaningful account of our own and other's behavior.

Finally, because second order consciousness is underdetermined by the data and events available to first order consciousness, other factors must contribute to our self-understandings. These other factors may be as benign as a naive or uninformed theory. However, more tendentious influences may also be at work to bias or distort second order consciousness—influences such as the need to maintain self-esteem and/or to disavow various ego-threatening ideas/impulses (Erdelyi, 1985). However, there is no need to assume that such factors must be well or fully represented in second order consciousness in order to influence it (Bowers, 1987; cf. Joseph, 1987).

To summarize my argument: It is the very nature of a theory

to be incomplete vis à vis the phenomenon it explains (e.g., Polkinghorne, 1983; Popper, 1979). Because an account of one's actions represented in second order consciousness is a theory of sorts, it is necessarily incomplete. Consequently, the action in question is inevitably subject to unconscious influences. By the same token, the unconscious influences operating on a particular action are often trivial and "safe" to disregard. However, it is not always easy to know when we are confronting such a benign set of circumstances and when we are not. The difficulties inherent in such a decision make it possible—even tempting—to assume that each and every action we take is transparently everything and only what it appears to be. Indeed, the temptation to so regard an action may be greatest when there is a defensive need to disavow threatening information and/or interpretations of reality that may nevertheless have some validity. This possibility raises the spectre of self-deception, to which we now turn our attention.

SELF-DECEPTION

Self-deception is frequently envisioned as an intrapersonal version of interpersonal deception (e.g., Martin, 1985; Sackeim & Gur, 1978). When this approach is taken, it immediately raises a paradox: How can the deceiver and the deceived be the same person? After all, in order to lie to oneself, one must know the truth in order to falsify it. Yet, how can one both know the truth, and be deceived by one's own misrepresentation of it? This kind of paradox has also emerged with respect to perceptual defense and repression (Erdelyi, 1985). The issue with perceptual defense is this: In order to defend against perceiving something, we must first perceive it—and, to paraphrase Sartre (1966), we must perceive it most precisely in order to avoid it more efficiently. Similarly with repression: In order to avoid remembering something, we must first recall it, the better to keep what is recalled outside awareness. Many critics are quite content to regard the paradoxical nature of self-deception, perceptual defense, and repression as sufficient reason to jettison them one and all.

It should be emphasized that the paradox vis à vis each of these notions depends entirely on a unitary concept of consciousness—that consciousness is consciousness is consciousness, and that different layers or levels of consciousness is a non sequitur, or at least a notion lacking in parsimony, and which will therefore not survive a few swipes of Occam's razor. I hope, however, that I have already persuaded the reader that there are at least two levels of consciousness—first and second order consciousness—and, by implication, two levels of unconscious influence—namely, perception without noticing, and noticing without a valid understanding of how one's thought and behavior are influenced by factors that may in fact be noticed—that is, represented in first order consciousness. Having proposed two levels of consciousness, however, the paradox implicit in the interpersonal model of self-deception disappears. First of all, perception without noticing enables a person to perceive a threatening stimulus without selectively attending it. Presumably, enough information can be extracted at this preliminary level to perceive the information as threatening, and to terminate any further processing of it (cf. Zajonc, 1980). By virtue of this self-initiated distraction, selective attention to the perceived information never takes place, and it therefore remains unnoticed—that is, it is never represented in first order consciousness. If information is not represented in first order consciousness, it cannot contribute to self-understanding, even though it might have had some measurable impact on the person—such as increasing activation or anxiety (cf. Lazarus, 1966; 1991).

But let us suppose that information is sufficiently salient or peremptory to be noticed—that is, selective attention to the information cannot be averted. Then what? Remember that observation and introspection underdetermine one's understanding of the events represented in first order consciousness. In other words, no particular theory or account of one's thought and action in second order consciousness is entailed by the events represented in first order consciousness. Thus, the subject in my conditioning experiment could deny that contingent reinforcement of her responses had any impact on her behavior. In that case, however, simple ignorance of the fact that trials are interdependent "legitimized" her belief that the response/reinforcement contingencies did not influence her behavior. Suppose, however, that mere ignorance cannot explain a person's implausible account of his or her behavior. Consider the following vignette.

Sarah is Jane's best friend. It is obvious beyond a reasonable doubt to Sarah that Jane's husband is having an affair, and that Sarah has come to this conclusion only on the basis of evidence available to both of them. Sarah is not unusually cynical or paranoid, and while she is concerned for the welfare of Jane, she is also the soul of discretion. Consequently, she does not try to convince Jane that her husband is cheating. But she cannot forebear drawing Jane's attention to the evidence at hand—not all at the same time, perhaps, but with an eye to assuring herself that Jane is in touch with the relevant data. All to no avail. And suppose that Sarah (who is, incidentally, a social psychologist) decides to create a scenario that includes all of the relevant data, suitably disguised to protect the innocent, and gives it as part of a research project in which subjects are asked to draw the most likely conclusions from a set of scenarios. And let us further suppose that, to the particular scenario of interest, all 100 subjects in the experiment conclude that the husband is having an affair. What are we to make of Jane's apparent inability to draw the same conclusion about her husband that any reasonable and informed person would?

One obvious possibility is that Jane knows full well what is going on and has simply decided to turn a blind eye—confiding this knowledge to herself, but not to her best friend. If this were the only conceivable interpretation of Jane's behavior, the very possibility of self-deception is precluded. In fact, what appears to be self-deception is a mild form of other deception—withholding from her best friend something that Sarah has reason to think Jane would mention if she were aware of it. The assumption that self-deception is always illusory, and consists merely of a reluctance to reveal one's knowledge to another person might conceivably be true, but I find it simplistic— and intuitively, it does not square with my own clinical experience, to say nothing of my own personal experience. However, I have neither the time nor the wit to prove the insufficiency of self-deception as mere reluctance to reveal to others what is consciously known.

Another possible interpretation of Jane's behavior is that she simultaneously holds two contradictory beliefs. Consciously she believes that her husband is faithful, but unconsciously she believes otherwise; further, the belief in his infidelity is unconscious because it is too threatening to be represented in second order consciousness. This is the classical model of self-deception that Sackeim and Gur (1978) forwarded in their empirical investigations of self-deception, and for which they found some support. It is a view based on an *inter*personal model of deception, in which the deceiver and the deceived are two people, and in that context, of course, there is no paradox. But when the deceiver and the deceived are one and the same person, we are flat up against the paradox that was mentioned earlier. Perhaps this classic concept of self-deception is true, even though it requires that two contradictory beliefs are held simultaneously, one of them conscious, the other motivated into an unconscious status. But I do not think this kind of mental jujitsu is necessary for a viable concept of self-deception.

The third possibility accounting for Jane's apparent inability to see her husband as others do is much simpler. It is not necessary to assume that Jane holds two simultaneous and contradictory beliefs— one conscious and the other unconscious. It is enough that she maintain only the belief in her husband's fidelity, that she does so tenaciously, and in the face of mounting evidence (so to speak) that would suggest otherwise to a reasonable, informed, and disinterested person (cf. Sarbin & Coe, 1979). But in this matter Jane is not disinterested, however reasonable and informed she may be in most respects. The available evidence, however well it may be represented in first order consciousness, does not entail personally threatening and unpleasant beliefs about it in second order consciousness. Jane is doubtless highly motivated to preserve a benign version of the facts represented in first order consciousness, but this is quite different from saying that she has an unconscious *belief* that is too painful to admit into second order consciousness. True, it may be increasingly necessary for Jane to invoke a series of ad hoc hypotheses to preserve the belief in her spouse's fidelity. This should not be too surprising, however, insofar as some scientists and most politicians do it all the time in order to preserve their favored version of reality. Why should we deny the same possibilities to the ordinary person trying to make sense of his or her personal life and relationships? And although this scenario of self-deception is not based on the interpersonal model of it, this is not in itself a good reason to deny the status of self-deception. Indeed, the motivated disavowal of a particular interpretation of "the facts," or even the denial of facts relevant to a threatening conclusion, seems very close to the common sense view of self-deception (cf. Goleman, 1985).

To summarize: The concept of self-deception suggests that the beliefs or theories comprising second order consciousness are often highly motivated versions of reality that stand in the face of contrary evidence, and that do not easily submit to tests of its validity.

Before leaving this section on self-deception, let me add only this. It can be difficult for the disinterested person to understand how a person has not drawn certain "obvious" conclusions from the available evidence. Perhaps this is why unconscious beliefs are so easily attributed to such a person. In other words, if the evidence fairly screams for certain conclusions about it, the impartial observer may find it easier to assume that the person did in fact come to the "obvious" belief or conclusion—but unconsciously—rather than to assume that the conclusion was not drawn at all. However, such an attribution perhaps *underestimates* how motivation can operate simply to preserve a comfortable and comforting version of reality in the face of contrary evidence, and *overestimates* the degree to which full-fledged beliefs can be unconscious. Indeed, according to the view I have proposed, second order consciousness is precisely a theory or belief about information represented in first order consciousness. I am not yet ready to take on the responsibility of proposing a notion of second order consciousness that permits it to consist of unconscious beliefs.

DISSOCIATION AND HYPNOSIS

Let us return to the possibility, mentioned earlier, that people may simply fail to mobilize selective attention to perceived information. We are not referring here to active inattention vis à vis threatening information; rather, it is the simple absence of attention that is at issue. Such an attentional lacuna is due to the fact that people simply do not have the will or the way to attend information that has been perceived.

To illustrate, Henry Bennett (1988) reviewed a series of studies involving surgical patients who were administered suggestive communications while under general anesthesia. In one such study, anesthetized patients were told to pull on their ear lobes in a subsequent postoperative interview with the investigator. On the average, patients in this experimental group manifested the suggested response six times more often than did a control group of surgical patients who did not receive the suggestive communication. What is more, none of the patients in the experimental condition were later able to recall the suggestive communication, even when hypnosis was employed to aid their recall (Bennett, Davis, & Giannini, 1981; see also Bonke, Fitch, & Millar, 1990).

Evans (1979) reviewed a somewhat similar series of studies not employing surgical patients. Subjects in alpha-free, Stage I sleep were provided suggestions for particular responses, together with a cue that was to trigger their subsequent occurrence. When the cue was administered to the sleeping subject later that night, or on a subsequent night up to 5 months later, it elicited an appropriate discriminative response a reasonably high proportion of the time; irrelevant cues, however, were ineffective in this regard (Evans, Gustafson, O'Connell, Orne, & Shor, 1966, 1970). All of this transpired without any evident waking memory for the original, sleep-administered suggestions.

Both the Bennett and the Evans et al. investigations establish, rather persuasively, that people need not be conscious (in any ordinary sense) of the suggested basis for discriminative and directed behavior. In other words, such behavior is dissociated from the ordinary means of initiating and monitoring it (Hilgard, 1977).

In the studies on both general anesthesia and normal sleep, people are unable to attend or appraise meaningful information that can, nevertheless, engender action in accordance with it. These behaviors are not planful enactments that derive from higher level executive initiative; rather, they occur because lower subsystems of control seem to be directly activated by the suggestive communications. However, such direct activation of lower centers of control does not require that a person be unconscious, inasmuch as fully alert people occasionally engage in fairly complex behaviors "mindlessly"—for example, dialing a more familiar telephone number instead of the intended one (cf. Norman, 1981). Such an "action slip" seems to occur spontaneously when vagrant thoughts of the familiar person insinuate themselves into the planned sequence of events, thereby derailing executive control of the intended act. Athough such spontaneous defections from executive plans and initiative may be relatively rare, hypnotic suggestions routinely activate subsystems of control without the full participation of, or undue interference from, higher executive functions (Hilgard, 1977).

Although hypnosis does not, contrary to popular myth, render a person unconscious in the way sleep and anesthesia do, it does share with them the ability to engender a loss of generalized reality orientation. According to Shor (1970):

In all of our waking life we carry around in the background of our awareness a kind of frame of reference or orientation to generalized reality which serves as a context or arena within which we interpret all of our ongoing conscious experiences. Under certain conditions—of which hypnosis is just one—this wide frame of reference or orientation to generalized reality can fade into the very distant background of our minds so that ongoing experiences are isolated from their usual context. (p. 91)

Reducing a person's generalized reality orientation by hypnosis (or, to an even greater degree, by sleep and certain drugs), diminishes the willingness or capacity to appraise and evaluate the suggested state of affairs. Consequently, subsystems of control are less subject to the guidance and monitoring of executive plans and intentions, and they therefore seem more susceptible to direct activation by suggestive communications (Miller, Galanter, & Pribram, 1960; Hilgard, 1977, 1979; Kihlstrom, 1984). How this neo-dissociative model of hypnosis (Hilgard, 1977) coordinates itself with my proposal for first and second order consciousness is the burden of the rest of this chapter.

Some Historical Considerations

The two-tier model of consciousness (with its implication for two levels of unconscious influence) has, for the most part, emphasized the unconscious impact of exogenous information. Traditionally, however, it has been endogenous conflicts, complexes, dissociated systems of ideas, impulses, fantasies, threats to self-esteem, defense mechanisms, and so on that clinicians have viewed as having an unconscious impact on thought and behavior (e.g., Nemiah, 1984). Historically, the two main, competing systems for coming to terms with these endogenous sources of unconscious influence have been proposed by Pierre Janet and Sigmund Freud (Perry & Laurence, 1984).

According to Janet (1965), dissociation involved an integrated subsystem of ideas and thoughts that split away (usually under stress) from consciousness, which was itself composed of an even larger, more differentiated, and interassociated network of ideas and thoughts. For a variety of reasons, Janet's views were eclipsed by Freud's more motivational and theoretical model of the unconscious, and Janet's contributions have only recently been resurrected.

The revival of interest in Janet has been multiply determined. First, Ellenberger's (1970) classic book on the unconscious included a lengthy chapter on Janet that superbly introduced an entire new generation of scholars and investigators to his seminal but largely forgotten work. Second, Ellenberger's book was soon followed by E. R. Hilgard's (1977) neo-dissociative model of mind, which was largely inspired by his research on hypnosis—a phenomenon which, in turn, had historic ties to Janet and the entire concept of dissociation. Third, Janet's concept of dissociation seems to fit the zeitgeist of current cognitive psychology better than does Freud's emphasis on sex and aggression as twin pillars of "the unconscious" (Kihlstrom, 1987; Robinson, 1984). Fourth, Janet's views, to a greater extent than Freud's, fit current theorizing about psychopathology—especially theorizing concerned with currently "hot" disorders such as post-traumatic stress syndrome (Spiegel, 1984) and multiple personality (Kluft, 1984a; see also Frankel, 1976; Spiegel & Spiegel, 1978). Finally, appreciation for Janet seems to have increased as an indirect consequence of some recent and quite critical reappraisals of Freud's views (e.g., Grunbaum, 1984, 1986;Masson, 1985). Freud's emphasis on imagined and fantasied events (rather than on actual historical events) as the basis for adult psychopathology has been particularly problematic in this regard (cf. Spence, 1982).

Whatever the reasons for the renaissance of interest in Janet's contributions, Hilgard's neo-dissociation account of mind and hypnosis reasserts and clarifies what Janet accepted as obvious—that unconscious influences need not be synonymous with id-dominated sexual and aggressive impulses. However, whereas Janet emphasized that subsystems of ideas could pathologically split off from primary consciousness, Hilgard's model has instead emphasized that subsystems of *control* were integrated into a hierarchically arrayed model of mind, the topmost level of which involved executive planning, initiative, and monitoring of lower levels of control and functioning. In other words, executive control is largely responsible for conscious and volitional behavior, whereas lower levels of control are more reactive and automatic. Moreover, there is an open-textured character to the control network, such that lower levels of control can be activated by information, perceptions, ideas, thoughts, expectations, and so forth that are not themselves completely subject to or governed by the highest level of executive control. This is especially true when the executive level of control has been rendered more or less inoperative by normal sleep or anesthesia, or when its efficiency has been reduced by hypnosis, fatigue, extreme emotional arousal, or drugs.

Evading Executive Control

When executive control is intact however, considerable sophistication is required to bypass its critical, reality-testing function. There are two general ways of "outsmarting" executive control—each way being associated with a particular research tradition in psychology. The first way of avoiding the critical functions of executive control is to introduce information to the subject that is unattended, and therefore unrepresented in first-order consciousness. Historically, this strategy has been the province of cognitive psychology. One research paradigm practiced by this tradition involves introducing information subliminally, in a manner already mentioned. But circumventing a person's attention and noticing can also be accomplished by supraliminal information from which attention is distracted because the subject is attending to another, simultaneously performed task. This is the strategy explored by investigations of dichotic listening (e.g., Glucksberg & Cowan, 1970; Govier & Pitts, 1982; MacKay,

1973; Norman, 1969), about which I have had more to say elsewhere (Bowers, 1984, 1987). The upshot of this research is that information that is unattended, and that is therefore unlikely ever to have been represented in first order consciousness, can nevertheless have a demonstrable impact on one's conscious experience and behavior (for a demurral from this view, see Newstead & Dennis, 1979, and Holender, 1986). In a more practical vein, I have previously mentioned several examples of how therapeutic interventions have been effective because they were unattended—the advantage being that patient resistance is thereby averted (Bowers, 1978).

The second research tradition that attempts to circumvent a fully functioning executive involves influences that may be readily noticed, but whose power to move and shape behavior is not easy for the target person to understand or appreciate. This latter tradition has largely been the province of social and applied psychology (e.g., Cialdini, 1985; Frank, 1973). An important ingredient of success in this domain is that the psychologist should be more sophisticated or knowledgeable than the target person regarding what is likely to alter the latter's attitudes, feelings, and behavior. It is consequently no accident that social psychologists often use relatively unsophisticated experimental subjects (e.g., freshmen in college) and, in addition, often need to use deception in order to maintain subjects' naiveté. The more sophisticated subjects are about the hypothesis under investigation, and the more informed their psychological theories, the more difficult it is to circumvent second order consciousness and the critical appraisals of high-level executive control.

Neither the cognitive nor the applied/social tradition has systematically dealt with alterations in consciousness that reduce the level at which the executive control functions. This is one reason why hypnosis, for example, has historically not been well integrated into the mainstream psychological literature. However, there is growing evidence that a more broadly based understanding of mind and behavior is evolving—one that considers normal as well as altered states of mind (e.g., Baars, 1988; Bowers, in press; Kihlstrom, 1984, 1987; Pettinati, 1988).

For present purposes, it is important to emphasize that hypnotic suggestions are fully attended, and therefore represented in first order consciousness. Moreover, suggestive communications seem to alter, at least temporarily, what the hypnotized subject believes; indeed, he or she is moved to experience the suggested state of affairs as a "believed-in-imagining" (Sarbin & Coe, 1972, 1979). In other words, by virtue of being hypnotized—with all that that implies by way of a temporary reduction in generalized reality orientation—a person uncritically accepts the validity of quite unrealistic and illogical experiences and beliefs (Bowers, 1983; Orne, 1959). Thus, far from preventing the development of beliefs in second order consciousness, hypnotic suggestions accentuate and emphasize the subject's belief in the reality of the suggested state of affairs.

Hypnosis Alters Third Order Consciousness.

All things considered, hypnosis does not seem to operate primarily on first or second order consciousness—though specifically hypnotic effects at these two levels may indeed occur. More characteristically, however, the reduced generalized reality orientation produced by hypnosis constrains and impairs a multiperspective view of reality— thereby rendering the hypnotized person more susceptible to an uncritical belief in the suggested state of affairs. Such constraints placed on a person's multiperspective orientation can perhaps be viewed as altering *third order consciousness*. In the ordinary course of events, third order consciousness emerges out of experiencing the difference between holding a particular belief, on one hand, and consciousness of oneself as holding that belief, on the other. In turn, this emerging distinction develops into a secure realization of oneself as distinct from any particular idea, belief, understanding, or theory held about oneself or the world (cf. Joseph, 1987). When, belief and believer are conflated however, the person does not readily bring alternative interpretations or beliefs to bear on the experience of oneself and the world. In other words, when a multiperspective orientation to reality is minimized or eliminated, a person is likely to become totally identified with a specific believed-in reality. This state of affairs is conceptually close to what Janet (1965) referred to as *idées fixes*, or fixed ideas. A hypnotically suggested state of affairs seems to engender just such a (temporarily) fixed belief or belief system, though it is by no means unique in its ability to do so (e.g., Conway & Siegelman, 1979; Delgado, 1977).

In sum, hypnosis erodes a multiperspective orientation toward the world, so that belief in the suggested state of affairs is not well embedded in consciousness of oneself as separate and distinct from this belief. Accordingly, we can speak of hypnotically suggested effects as being dissociated from third order consciousness. In other words, deeply hypnotized individuals display a temporarily reduced ability or inclination to evaluate and appraise the suggested state of affairs in terms of background considerations, and in terms of alternative beliefs and hypotheses, which together constitute third order consciousness.

Incidentally, this view of dissociation as involving a reduction or alteration in third order consciousness squares very nicely with Pierre Janet's early theorizing about the action of suggestion in hypnosis and hysteria. For example, he asserted that, "In order that there may be suggestion, . . . the idea should seem to develop to the extreme, *without any participation of the will or of the personal consciousness of the subject*" (Janet, 1965, p. 285; italics added). To thrust my current terminology onto Janet, the suggested idea is dissociated from the panoply of other ideas, beliefs, associations, and related background considerations that together secure and constitute third order consciousness.

Although I have emphasized dissociation in the context of hypnosis, dissociation in the context of psychopathology is somewhat more complex. For example, as implied in Janet's original contributions, the pathologically dissociated ideas that produce hysterical symptoms are not well represented in first or second order consciousness. Recall, by way of contrast, that suggestive communications delivered to the hypnotized subject are ordinarily quite accessible to both first and second order consciousness; it is third order consciousness that seems most affected by hypnosis.

According to the present analysis, then, the dissociations involved in "garden variety" hysterical symptoms tend to be restricted to the first and second order consciousness. On the other hand, influences that are dissociated from first and second order consciousness are not necessarily pathogenic. Indeed, with respect to second order consciousness, I have argued that unconscious (dissociated) influences are logically necessary. Thus, no one escapes unconscious influences operating on second order consciousness, and the same is probably true vis à vis first order consciousness as well. When do such dissociated influences become pathological? The simplest answer is that dissociated ideas and beliefs are pathogenic when they engender recognizable symptoms, which impair and disrupt the person's quality of life.

However, there is one particular dissociative disorder that requires special comment—namely, multiple personality disorder (MPD). While I accept the genuineness of the disorder, I am frankly quite skeptical of recent reports indicating a quite extraordinary proliferation of the number of patients who have received an MPD diagnosis (e.g., Bliss, 1984, 1986; Kluft, 1984b) (to say nothing of the proliferation of the number of personalities "discovered" in individual patients). However, this chapter is limited to making sense of how genuine (or even pseudo) MPD may arise, in terms of the tripartite model of consciousness proposed herein.

As indicated earlier, third order consciousness involves a multiperspective view of the world and oneself. Ordinarily, people can switch back and forth between several different ways of viewing things, in an attempt to get the most complete and best informed version of reality. However, as we have seen, a particular version of, or belief about, the world can become dissociated from third order consciousness under certain (e.g., hypnotic) circumstances—so that belief and believer are conflated. Such a conflation means that the person loses sight of himself or herself as distinct from the currently ascendant belief or belief system. MPD can be understood as a pathological fusing of belief and believer. As already mentioned, a nonpathological form of such fusion occurs in hypnosis, where the situation is considerably tempered by the fact that the hypnotized individual remains aware, in both first and second order consciousness, of the suggestive communications and their role in creating the temporarily fixed belief. However, in MPD, the origin of the ascendant belief or belief system is obscure—that is, the etiologic factors producing the fixed belief are not well represented in first or second order consciousness. In other words, the dissociations involved in MPD occur at all three levels of consciousness at once. Not only is the person "stuck" in a fixed belief system, there is no awareness of how he or she got there, let alone awareness of alternative belief possibilities.

Ordinarily, we retain some flexibility and control regarding how the world is viewed, precisely because the individual remains distinct from any particular belief or belief system—which is to say, third order consciousness remains intact. However, third order consciousness is precisely what is most impaired in MPD. Consequently, an MPD patient has relatively little belief-independent identity as a secure base for "trying out" alternative views or versions of himself or herself. This does not mean that alternative views or belief systems are unavailable. However, when firmly embedded in one belief system, there is (so to say) relatively little of the person left over to initiate a shift to another, perhaps more (or perhaps less) adaptive belief system. Shifts to another belief system do occur, of course, but the initiative for such shifts is often experienced as outside the patient's control. When such a shift occurs, there is, again, little belief-independent identity that can serve as an autonomous control center from which to monitor and/or reactivate the original belief system. In effect, total investment in one belief system impairs ready access to alternative beliefs.

To summarize, dissociation of beliefs from third order consciousness conflates the believer and the belief in a manner that can engender MPD. The impairment of third order consciousness is aided and abetted by the fact that etiologic factors leading to a particular belief system are not well represented in first or second order consciousness.

Obviously, this brief attempt to understand MPD in terms of the tri-partite level of consciousness is highly schematic, and does not begin to address the developmental or defensive character of the disorder. Other contributions to this volume will, I am sure, be more sufficient in that regard. There is something to be said, however, for building a conceptual model of the mind within which various phenomena can be understood and inter-related, and it is in that spirit that this chapter has been written.

CONCLUSION

In the brief course of this chapter, three levels of consciousness have been forwarded and, as well, three corresponding levels of unconscious (dissociated) influence. It is fair to say that clinicians and research psychologists often have trouble communicating with each other about conscious and unconscious aspects of human functioning, partly because they are referring to different levels of consciousness—usually without realizing it. Perhaps the present, multilevel account of consciousness will help remedy an intellectual chauvinism that all too often characterizes discussions of consciousness, and of unconscious influences on human thought, feeling, and behavior.

In addition, we have seen that dissociation is a complex, multidimensional concept that differs in the form it takes vis à vis first, second, and third order consciousness. We should be prepared to qualify the word appropriately as it is employed in different contexts for different purposes. One thing is certain: A great deal of theoretical and empirical work is needed to specify the meaning of dissociation with ever greater precision and clarity, so that use of the word will promote thought, rather than replace it.

Finally, I appreciate that this prolegomenon to a multilevel model of consciousness is brief and schematic, but it will have to do for now. What I would like to stress in conclusion is that hypnosis is a dissociative phenomenon, and that it was Hilgard's point of entry into the entire domain of dissociation and divided consciousness (Hilgard, 1973, 1977) that so fascinated Hebb toward the end of his career. As someone who is committed to the investigation of dissociative phenomena in general, and hypnosis in particular, I can only regret that Hebb came so late in his life to an appreciation of this rich and complex domain of investigation. It would have been wonderful to have had his imagination and intelligence contributing to our understanding of such puzzling phenomena.

REFERENCES

Baars, B. (1988). *A cognitive theory of consciousness.* Cambridge: Cambridge University Press.

Bennett, H. L. (1988). Perception and memory for events during adequate general anesthesia for surgical operations. In H. Pettinati (Ed.), *Hypnosis and memory* (pp. 193-231). New York: Guilford Press.

Bennett, H. L., Davis, H. S., & Giannini, J. A. (1981). Nonverbal response to intraoperative conversation. *British Journal of Anesthesia, 57,* 174-179.

Bliss, E. L. (1984). A symptom profile of patients with multiple personalities, including MMPI results. *Journal of Nervous and Mental Diseases, 172,* 197-202.

Bliss, E. L. (1986). *Multiple personality, allied disorders, and hypnosis.* New York: Oxford University Press.

Bonke, B., Fitch, W., & Millar, K. (1990). *Memory and awareness in anethesia.* Amsterdam: Surets and Zeitlinger.

Bowers, K. S. (1975). The psychology of subtle control: An attributional analysis of behavioral persistence. *Canadian Journal of Behavioral Science, 7,* 78-95.

Bowers, K. S. (1978). Listening with the third ear: On paying inattention effectively. In F. H. Frankel & H. S. Zamansky (Eds.), *Hypnosis at its bicentennial.* (pp. 3-14). New York: Plenum.

Bowers, K. S. (1983). *Hypnosis for the seriously curious.* New York: Norton.

Bowers, K. S. (1984). On being unconsciously influenced and informed. In K. S. Bowers & D. Meichenbaum (Eds.), *The unconscious reconsidered* (pp. 227-272). New York: Wiley.

Bowers, K. S. (1987). Revisioning the unconscious. *Canadian Psychology, 28,* 93-104.

Bowers, K. S. (1990). Unconscious influences and hypnosis. In J. L. Singer (Ed.), *Repression and dissociation: Implications for personality theory, psychopathology and health (pp. 142-179).* Chicago: U. Chicago Press.

Cheesman, J., & Merikle, P. M. (1986). Distinguishing conscious from unconscious processes. *Canadian Journal of Psychology, 40,* 343-367.

Cialdini, R. B. (1985). *Influence: Science and practice.* Glenview, IL: Scott, Foresman.

Conway, F., & Siegelman, J. (1979). *Snapping.* New York: Dell.

Delgado, R. (1977). Religious totalism: Gentle and ungentle persuasion under the first amendment. *Southern California Law Review, 51,* 1-98.

Dixon, N. F. (1971). *Subliminal perception: The nature of a controversy.* London: McGraw-Hill.

Dixon, N. F. (1981). *Preconscious processing.* New York: Wiley.

Dixon, N. F. (1987). Unconsciousness reconsidered. *Canadian Psychology, 28,* 118-119.

Dulany, D. E. (1962). The place of hypotheses and intentions: An analysis of verbal control in verbal conditioning. In C. W. Eriksen (Ed.), *Behavior and awareness* (pp. 102-129). Durham, NC: Duke University Press.

Ellenberger, H. F. (1970). *The discovery of the unconscious: The history and evolution of dynamic psychiatry.* New York: Basic Books.

Erdelyi, M. (1985). *Psychoanalysis: Freud's cognitive psychology.* New York: W.H. Freeman.

Eriksen, C. W. (1959). Unconscious processes. In M. R. Jones (Ed.), *Nebraska symposium on motivation: 1958* (pp. 169-227). Lincoln: University of Nebraska Press.

Eriksen, C. W. (1960). Discrimination and learning without awareness: A methodological survey and evaluation. *Psychological Review, 67,* 279-300.

Evans, F. J. (1979). Hypnosis and sleep: Techniques for exploring cognitive activity during sleep. In E. Fromm & R. E. Shor (Eds.), *Hypnosis: Developments in research and new perspectives* (2nd ed. pp. 139-183). New York: Aldine.

Evans, F. J., Gustafson, L. A., O'Connell, D. N., Orne, M. T., & Shor, R. E. (1966). Response during sleep with intervening waking amnesia. *Science, 197,* 687-689.

Evans, F. J., Gustafson, L. A., O'Connell, D. N., Orne, M. T., & Shor, R. E. (1970). Verbally induced behavioral responses during sleep. *Journal of*

Nervous and Mental Disease, 148, 467-476.

Frank, J. D. (1973). *Persuasion and healing: A comparative study of psychotherapy.* Baltimore: Johns Hopkins University.

Frankel, F. (1976). *Hypnosis: Trance as a coping mechanism.* New York: Plenum.

Glucksberg, S., & Cowan, G. N. (1970). Memory for nonattended auditory material. *Cognitive Psychology, 1,* 149-156.

Goleman, D. (1985). *Vital lies, simple truths: The psychology of self-deception.* New York: Simon & Schuster.

Govier, E., & Pitts, M. (1982). The contextual disambiguation of a polysemous word in an unattended message. *British Journal of Psychology, 73,* 537-545.

Greenwald, A. G. (1992). New look 3: Unconscious cognition reclaimed. *American Psychologist, 47,* 766-779.

Grunbaum, A. (1984). *The foundations of psychoanalysis: A philosophical critique.* Berkeley, CA: University of California Press.

Grunbaum, A. (1986). Precis of the foundations of Psychoanalysis: A philosophical critique. *Behavioral and Brain Sciences, 9,* 217-228.

Hilgard, E. R. (1973). A neo-dissociation interpretation of pain reduction in hypnosis. *Psychological Review, 80,* 396-411.

Hilgard, E. R. (1977). *Divided consciousness: Multiple controls in human thought and action.* New York: Wiley.

Hilgard, E. R. (1979). Divided consciousness in hypnosis: The implications of the hidden observer. In E. Fromm & R. E. Shor (Eds.), *Hypnosis: Developments in research and new perspectives* (2nd ed., pp. 45-79). New York: Aldine.

Holender, D. (1986). Semantic activation without conscious identification. *Behavioral and Brain Sciences, 9,* 1-23.

Janet, P. (1965). *Major symptoms of hysteria.* New York: Hafner. (Original work published 1929)

Joseph, E. D. (1987). The consciousness of being conscious. *Journal of the American Psychoanalytic Association, 35,* 5-22.

Kahneman, D., Slovic, P., & Tversky, A. (1982). *Judgment under uncertainty: Heuristics and biases.* Cambridge: Cambridge University Press.

Kihlstrom, J F. (1984). Conscious, subconscious, unconscious: A cognitive perspective. In K. S. Bowers & D. Meichenbaum (Eds.), *The unconscious reconsidered* (pp. 149-211). New York: Wiley.

Kihlstrom, J. F. (1987). The cognitive unconscious. *Science, 237,* 1445-52.

Kluft, R. P. (1984a). An introduction to multiple personality disorder. *Psychiatric Annals, 14,* 19-24.

Kluft, R. P. (1984b). Treatment of multiple personality disorder: A study of 33 cases. *Psychiatric Clinics of North America, 7,* 9-29.

Kruglanski, A. (1980). Lay epistemo-logic-processes and contents: Another look at attribution theory. *Psychological Review, 87,* 70-87.

Lakatos, I. (1970). Falsification and methodology of scientific research programmes. In I. Lakatos & A. Musgrave (Eds.), *Criticism and the growth of knowledge* (pp. 91-196). Cambridge: Cambridge University Press.

Lazarus, R. S. (1966). *Psychological stress and the coping process.* New York: McGraw-Hill.

Lazarus, R. S. (1991). *Emotion and adaptation.* Oxford: Oxford University Press.

Lazarus, R. S., & McCleary, R. A. (1951). Autonomic discrimination without awareness: A study of subception. *Psychological Review, 58,* 113-122.

Luborsky, L., Blinder, M., & Schimek, J. (1965). Looking, recalling, and the GSR as a function of defense. *Journal of Abnormal and Social Psychology, 20,* 270-280.

Lundh, L. G. (1979). Introspection, consciousness, and human information processing. *Scandinavian Journal of Psychology, 20,* 223-238.

Lyons, W. (1986). *The disappearance of introspection.* Cambridge, MA: Bradford.

MacKay, D. G. (1973). Aspects of the theory of comprehension, memory and attention. *Quarterly Journal of Experimental Psychology, 5,* 22-40.

Masson, J. M. (1985). *The assault on truth: Freud's suppression of the seduction theory.* New York: Penguin.

Martin, M. W. (1985). General introduction. In M. W. Martin (Ed.), *Self-deception and self-understanding* (pp. 1-27). Lawrence, KS: University of Kansas Press.

Miller, G. A., Galanter, E., & Pribram, K. H. (1960). *Plans and the structure of behavior.* New York: Holt.

Nemiah, J. C. (1984). The unconscious and psychopathology. In K. S. Bowers & D. Meichenbaum (Eds.), *The unconscious reconsidered* (pp. 49-87). New York: Wiley.

Newstead, S. E., & Dennis, I. (1979). Lexical and grammatical processing of unshadowed messages: A reexamination of the MacKay effect. *Quarterly Journal of Experimental Psychology, 31,* 477-488.

Nisbett, R., & Ross, L. (1980). *Human inference: Strategies and shortcomings of social judgment.* Englewood Cliffs, NJ: Prentice-Hall.

Nisbett, R., & Wilson, T. D. (1977). Telling more than we can know: Verbal reports on mental processes. *Psychological Review, 84,* 231-254.

Norman, D. A. (1969). Memory while shadowing. *Quarterly Journal of Experimental Psychology, 21,* 85-93.

Norman, D. A. (1981). Categorization of action slips. *Psychological Review, 88,* 1-15.

Orne, M. T. (1959). Hypnosis: Artifact and essence. *Journal of Abnormal and Social Psychology, 58,* 277-299.

Perry, C., & Laurence, J.-R. (1984). Mental processing outside awareness: The contributions of Freud and Janet. In K. S. Bowers & D. Meichenbaum

(Eds.), *The unconscious reconsidered* (pp. 9-48). New York: Wiley.

Pettinati, H. M. (1988). *Hypnosis and memory.* New York: Guilford.

Polkinghorne, D. (1983). *Methodology for the human sciences.* Albany, NY: SUNY Press.

Popper, K. (1979). *Objective knowledge: An evolutionary approach.* Oxford: Oxford University Press.

Robinson, D. N. (1984). Psychobiology and the unconscious. In K. S. Bowes & D. Meichenbaum (Eds.), *The unconscious reconsidered* (pp. 212-216). New York: Wiley.

Sackeim, H. A., & Gur, R. C. (1978). Self-deception, self-confrontation, and consciousness. In G. E. Schwartz & D. Shapiro (Eds.), *Consciousness and self-regulation* (pp. 139-197). New York: Plenum.

Sarbin, T. R., & Coe, W. C. (1972). *Hypnosis: A social psychological analysis of influence communication.* New York: Holt, Rinehart & Winston.

Sarbin, T. R., & Coe, W. C. (1979). Hypnosis and psychopathology: Replacing old myths with fresh metaphors. *Journal of Abnormal Psychology, 88,* 506-526.

Sartre, J. P. (1966). *Being and nothingness.* New York: Washington Square Press.

Shor, R. E. (1970). The three-factor theory of hypnosis as applied to the book-reading fantasy and to the concept of suggestion. *International Journal of Clinical and Experimental Hypnosis, 28,* 89-98.

Skinner, B. F. (1963). Behaviorism at fifty. *Science, 140,* 951-958.

Spence, D. S. (1982). *Narrative truth and historical truth: Meaning and interpretation in psychoanalysis.* New York: Norton.

Spiegel, D. (1984). Multiple personality as a post-traumatic stress disorder. *Psychiatric Clinics of North America, 7,* 101-110.

Spiegel, H., & Spiegel, D. (1978). *Trance and treatment: Clinical uses of hypnosis.* New York: Basic Books.

Spielberger, C. D. (1962). The role of awareness in verbal conditioning. In C. W. Eriksen (Ed.), *Behavior and awareness* (pp. 73-101). Durham, NC: Duke University Press.

Tulving, E. (1985). Memory and consciousness. *Canadian Psychology, 26,* 1-12.

Velmans, M. (1991). Is human information processing conscious? *Behavioral and Brain Sciences, 4,* 651-669.

Wilson, T. D. (1985). Self-deception without repression: Limits on access to mental states. In Martin, M. W. (Ed.), *Self-deception and self-understanding* (pp. 95-116). Lawrence, KS: University of Kansas Press.

Zajonc, R. B. (1980). Feeling and thinking: Preferences need no inferences. *American Psychologist, 35,* 151-175.

6
Dissociative Effects of Mood on Memory

Carolyn Szostak
Rotman Research Institute
Baycrest Centre for Geriatric Care

Richard Lister
Michael Eckardt
Herbert Weingartner
National Institute on Alcohol Abuse
and Alcoholism

The retrieval of information acquired in one mood state, under some conditions, is greatest if the same mood state is present when events are retrieved from memory (Bower, 1981; this volume). This has been demonstrated in a number of different types of studies, including manipulation of mood in normal volunteers, drug-induced changes in mood, and assessment of dissociative effects on retrieval in psychiatric populations (e.g., bipolar depressives and patients with multiple personality disorder). A typical finding of such experiments was reported by Teasdale and Fogarty (1979), who noted that unhappy or sad experiences were remembered more readily by subjects in a sad or depressed mood than in an elated mood. Such results have been interpreted as reflecting state-dependent learning (SDL) or state-dependent retrieval (SDR) (Overton, 1984), wherein the differential states underlying the dissociative effects observed on remembering are characterized by changes in mood.

In this chapter, the phenomenon of mood-dependent retrieval is discussed within the framework provided by the literature on state-dependent learning and retrieval. That is, the dissociative effects of disparate mood conditions on retrieval processes may reflect the specificity of encoding and retrieval processes related to the stimulus context in which learning and remembering occurred. In addition, a preliminary description of the mechanisms and cognitive structures that might modulate the phenomena of mood-dependent learning and retrieval is presented. To this end, two types of studies from our laboratory that assessed mood-dependent retrieval of information are reviewed.

OVERVIEW OF SDL-SDR PHENOMENA

It is well documented that retrieval of previously acquired information is facilitated if the state of the subject is consistent across acquisition and retrieval conditions. For example, if learning takes place under the influence of alcohol, then recall of that information will be greater if alcohol is readministered to the subjects when trying to remember than if they are tested while sober (e.g., Goodwin, Powell, Bremer, Hoine, & Stern, 1969). Whereas early research focused on pharmacological manipulations of state (e.g., administration of alcohol, barbiturates), more recent research suggests that a variety of manipulations, including environmental (Smith, 1979) and affective (for a review see Bower, 1981) factors, can alter state conditions such that SDL and SDR are observed.

Although SDL-SDR can be reliably produced, the dissociative effects on memory induced by both drug and mood manipulations are often subtle and fragile. For example, most reports of SDL-SDR consist of only slight to modest deficits in recall performance. Subjects tested in a different state are typically able to recall some information from the acquisition session, but not as much as subjects who are tested for recall in the same state. In addition, SDL-SDR effects are often found to be asymmetrical. That is, dissociative effects are obtained when acquisition occurs in a drugged state and retrieval is tested for in a drug-free state. However, dissociations of memory are not as frequently observed when the conditions are reversed (e.g., No-drug -> Drug). It has been suggested that the asymmetrical SDL-SDR phenomena induced by pharmacological manipulations occurs because many of the cues associated with the no drug state are also present in a drugged state, permitting generalization from the no drug to the drugged state. However, when learning occurs in the drugged state, the cues associated specifically with the drug are noticeably absent during subsequent testing in the no drug state (Overton, 1984). Whether dissociations of memory that occur in response to changes in mood state are also asymmetrical is not known.

The occurrence of state-dependent dissociations is also highly dependent on the specific experimental parameters and procedures employed. In general, the pattern of findings that define the determinants of mood-related SDL-SDR are similar to those that have been identified in the literature on drug-induced SDL-SDR. Three broadly defined factors seem to determine the likelihood of demonstrating state-dependent dissociations in memory: (a) treatment variables (e.g., drug dose; intensity of mood); (b) procedures used for the assessment of acquisition and retrieval (e.g., free recall versus recognition; stimulus encoding conditions); and (c) types of cognitive processes examined (e.g., episodic vs. semantic knowledge).

The type of treatment used to manipulate state and its "intensity" (e.g., dose of drug; rate of administration) are clearly important in determining the likelihood of obtaining dissociative effects (Overton, 1984). The drugs studied most frequently include alcohol, marijuana, and barbiturates. Dissociative effects on retrieval processes are typically obtained only if the experimental manipulation is potent or strong. That is, large doses are more likely to produce SDL-SDR than small doses. In general, a dose larger than needed to produce observable behavioral changes but not sufficient to render the subject unconscious is required to produce drug-induced dissociation of retrieval (Overton, 1984). The issue of intensity of the manipulation may be particularly important in assessing mood SDL-SDR. Subtle changes in mood may not alter a subject's state sufficiently, such that dissociative effects on retrieval can be observed readily. As such, how mood is manipulated may also have implications for the establishment of SDL-SDR.

Several methods have been used to alter mood states. For example, changes in the mood of normal volunteers have been produced by behavioral methods, such as varying the information subjects are asked to react to or process before testing for acquisition and retrieval (e.g., Velten's Mood Induction procedure or music, see Clark, 1983, for a review). Other studies have employed hypnosis to induce elated or depressed moods (Bower, 1981). Mood states have also been purported to be altered by giving unknowing subjects a small gift (Isen & Daubman, 1984) or by exposing subjects to a situation where they are either successful or unsuccessful (Isen, Shalker, Clark, & Karp, 1978). There have also been a few investigations that have used drugs to deliberately alter mood acutely in normal volunteers (Weingartner, Snyder, Faillace, & Markley, 1970). Finally, it is possible to assess mood SDL-SDR in various psychiatric populations, taking advantage of the shifts in mood state associated with disorders such as bipolar depression (Teasdale, 1983b; Weingartner, Murphy, & Stillman, 1978).

It is not known the extent to which mood must be altered so that mood-dependent retrieval of memories will be observed. Nor is it clear whether all moods are equally sensitive to state-dependent effects on retrieval functions. Thus, regardless of the method used to influence mood state, it is essential that the extent to which a subject's mood is altered be determined objectively. Advances have been made with respect to quantifying mood states and, more importantly, shifts in moods (Matthews, Jones, & Chamberlain, 1990; McCormack, Horne, & Sheather, 1988 ;Watson & Tellegen, 1985).

The expression of SDL-SDR is also dependent on the characteristics of the experimental stimuli and the methods used to test memory. For example, dissociative effects on memory are highly dependent on how the events to be remembered have been encoded. Information or stimuli that have been processed extensively are less sensitive to the effects of disparate state conditions than are poorly encoded events (Eich & Birnbaum, 1982; Weingartner, Adefris, Eich, & Murphy, 1976). This is demonstrated by the observation that the likelihood of remembering words that are highly imageable does not vary across state conditions (Weingartner et al., 1976). Moreover, items that have been presented repeatedly are more likely to be retrieved across disparate mood states than are events that have only been presented a single time.

The manner in which memory is tested is also a crucial factor in demonstrating memory dissociations. In general, SDR effects are apparent when subjects must generate their own strategies for searching memory and retrieving appropriate information, as with tests of free recall. In contrast, dissociative effects on retrieval are not usually obtained when subjects are provided with cues or prompts that can facilitate attempts to search memory (e.g., cued recall or recognition tests). The role of these factors in the establishment of SDR effects has been reasonably well established (Eich, 1980; Eich, Weingartner, Stillman, & Gillin, 1975). It should be noted that, although dissociative effects are typically observed with free recall tests, it remains possible that the subject will, at times, access information acquired in a different state – even under such test conditions. For example, if the subject, when asked to freely recall test items, "stumbled" upon a correct response, that response may then act as an effective cue for the retrieval of other items. The likelihood of this occurring would, however, still be greater in same-versus different-state conditions.

Finally, the types of memory presentations that are to be retrieved under congruent versus disparate acquisition-retrieval test conditions constitute the third class of variables that may be important in determining mood SDL-SDR effects. Most pharmacological SDL-SDR studies have been concerned with the remembering of sequentially bound, recently acquired events that are linked to a unique context (i.e., episodic memory). Although retrieval of semantic information (e.g., information that is impersonal, undated; Tulving, 1983) has not frequently been studied in such experiments, there is some evidence to suggest that access to semantic memory may also be sensitive to changes in state. A review of the published clinical SDL-SDR findings also suggests pronounced mood-dependent effects on retrieval in situations in which subjects must retrieve information from semantic memory (Fogarty & Hemsley, 1983; Mathews & Bradley, 1983; Natale & Hantas, 1982; Teasdale, 1983a; Teasdale, Taylor, & Fogarty, 1980). For example, Teasdale and associates reported that the probability of recalling happy and unhappy personal experiences is mood dependent in both male and female subjects. In contrast, mood-dependent retrieval of pleasant versus unpleasant trait words was evident only in females (see Teasdale, 1983a). This suggests that mood states may function as discriminative stimuli that, like drugs, have cuing functions, eliciting stimulus-specific hierarchies of responses. We suggest that the stimulus properties of a mood state elicit a hierarchy of information that is part of semantic memory. This state-specific hierarchy of information may serve to modulate mood-specific encoding of recent episodic events and, as such, may provide a more direct and effective means of examining the subjective sense that we somehow experience our historical selves and the events around us in a mood-dependent manner.

MOOD SDL-SDR EFFECTS IN PATIENTS WITH BIPOLAR AFFECTIVE DISORDER

Two types of studies from our laboratory support the latter conceptualization. First, rapidly cycling bipolar affective disorder patients were examined using procedures tailored to the clinical limitations set by the profound changes in mood evident in these patients. Patients served as their own controls and were studied during documented periods of mania, depression, and euthymia. In each of these studies, the degree to which self-generated events were reproducible was examined as a function of the extent of change in mood state from time of information generation to the time of retrieval from memory. In one study, a pharmacological manipulation of mood was superimposed on the mood state of these patients at various points in their cycle of changing affect. In this study, the types of responses subjects generated while in one state were directly compared with the type of responses generated in either the same or altered mood state condition. Discussion of these results is followed by a description of the effects of amphetamine-induced alterations in mood on the types of responses elicited from semantic memory in normal volunteers. The results from these studies suggest that mood can serve as a context for selectively altering how and what information is acquired and retrieved from memory.

In the first experiment, bipolar patients (n = 8) were asked to generate a single word in response to each of 20 standard noun stimuli for which normative data (n= 500) were available (Weingartner, Miller, & Murphy, 1977). Patients were tested over a period of several months using different sets of equivalent stimuli. During the course of the experiment, the task was administered during periods of normal affect and of mania. It should be noted that patients were able to complete this task even during manic episodes. Associative responses were scored according to their frequency of occurrence in a normative population (Palermo & Jenkins, 1968). During manic periods, as defined by standardized and validated National Institute of Mental Health (NIMH) affective rating scales (Bunney & Hamburg, 1963), 33% of patients' responses, although appropriate, were judged to be idiosyncratic. That is, they occurred less than once in 500 responses (p < .001, Fisher exact probability test). In contrast, less than 5% of responses were unusual or idiosyncratic when these same patients were tested in a "normal" mood state. This finding suggests that the altered thought processes that are characteristic of mania may reflect the association of different sets of responses with common stimuli (Weingartner & Silberman, 1984).

The issue of the state-specific stability of responses was examined in a second study, wherein eight hospitalized patients with bipolar affective disorders were repeatedly tested for 4 to 9 weeks (Weingartner, Miller, & Murphy, 1977). During this time, they exhibited periods of mania, depression, and normal affect. Patients were asked to generate 20 single-word responses to standard stimuli and then reproduce these associations 4 days later. Clinical changes in mood were determined by the clinical staff using pretested and validated, behaviorally defined, standardized rating instruments (Bunney & Hamburg, 1963). Over 150 pairs of observations were collected from these eight patients. Acquisition and retrieval phases of the experiment were conducted across a broad range of altered mood states. The extent of the change in mood was inversely related to the number of associations that could be reproduced (r = -0.48, p < .002). Analysis of patient-specific clusters of mood-relevant behaviors yielded significantly stronger relationships between the absolute change in mood and consistency of the generated and reproduced words. Specifically, responses were recalled less frequently when large changes in mood state differentiated the generation and regeneration phases of this word-association task.

The occurrence of mood SDL-SDR was also tested pharmacologically, using a similar patient population (Weingartner et al., 1978). Specifically, manic-depressive patients were tested for serial learning and retrieval following the administration of d-amphetamine; d-amphetamine in conjunction with lithium; lithium alone; and placebo. Two interrelated issues were examined in this experiment. Does amphetamine, a prototypic psychostimulant, induce state-dependent learning and retrieval of information; and, if so, are these effects dependent on the presence of a robust alteration of mood? It was also hypothesized that lithium would block the mood-altering effects of amphetamine. Accordingly, if the dissociative effects observed with amphetamine are dependent on changes in mood, then one would expect that these changes would be blocked by the coadministration of lithium.

Each pharmacological treatment was administered twice, in a double-blind manner and in a randomized sequence, to each of nine bipolar depressed patients hospitalized in the Clinical Center at NIMH, Bethesda, MD. One and one-half hours after drug administration (the time at which a peak drug effect was expected using methods tested and validated in previous studies), subjects attempted to learn a fixed sequence of 12 common words. Eight hours later, subjects were asked to freely remember these serial lists by attempting to reconstruct them in the same order in which they were learned.

A clinically meaningful and measurable (as assessed by a NIMH standardized mood assessment inventory; Weingartner & Silberman, 1984) change in mood and level of activation occurred in response to the amphetamine treatment ($p < .01$). Amphetamine-induced mood alterations were blocked by lithium. Amphetamine did not reliably alter characteristics of list learning during the acquisition phase of the study. However, regeneration of the list (i.e., number of responses that could be correctly remembered in the appropriate serial order) was less complete if learning had occurred after being administered amphetamine, relative to control levels of performance ($p < .01$). The most striking feature of the amphetamine-induced memory dissociation was that it was largely dependent on the presence of changes in mood from the time of learning to the time of retrieval, 8 hours later. That is, patients who were less depressed and more activated in response to amphetamine *and* who had returned to their baseline depressed state when drug effects had dissipated at the time of retrieval, showed a large dissociation of previously learned information ($r = -0.72$, $p < .01$). In other words, mood changes that differentiated state at time of acquisition and retrieval were negatively correlated with recall of serial information. Moreover, the dissociative effects of amphetamine were not apparent when lithium was administered in conjunction with the amphetamine. Thus, lithium was found to block both the mood-enhancing properties of amphetamine and the dissociative effects of amphetamine on retrieval processes as well.

DRUG-INDUCED MOOD-STATE DEPENDENT RETRIEVAL IN NORMAL VOLUNTEERS

A series of experiments, in which several mescaline- and amphetamine-like drugs were investigated with respect to their psychotropic properties, was conducted several years ago by Snyder, Faillace, and Weingartner. One of the aims of these studies was to define the typography of specific cognitive changes mapped on the neurochemical variations of these agents (Snyder, Richelson, Weingartner, & Faillace, 1970). Specific drugs were observed to have differential responses. For example, one drug (DOM, 2.5-dimethoxy, 4-methylamphetamine) resulted primarily in changes in perception, whereas another (DOET, 2.5-dimethoxy, 4-ethylamphetamine) seemed to alter how subjects interpreted the world around them through changes in cognition (Snyder & Faillace, 1970; Weingartner et al., 1970). It is the cognitive response to this latter drug that is of renewed interest because it appears that the observed effects can be interpreted in terms of changes in the accessibility of semantic memory. Moreover, it is possible that the abuse potential of DOET is related to its mood-altering properties.

The types of responses that subjects would retrieve from semantic memory in response to standard stimuli (as previously described) following the administration of DOET and placebo were determined initially (Weingartner et al., 1970). Ten young normal volunteer college graduate males were administered an oral dose of DOET (1.5 mg/70 kg body weight) on one occasion and an active placebo treatment (10 mg amphetamine) on another in a double-blind, cross-over design. Immediately following the administration of either DOET or placebo, and every 2 hours thereafter for 6 hours, subjects were administered mood scales, as well as a cognitive procedure that was designed to measure access to previously acquired knowledge. Specifically, subjects were read lists of 25 words and were asked to respond with a single word association that was felt to be related to the stimulus word. The stimulus words in each list were matched with respect to the occurrence of frequency of the stimuli in the English language (Palermo & Jenkins, 1968). In addition, the stimuli in each list were matched in terms of the pattern of free-associated responses normally given to these words. For example, each list contained the same number of stimuli that produced a single, very high frequency associate, and the same number of stimuli that produced a distribution of responses, in which several words, rather than a single word, were frequently given in the free-association tests. After the subjects had responded with a free association to each of the 25 stimuli, mood was assessed; this took approximately 5 minutes. Afterward, the previously presented stimuli were again read to subjects in a different, random sequence. Subjects were instructed to reproduce their previous associative responses.

Following DOET treatment, subjects reported mild euphoria (a notably pleasant experience), a slight difficulty in concentration, and increased talkativeness. No marked changes in pulse, blood pressure, or oral temperature occurred with either treatment.

Free-association responses generated by subjects were categorized as either (a) high frequency responses, occurring in a normative population at least 10% of the time; (b) medium strength associates, occurring from 1% to 10% of the time; (c) low probability associative responses, occurring 5 or less times per 500 responding subjects; and (d) idiosyncratic responses, occurring less than 1 time per 500. Subjects' associations to stimuli were, as expected, remarkably similar during familiarization to the study and at baseline assessment. During baseline testing, all subjects generated at least 50% but no more than 70% high-frequency free associations. Few idiosyncratic responses were generated at baseline or under placebo conditions. All subjects also demonstrated that their free associations could be reliably reproduced. Five minutes after generating their responses, subjects could regenerate at least 94% of their free associations given at baseline or following placebo administration.

The effects of DOET on the production and reproduction of free associations were examined at 2 hour intervals. The proportion of high-frequency associations at 0, 2, 4, and 6 hours after drug administration were ranked and analyzed using a Friedman two-way analysis of variance for ordinal, ranked data. Following DOET treatment, a reliable decrease in the proportion of emitted high-frequency associations, with the nadir occurring at 4 hours, was observed ($X^2 = 13.7$, $p < .01$). The maximum effect of the drug on the types of associative responses generated from semantic memory corresponded to the time of peak drug effect based on the physiological effects of the drug and the elevation in mood produced by the drug.

The decrease in the production of high-frequency associations under DOET conditions corresponded to an increase in the proportion of low- and medium-strength associations that were emitted but *not* an increase in idiosyncratic associations generated by the subjects ($p < .01$). Thus, DOET did not induce the generation of irrelevant associations, but rather elicited responses that were less common. The unique responses associated with the presented stimuli were nevertheless appropriate.

All of the generated associations were at least as reproducible under DOET conditions as at baseline or following placebo. In fact, associations generated in a DOET-altered state were somewhat more reproducible (97.5 %), as compared to a baseline reproducibility of 94.0%. However, this difference did not reach statistical significance. The reproducibility data support the notion that the associations produced under DOET conditions were stable and tightly bound to the stimuli that elicited them, despite the increased occurrence of low- and medium-strength associations. This interpretation must, however, be viewed in the context of the task that required subjects to reproduce their associations and, as such, does not reflect the "spontaneous" recurrence of the original associations. As such, the task probably involved access to both semantic and episodic memory.

The pattern of reproduction of responses generated from semantic memory under DOET conditions was also qualitatively different from that observed under placebo conditions. Normally, high-frequency responses are more likely to be regenerated than either low-frequency or idiosyncratic responses. This was the case both at baseline and under placebo conditions in the present experiment. For example, at baseline a total of 14 responses could not be reproduced (across all subjects), only 4 of which were high-frequency associations. Because 60% of subjects' associations were high-frequency associations, the expected number of irreproducible responses should have been twice as great as the number actually observed. In contrast, under DOET conditions, the relationship between frequency of occurrence of associations to stimuli and their reproducibility was not apparent. Subjects were able to reliably reproduce almost all of their associations, including low-frequency responses. The low-frequency associations were just as likely to be reproduced, as were commonly elicited associations. In effect, these low-frequency responses appeared to be as tightly bound to the stimuli that elicited them as the high-frequency responses that were so readily produced in the unaltered state. In addition, the low-frequency responses elicited in the presence of DOET appeared to be an accessible aspect of semantic memory.

Changes in the types of responses elicited in the different mood states were not associated with concurrent changes in the speed with which these less common items were retrieved. This finding is consistent with the observations that changes in the commonality of responses associated with alterations of mood by DOET were not associated with a decrease in the consistency with which these responses were reproduced. These results suggest that distinct mood states are associated with at least partially nonoverlapping response hierarchies, representing state-specific or differentiated knowledge about past experiences.

Similar results to those described have been reported following the administration of other drugs of abuse. For example, Block and Wittenborn (1985) examined the effects of marijuana on associative responses elicited to standard stimuli. Subjects who freely generated word associations produced more uncommon or atypical responses during a marijuana-induced change in mood. These findings, however, have not generally been viewed as reflecting changes in the kinds of information accessed from semantic memory. When such alterations in response hierarchies appear, such a model is appropriate and consistent with an SDL-SDR interpretation of these drug effects.

POSSIBLE MECHANISMS UNDERLYING STATE-DEPENDENT RETRIEVAL

For most common stimuli, the elicitable response hierarchies within semantic memory are highly structured, overlearned, reproducible, and, hence, insensitive to changes in internal and external environments. These stimuli are not likely to be interpreted or responded to very differently as a function of changes in state. For this reason, the meaning and interpretation of many types of events are relatively invariant across many conditions. However, under some conditions, such as those situations that are inherently less structured, what is retrieved from a previously acquired knowledge base is in fact state- or mood-context dependent.

Thus far, the phenomenology of mood-dependent learning and

retrieval has been described, and the potential mechanisms underlying this phenomenon have been undefined. We propose that the dissociative effects on retrieval may occur with or without the individual being aware of these changes.

Working within an "explicit" framework, "states of mind" can bias those processes and operations employed intentionally by a subject in encoding, organizing, and rehearsing ongoing experience. Within such a scheme, states of mind induce conscious encoding operations, which subjects use in a controlled manner, to organize and relate on-going experiences to past experiences and previously acquired knowledge. States of mind would similarly influence the controlled search strategies employed to scan what is in memory, regardless of whether that memory was established recently or a long time ago. According to this viewpoint, subjects are aware of the fact that they are thinking about and doing things differently than normal. Moreover, they can tell us what they are doing, including how they are rehearsing information. Thus, what may be altered in a state-specific manner is a part of the conscious monitoring system. To this end, it is interesting to note that Block and Wittenborn (1985) reported that when subjects, who had been given marijuana, were constrained in how they were asked to search their previously acquired knowledge (e.g., think of a fruit that starts with the letter "a"), state-specific retrieval was not evident. A possible interpretation of this finding is that cuing effectively restricted and structured subjects' memory search plan(s), thereby overriding the selection of any state-specific retrieval strategies. Thus, when processing constraints are minimized (e.g., "tell me whatever comes to mind," or "try to freely remember a set of experiences") stable patterns of responses that are state specific can emerge.

Alternatively, it is possible that the major effect of changes in state is to bias the types of cognitive processes that are carried out implicitly. Although these operations are normally conducted outside of awareness, they can, nevertheless, influence or determine what aspects of experience are stored or accessed at a later point in time.

These processes can, and do, have a powerful impact on how the world is viewed and how experiences are organized. For example, at times, certain types of stimuli can elicit memories of discrete events, places, or people - things that have not been thought of for a long time. Instances of déjà vu may also reflect the influence of implicit cognitive processes on interpretation of the present situation. Working within this framework, different states could function to prime past experiences differentially, thereby biasing the way things are presently viewed.

It is also possible that stimuli that elicit discriminable associative structures also influence pre-encoding operations that may, for example, be involved in determining how to attend to information and/or defining focus of attention. Pre-encoding processes could be one class of cognitive operations that function outside of awareness but, nevertheless, influence on-going information processing. For example, using both classical and operant conditioning paradigms, it has been demonstrated that subjects are not necessarily aware of the establishment of new responses (Dawson & Schell, 1987). Moreover, instances of parallel processing, as assessed, for example, in shadowing experiments, indicate that events that are purported to be outside of awareness can bias overt or conscious behavior. To date, little research has been conducted that addresses this potential aspect of state dependency. However, this possibility merits attention as it may have implications for the interpretation of state-dependent effects on cognitive processes. For example, it would be of interest to determine whether, in different mood states, subjects scan visual fields differentially and whether these strategies are adopted consistently within a given state. To this end, it is interesting to note that different aspects of information (e.g. central vs peripheral detail) are attended to differently as a function of whether the information was neutral, unexpected or emotionally toned (Christianson, E.F. Loftus, Hoffman & G.R. Loftus, 1991). If consistent changes do occur, then one could assess whether these changes are systematically related to the observed changes in the types of associative structures accessed from semantic memory.

Although these two hypotheses are purely speculative and not necessarily mutually exclusive, it is possible to test the predictive value of each position. A growing body of cognitive research has focused on the mechanisms that account for performance differences on explicit and implicit tasks of cognition and, in particular, memory functions (Nissen, Ross, Willingham, Mackenzie, & Schacter, this volume; see also Schacter, 1987, for a review). This body of research has resulted in the generation of many methods and procedures that can be applied to the study of dissociative effects on retrieval.

To this end, it is interesting to note that Nissen, Ross, Wellingham, Mackenzie, & Schacter (1988; see also this volume) have recently examined a single patient with a multiple personality disorder using these experimental procedures; that is, a patient who had been diagnosed as having several alter personalities (each of which was unaware of the others), was tested using several implicit and explicit tests of retrieval. The personality that was present under training and/or testing conditions was manipulated so that potential dissociative effects on performance could be ascertained. Dissociative effects on some, though not all, of the implicit and explicit retrieval tasks were observed. They suggested that the critical factor in determining the occurrence of SDL-SDR effects was the relative ambiguity or degree of structure associated with the test stimuli. Further research is required in order to clearly understand the profile of their results.

Although the study by Nissen et al. (1988) directly compared performance on implicit and explicit tasks, the study did not provide unequivocal support for either of the two positions outlined previously. In order to test the two proposed hypotheses more directly, it may be helpful to test for dissociative effects using a manipulation of state that ensures more experimenter control than is the case in the study of multiple personality disorders. For example, a drug with strong discriminative properties and one that has been found to induce SDL-SDR effects might prove to be particularly useful in assessing the relative involvement of these two types of processes.

REFERENCES

Block, R. I., & Wittenborn, J.R. (1985). Marijuana effects on associative processes. *Psychopharmacology, 85*, 426-430.

Bower, G. H. (1981). Mood and memory. *American Psychologist, 36*, 129-148.

Bunney, W. E. Jr., & Hamburg, D. A. (1963). Methods for reliable longitudinal observation of behavior. *Archives of General Psychiatry, 9*, 280-294.

Christianson, S., Loftus, E. F., Hoffman, H., & Loftus, G. R. (1991). Eye fixations and memory for emotional events. *Journal of Experimental Psychology: Learning, Memory, and Cognition, 17*, 693-701.

Clark, D. M. (1983). On the induction of depressed mood in the laboratory: Evaluation and comparison of the Velten and musical procedures. *Advances in Behavior Research and Therapy, 5*, 27-49.

Dawson, M. E. , & Schell, A. M. (1987). Human autonomic and skeletal classical conditioning: The role of conscious cognitive factors. In G. Davey (Ed.), *Cognitive processes and Pavlovian conditioning in humans,* (pp 27-55). Chichester, England: Wiley.

Eich, J. E. (1980). Cue-dependent nature of state-dependent retrieval. *Memory and Cognition, 8*, 157-173.

Eich, J. E., & Birnbaum, I. M. (1982). Repetition, cueing and state-dependent memory. *Memory and Cognition, 10*, 103-114.

Eich, J. E., Weingartner, H., Stillman, R. C., & Gillin, J. C. (1975). State-dependent accessibility of retrieval cues in the retention of a categorized list. *Journal of Verbal Learning and Verbal Behavior, 14*, 408-417.

Fogarty, S. L., & Hemsely, D. R. (1983). Depression and the accessibility of memories. *British Journal of Psychiatry, 142*, 232-237.

Goodwin, D. W., Powell, B., Bremer, D., Hoine, H., & Stern, J. (1969). Alcohol and recall: State-dependent effects in man. *Science, 163*, 1358-1360.

Isen, A. M., & Daubman, K. A. (1984). The influence of affect on categorization. *Journal of Personality and Social Psychology, 47*, 1206-1217.

Isen, A. M., Shalker, T. E., Clark, M., & Karp, L. (1978). Affect, accessibility of material in memory and behavior: A cognitive loop? *Journal of Personality and Social Psychology, 36*, 1-12.

Mathews, A., & Bradley, B. (1983). Mood and the self-reference bias in recall. *Behavior Research and Therapy, 21*, 233-239.

Matthews, G., Jones, D. M., & Chamberlain, A.G. (1990). Defining the measurement of mood: The UWIST mood adjective checklist. *British Journal of Psychology, 81*, 17-42.

McCormack, H. M., Horne, D. J. & Sheather, S. (1988). Clinical applications of visual analogue scales: A critical review. *Psychological Medicine, 18*, 1007-1019.

Natale, M., & Hantas, M. (1982). Effect of temporary mood states on selective memory about the self. *Journal of Personality and Social Psychology, 42*, 927-934.

Nissen, M. J., Ross, J. L., Willingham, D. B., MacKenzie, T. B., & Schacter, D. L. (1988). Memory and awareness in a patient with multiple personality disorder. *Brain and Cognition, 8*, 117-134.

Overton, D. A. (1984). State-dependent learning and drug discriminations. In L.L. Iversen, S. D. Iverson, & S. H. Snyder (Eds.), *Handbook of psychopharmacology, Vol. 18* (pp. 59-127). New York: Plenum.

Palermo, D. S., & Jenkins, J. J. (1968). *Word association norms: Grade school through college.* Minneapolis: University of Minnesota Press.

Schacter, D. L. (1987). Implicit memory: History and current status. *Journal of Experimental Psychology: Learning, Memory, and Cognition, 13*, 501-518.

Smith, S. M. (1979). Remembering in and out of context. *Journal of Experimental Psychology: Learning, Memory and Cognition , 5*, 460-471.

Snyder, S. H., Richelson, E., Weingartner, H., & Faillace, L. A. (1970). Psychotropic methoxyamphetamines: Structure and activity in man. In E. Costa & S. Garrattini (Eds.), *Amphetamine and related compounds* (pp. 905-928). New York: Raven.

Snyder, S. H., Weingartner, H., & Faillace, L. A. (1970). DOET and DOM psychotropic agents: Their effects in man. In D.H. Efron (Ed.), *Psychomimetic drugs* (pp. 247-263). New York: Raven.

Teasdale, J. D. (1983a). Affect and accessibility. *Philosophical transactions of the Royal Society of London, 302*, 403-412.

Teasdale, J. D. (1983b). Negative thinking in depression: Cause, effect, or reciprocal relationship? *Advances in Behavior Therapy, 5*, 3-25.

Teasdale, J. D., & Fogarty, S. J. (1979). Differential effects of induced mood on retrieval of pleasant and unpleasant events from episodic memory. *Journal of Abnormal Psychology, 88*, 248-257.

Teasdale, J. D., Taylor, R., & Fogarty, S. J. (1980). Effects of induced elation-depression on the accessibility of memories of happy and unhappy experiences. *Behavior Research and Therapy, 18*, 339-346.

Tulving, E. (1983). *Elements of episodic memory.* Oxford University Press.

Watson, D., & Tellegen, A. (1985). Toward a consensual structure of mood. *Psychological Bulletin, 98*, 219-235.

Weingartner H., Adefris, W., Eich, J. E., & Murphy, D. L. (1976). Encoding imagery specificity in alcohol state-dependent learning. *Journal of Experimental Psychology: Human Learning, and Memory, 2*, 63-67.

Weingartner, H., Miller, H. & Murphy, D. (1977). Mood-state-dependent retrieval of verbal associations. *Journal of Abnormal Psychology, 86*, 276-284.

Weingartner, H., Murphy, D. L., & Stillman, R. C. (1978). Mood state dependent learning. In F. C. Colpaert & J. C. Rosecrans (Eds.), *Stimulus properties of drugs: Ten years of progress* (pp. 445-453). Amsterdam: Elsevier/North-Holland.

Weingartner, H., & Silberman, E. (1984). Cognitive changes in depression. In R. Post & J. Ballenger (Eds.), *Neurobiology of mood disorders* (pp. 121-135). Baltimore, MD: Williams & Wilkins.

Weingartner, H., Snyder, S. H., Faillace, L. A., & Markley, H. (1970). Altered free associations: Some cognitive effects of DOET (2.5-dimethoxy, 4-ethylamphetamine). *Behavioral Science, 15*, 297-303.

7
Temporary Emotional States Act Like Multiple Personalities

Gordon Bower
Stanford University

In this chapter, I report on my research on how variations in people's temporary mood states influence their memory, thoughts, judgments, and self-image. All of my studies use normal adults, usually college students; however, I try to relate my findings to clinical phenomena of dissociation and multiple personality. I have no personal knowledge of multiple personality patients. What I know of the disorder I have learned from watching Joanne Woodward's acting in "The Three Faces of Eve" and from reading about it. For example, I've learned that 92% of multiples are women, that 97% report having suffered through a history of childhood incest, torture, trauma, or other abuse in a disturbed family, and that patients are typically very hypnotizable, suggesting a genetic predisposition towards dissociation (Kluft, 1984).

I've also learned that the four major theories of multiple personalities are:

1. that it reflects a series of self-hypnosis episodes (Bliss, 1980);

or

2. it reflects the deep involvement of the patients in enacting multiple social roles that enable them to cope with warded-off

impulses and conflicts, with the role-playing encouraged and legitimated by the therapist (Spanos, Weekes, & Bertrand, 1985); or

3. it is caused by epileptiform activity in the temporal lobe and the limbic system (Schenk & Bear, 1981); or

4. it reflects a coherent series of state-dependent memory phenomena (Braun, 1984; Kluft, 1984).

It is with this latter theory that I am most at home. I have conducted experimental studies of state-dependent memory, and I review herein those most relevant to multiple personalities.

For most of my professional life, I have studied human memory. For a memory theorist, the clinical phenomena of memory dissociation is wondrous, magical, and utterly incredible—the stuff of dreams and dramas. State-dependent memory shares some of that same mystery and allure: A person learns something in one psycho-neuro-physiological state, is unable to retrieve it while in a different state, yet can recover it later if the original state is reintroduced. When I began my studies in the late 1970s, I knew about the experiments showing a kind of state-dependent learning in rats when they were given different drugs such as alcohol, phenobarbital, or amphetamine. But the work on drug-state dependent memory in humans was sparse, and yielded inconsistent and inconclusive results. I wanted to see whether we could produce state-dependent memory using different emotions or moods, such as happiness, sadness, fear, or anger. And so we began our experiments.

A first successful demonstration of mood-state dependent memory was carried out in 1977 by me and my student, Stephen Gilligan (see Bower, Monteiro, & Gilligan, 1978). To induce the mood-states, we used hypnosis: We first selected highly hypnotizable college students; then, during the experiment, we hypnotized them and suggested that they get themselves into happy moods by recalling and reliving in imagination happy experiences from their lives. After 2 or 3 minutes of this mood induction, we had them memorize a list of 16 unrelated words for about 6 minutes while they continued to feel happy. The words would be read to them and then the subjects would try to recall them, in any order they could; this went on for several trials.

We then had the subjects switch moods, asking them to feel sad by reliving some episodes from their lives when they had felt sad. We told them to not get themselves too overwhelmingly sad, because we wanted them functional for our experiment. As they continued to feel sad, they memorized a second list of words for several minutes.

I've described a condition in which subjects learned a first word list while happy and a second list while sad. Other subjects learned the lists in the reverse mood order—first sad, then happy. We then had the subjects rest and read a book for 20 minutes to cause some forgetting. We then hypnotized them again, placed half in a sad mood, half in a happy mood, and asked them to recall both lists of words they had learned earlier.

The results are shown in Fig. 7.1 giving the average percentage of words from each list that the subjects retained and could recall later. We see here a strong mood-dependency: People who were tested when they were happy recalled more of the list they had learned when they were happy; people who were sad when tested recalled more of the list they had learned when they were sad. This is due to mood matching: If the mood during retrieval matches that during learning, then the memories are far more available than if the two moods mismatch. In this experiment, it was not important whether subjects were happy or sad during learning or during testing; what was important was the matching between the input state and the output state. It is that matching that causes state-dependent memory.

The forgetting shown here is a kind of *dissociation* between memories learned in these two states. When people are sad, they have something like selective amnesia for events that happened to them earlier when they were happy. It is as though their memories have several different directories, much like directories in a computer database or different suburban telephone directories. The directories are compartmentalized according to the dominant mood, emotion,

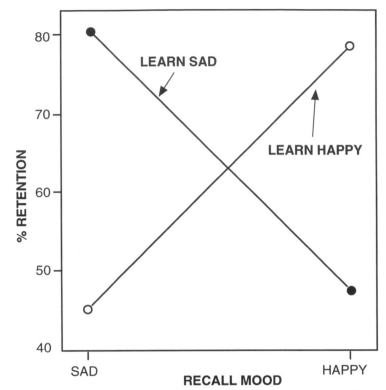

FIG. 7.1. Percent retention related to learning mood and
recall mood (from Experiment 3 of Bower, Monteiro,
& Gilligan, 1978; reprinted by permission).

or thematic relationship that prevailed during the original
experiences. A given memory directory can be easily entered and its
information accessed only by the person re-entering the
corresponding emotional state. Obviously, these mood directories
are similar to multiple personalities.

A follow-up experiment was carried out with another associate,
Bret Thompson, who demonstrated state-dependency with four
different emotions (cited in Bower, 1981). Our subjects were
hypnotized and taught four different lists of words, each list under a
different emotion—either joy, sadness, fear, or anger. After studying
the four lists, subjects were tested for recall of them. Before each

recall, however, subjects were again put in one of the four moods. The testing moods were selected so that, across subjects, each of the four learning moods was tested in each of the four retention moods. The experiment was hard work for subjects and experimenter alike, but it illustrates the utility of hypnosis for altering emotional moods.

Figure 7.2 shows the percentage retention scores for a list learned in the mood shown in the row when it was tested in the mood shown in the column. The main diagonal is shaded and shows same-mood retention scores. These scores are the highest in each row: They are not 100%, of course, because much forgetting occurs in such experiments. The opposite-mood entries are circled, for these were expected to yield the poorest recall, and they do so in all four rows. The other entry in each row represents medium generalization of learning between the two opposites, and the percentage recall scores do appear to be intermediate between the shaded diagonal entries and the circled entries. In order to make the relationships clearer, I have averaged the retention scores for the three types of test condition. The average percentages are 0.85 for same-mood testing, 0.70 for

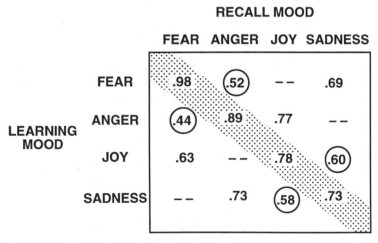

FIG.7.2. Percent retention of items learned in the Row mood and tested in the Column mood. (Experiment by Thompson cited in Bower, 1981; reprinted by permission.)

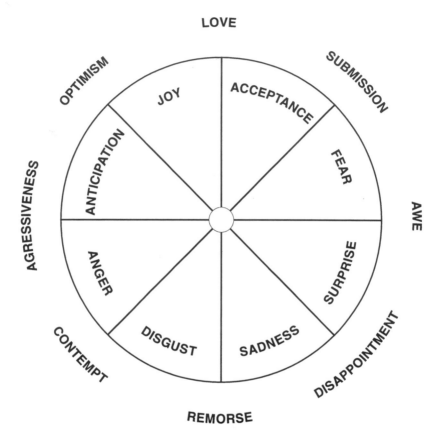

FIG. 7.3. Plutchik's theory of the similarity of eight primary emotions, listed inside the circle. Two emotions are more similar the closer they are around the circle. (From Plutchik, 1980, reprinted by permission.)

"intermediate mood" testing, and 0.54 for opposite-mood testing.

These data appear to be consistent with a proposal by Robert Plutchik (1980) regarding the similarity of different emotions. Plutchik's proposal is summarized in Fig. 7.3, which shows his proposed eight primary emotions on the inner circle—joy, acceptance, fear, surprise, sadness, disgust, anger, and anticipation. The similarity of two emotions is reflected in how near they are around the edge of the circle. Thus, joy and sadness are distant opposites, as are fear and anger, while anger and fear are half-way similar to sadness. This chart suggests that in multiple personalities, clinicians are more likely to observe amnesia between two personalities that display totally opposite emotional styles.

State dependency arises not only with such memories created in the laboratory, but also in people's memory for real-life events. In several experiments, subjects have been made happy or sad, and then asked to recall an unselected sample of memories from their past— in one experiment, to recall events from their childhood (see Bower, 1981); in another experiment, to recall events from the past few weeks. Mark Snyder and Phyllis White (1982) reported the results shown in Fig. 7.4: Their happy subjects recalled more happy events

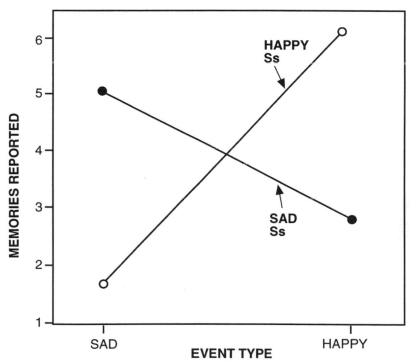

FIG 7.4. Number of memories of happy and sad events reported by subjects induced to feel happy or sad during the report. (Based on data reported by Snyder & White, 1982, adapted by permission.)

from their recent life, whereas sad subjects reported more sad events. This is a form of mood-dependent memory, because these people presumably felt appropriately happy or sad at the time these events originally occurred. One observes this sort of biased memory reporting, of course, from psychiatrically depressed patients or chronically anxious worriers.

Similar mood-dependent retrieval has been observed in manic-depressive patients who are cycling through different moods over days. Weingartner, Miller, and Murphy (1977) gave a series of memory tests to hospitalized manic-depressive patients whom they observed every 4 days over a period of many weeks that included many mood cycles. Figure 7.5 illustrates a hypothetical patient's mood swings over days. Every 4 days, at points marked A, B, C, and so forth, the patient's mood was assessed and he received two tests:

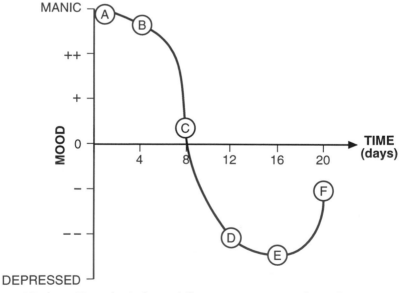

FIG. 7.5. Hypothetical mood fluctuations over 20 days of a manic-depressive patient. Every 4 days, at points marked A, B, C, D, E, and F, the patient's memory would be tested for material he or she had generated 4 days earlier. Based on a procedure developed by Weingartner, Miller, and Murphy (1977).

first, he generated 20 free associations to each of two novel stimulus words; then he tried to remember the 20 free associates he had given to two other stimulus words he had seen 4 days before. Thus, at point B, the patient would try to remember the words he had produced earlier at point A; and also at point B, he would generate new associates that he would have to remember when tested at point C; this procedure was repeated every 4 days.

The question is: How does the patient's memory for the previous session's associates relate to his change of mood? The results in Fig. 7.6 show that, as the mood changes more between one session and the next, the patient forgot more of the associates he had generated the previous session. Thus, in terms of Fig. 7.5, there

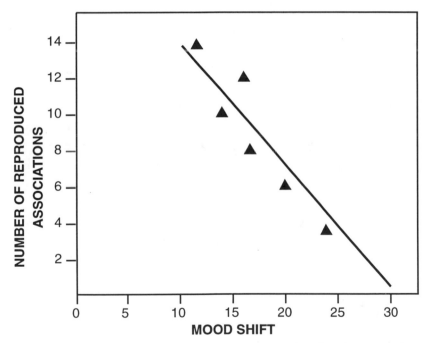

FIG. 7.6. The lower number of associations remembered as the patients' mood changed more between initial generation and the memory test. (From Weingartner, Murphy, & Sullivan, 1978, reprinted by permission.)

would have been little forgetting between days A and B, or D and E, but much forgetting between B and C, and C and D. So, the decreasing memory in Fig. 7.6 is exactly what we would expect from mood-state dependent memory.

I have heard that Dr. Edward Silberman of the National Institute of Mental Health has investigated state-dependent memory in multiple-personality patients. I have not seen his report, but I gather that he observed considerable dissociation in memory across the different personalities. In a secondary source (Institute of Noetic Sciences, 1985), he was quoted as having concluded that "different personality configurations associated with Multiple Personality Disorder may serve to provide contexts and stimulus markers for uniquely storing and retrieving previous experience in much the same way that a drug or mood state serves to mark experience" (p. 17).

Once one notices mood-state dependent memory, one begins to examine other phenomena from this perspective. For instance, let us look at state-dependent memory caused by certain drugs. It is an interesting fact that most of the drugs that produce state-dependent memory also produce radical shifts in mood. Successful state-dependent drugs are ones like marijuana, amphetamine, alcohol, diazepam, phenobarbitol, and opiate derivatives, all of which are mood altering. In fact, it is because they do alter moods that they are frequently abused. Thus, we might guess that these drugs produce state-dependency because they change moods.

There is some suggestive evidence for this view. In two different experiments, one using amphetamine with depressed patients (see Weingartner, Murphy, & Stillman, 1978), another using alcohol with college students (Eich & Birnbaum, 1988), state-dependent forgetting turned out to be predicted not so much by the drug dose as by the change in subjective mood state reported by the subject when, in a double-blind experiment, he or she was given the drug or placebo. For example, subjects who learned a word list while drunk were tested without alcohol but were led to believe that they had received vodka in tonic water; those who reported greater subjective feelings of intoxication recalled more of the items they had learned when drunk. Such results suggest that memory dissociations induced by centrally active drugs may often be achieving their effects by way of altering the person's mood.

The results reviewed have demonstrated mood-dependency for a variety of conditions—for different types of memories, autobiographic ones as well as laboratory-created memories, for different moods (anger, fear, sadness, happiness) that have been aroused in different ways—by hypnotic suggestions, by normal events like successes or failures, or fantasies and watching movies, by drugs, and by whatever biochemical changes underlie shifts in manic-depressive patients.

What kind of theory can explain these mood-dependent effects? My theory (Bower, 1981) explains things in terms of the person's current emotional state entering into association with on-going events. The basic idea is diagrammed in Fig. 7.7. An emotion—say, #3, sadness—is characterized by its connections to facial expressions,

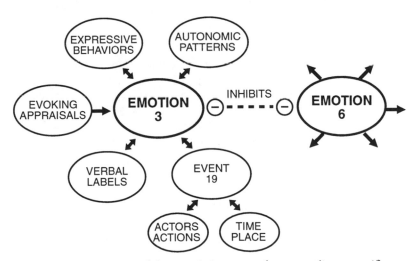

FIG. 7.7. Fragment of the associative network surrounding a specific
emotion node, say, sadness for Emotion 3. Arrows indicate links
along which activation can flow in either direction. (From Bower,
1981, reprinted by permission.)

to behavioral scripts and themes, to autonomic arousal patterns, and finally to ideas and memories of events that have occurred in association with that emotion.

When this emotion is aroused by whatever means, excitation or activation will spread out along its connections, turning on its physiological indicators and also priming and bringing into readiness these associated ideas and memories. Thus, when the person is sad and is asked to recall events from his or her childhood, that set of sad childhood memories will be receiving more total activation than others, so these sad memories become conscious and available for recall. Thus, individuals can better recall those events learned earlier when they were in the same mood.

Later experiments have added some amendments to this theory. For example, mood-dependent memory is not always found in such experiments, especially if the subjects' mood is *not* a salient part of their experience and they do not relate it to the on-going events (see Bower & Mayer, 1985, 1989). We have found that mood dependency is more probable if subjects see the to-be-learned events as *causing* their emotional reaction. If the emotion is seen as causally belonging to the on-going events, then a somewhat stronger associative bond seems to be formed between them, so that mood-dependent retrieval is more likely to follow. And this is the typical arrangement in real life: Life events that cause emotional reactions are the ones that are remembered in association with those emotions.

I now present several extensions of mood dependency. When emotions are strongly aroused, then the spreading of that activation will prime and bring into readiness associated concepts, themes, and rules for interpreting experience. Thus, emotional people will interpret their world and bias their judgments in a manner that is congruent with their feelings. Here is a list of some of these effects of spreading emotional activation:

- Free associations
- Themes of fantasies (T.A.T. stories)

- Snap judgments of other people
- Judgments of event likelihood
- Inter-personal judgments
- Self-perception
- Self-image

The first effect listed is that emotion influences our associative thinking, our reveries and fantasies. For example, happy or sad subjects give appropriately happy or sad free associations to words. When freely associating to a stimulus word like "life," the happy subject will say "wonderful, freedom, openness," whereas to "life" the depressed subject will say "death, misery, toil, struggle." That's understandable. A word like "life" has many associations, some pleasant, others not so pleasant. We theorize that our current emotional feeling stimulates into readiness certain ideas, so that words like "wonderful" and "freedom" receive the most activation from the stimulus word "life" when the person is happy, whereas "death" and "disaster" receive the most activation when the individual is sad.

Such word associations have been used to identify different multiple personalities. An early study of Eve White's three personalities was by psychologists Charles Osgood and Zella Luria (1954), who published a blind analysis of the semantic differential test given to Eve in each of her three different personalities. In that test, the patient rates along many dimensions the emotional connotation of certain key concepts such as "my mother, my spouse, myself, sex," and so on. Osgood and Luria came up with a surprisingly astute and accurate description of Eve's three personalities just by detailed analysis of the associations to such key concepts by Eve's three personalities. Thus, people's feelings alter the associations and emotional connotations aroused by key concepts (see also Osgood, Luria, Jeans, & Smith, 1976).

A similar emotional bias can be shown when happy, angry, or sad subjects daydream or make up imaginative stories for ambiguous pictures of the Thematic Apperception Test (see Bower, 1981).

Happy subjects compose stories of achievement and love, whereas angry subjects tell stories filled with conflict, frustrations, and fights. Again, my theory would assume that the subject's current emotion will activate the same themes that have, in the past, caused the person to react with just that emotion, and so he or she gives them back. This theme activation is relevant to the daydreams, ego-ideals, and fantasies of the alternative multiple personalities.

Third, mood biases people's snap judgments about familiar people and topics. We find that subjects who are temporarily happy give very friendly, charitable descriptions of their acquaintances, whereas angry subjects give uncharitable, critical assessments (see Bower, 1981). This bias may be explained by supposing that people have stored a variety of impressions about familiar persons, and the subject's current mood causes retrieval of primarily positive or negative memories of that person. Thus, a quick evaluation of that person will be biased by the preponderance of one-sided opinions that come to mind (see the "availability heuristic" of Tversky & Kahneman, 1973). This bias is like that of a multiple who has completely different opinions about some person or topic depending on which personality is dominant at the moment.

To continue listing the effects of emotional activation, we find that emotion influences people's forecasts or judgments of the likelihood of future events. In one of our experiments (cited in Bower, 1983), we found that subjects who were made momentarily happy tended to be optimistic—overestimating the likelihood of blessings in the future and underestimating that of future disasters—whereas subjects who were made temporarily sad were pessimistic in their likelihood estimates of positive or negative events in the future (see Fig. 7.8). Thus, temporarily happy people believe in a rosy future that will be filled with excitingly positive successes, whereas sad people construct for themselves a bleak future filled with anticipated failures, losses, frustrations, and gloom. These distorted forecasts also arise when people under an emotional spell predict their own performance capabilities, whether they will succeed or fail in some project (see

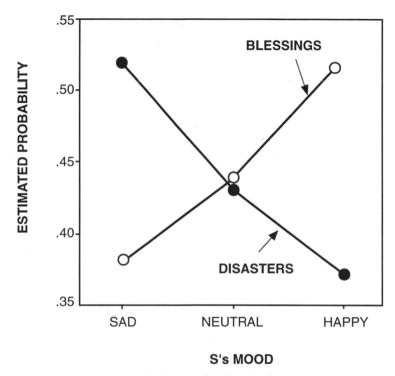

FIG 7.8. Estimates of subjective likelihood of positive (blessings) or
negative (disasters) events in the future for subjects induced to feel
happy or sad before they gave their estimates. (From Bower,
1983, reprinted by permission.)

Kavanagh & Bower, 1985). And such forecasts influence the kind
of decisions and plans people make in preparation for that future.

Thus, prevailing moods affect our judgment of our competence,
and that judgment affects the quality of our performance. Thus, in
social interactions, our sad mood may cause inept performances
which will indeed provoke from others the very reactions that will
fulfill our prophecy and maintain our prevailing mood. Reciprocity
in social interactions is the root cause of emotional contagion: happy,
up-beat people spread their joy to others, so that they attract friends;
depressed people spread gloom, so everyone avoids them; angry
people provoke anger from others, so they conclude that they live in

a world of hostile sharks. Thus, with a multiple personality, reciprocal reactions from others will serve to create a social reality that can maintain whatever ego is momentarily dominant.

As this suggests, we find that a person's mood strongly affects his or her social judgments and the impressions he or she forms of other people. Social perception is highly subjective and evaluative, because we have to read the intentions hidden behind people's words and actions. In that reading, our current emotional premise strongly influences how we interpret others' behavior. Thus, happy people tend to to be charitable and positive in their interpretation and impressions of others they are meeting. Angry people tend to be overly critical, ready to find fault and take offense. They may take out their anger on innocent bystanders as convenient scapegoats.

These emotional influences on personal judgments also apply when people judge themselves and their own behavior. For instance, depressed patients criticize themselves unjustly for what they perceive as their incompetent actions. In an experiment with Joe Forgas and Susan Krantz (Forgas, Bower, & Krantz, 1984), we investigated whether someone's emotional state would influence their moment-by-moment perception of their own behavior. Specifically, we asked whether fairly well-adjusted college students would see themselves as incompetent and socially unskilled if they viewed themselves on video-tape while feeling sad and rejected, but see themselves as competent and socially skilled if they looked at themselves while feeling happy.

In a 2-day experiment, we first interviewed subjects for 20 minutes about personal topics as they were video-taped with their knowledge and consent. The next day they learned how to score video-taped interviews for positive prosocial or negative antisocial behaviors. Examples of positive behaviors were smiling, leaning forward, and contributing friendly remarks; negative behaviors were frowning, looking away, and so on. Following this training, they were hypnotized. Half of them were asked to remember and replay in imagination a moment of social success when they had performed

FIG. 7.9. Proportions of observations where people perceive themselves
on video as emitting positive, prosocial or negative, antisocial
behaviors when the perceivers themselves are in a good or bad mood.
(Based on data reported by Forgas, Bower, & Krantz, 1984, adapted
by permission.)

well and felt good about themselves. The others were asked to recall
and replay a moment of social failure when they had felt embarrassed
or socially rejected because of something they had done that they
deemed awkward or shameful. Subjects were then asked to maintain
their mood while they looked at the 20-minute video-tape of
themselves being interviewed the previous day. Every 5 seconds they
marked at least one positive, negative, or neutral behavior they
observed in themselves.

Figure 7.9 shows the percentages of their observations that fell
into the prosocial and antisocial categories. People in bad moods saw

themselves in the video-taped interview as exhibiting many more negative, socially inept actions than positively skilled ones. In contrast, subjects in good moods saw themselves exhibiting more positive, prosocial actions. These differences are "all in the eye of the beholder," insofar as neutral judges rated the two groups as having equal proportions of positive and negative behaviors. Remember that these are moment-by-moment perceptual judgments, so the fact that they vary with the observer's mood tells us that whether actions are seen as positive or negative depends more on the observer than on the stimulus; and that just underscores the ambiguity of body language and normal conversations. It thus appears that social behavior is almost a blank screen where viewers project a picture according to their mood. They can even project a picture onto themselves, one that matches their current feelings.

Such emotional influences on social judgments can be explained by the associative network theory. The perceiver's mood activates and primes into readiness certain mood-congruent concepts, hypotheses, and inference rules that are then used for classifying the ambiguous gestures, phrases, and expressions of a person during conversation, whether that person is a stranger or oneself.

I have been discussing how our emotions alter our thinking, judgments, and ways of viewing the world and ourselves. Now, to relate this work to multiple personalities, I present one more result, namely, the ways emotions influence the way we think about our own personality and identity.

An especially interesting variant of an emotional bias arises when subjects describe themselves. Several different types of self-ratings can be taken. One is to ask subjects to estimate their subjective state of well-being or their satisfaction with themselves and their life situation. It turns out that people who are temporarily happy report far greater satisfaction than do sad people, even if the cause of their current mood is a passing irrelevancy such as whether it is a sunny, beautiful day or a dull, overcast day (Schwarz & Clore, 1983a). Also, if you take a medical history or health-status report, people who are temporarily sad will find more things wrong with themselves, have more symptom complaints, and rate their health status far lower than will people who are temporarily happy, despite the fact that their emotions may be due to some irrelevancy such as their favorite football team having just won or lost a crucial game.

Of special interest here is that people's reports of their so-called stable personality characteristics can be significantly altered depending on their passing mood. The simplest way to conduct these experiments is to first induce a mood in subjects by some means, such as having them write about some happy or sad events from their lives. Then, using a bogus cover story to mask the true purpose, subjects are led to believe that, as part of a second, unrelated study, they should fill out a personality questionnaire, checking those stable, enduring personality traits that describe what they are really like.

The mood-related effects can be quite dramatic (see Wright & Mischel, 1982). If we compare the trait adjectives people choose to describe themselves, the temporarily happy subject is likely to check such traits as "confident, worthy, socially skilled, lovable, successful, lively, and strong." In contrast, temporarily sad subjects are likely to describe themselves as "helpless, cautious, weak, incompetent, apathetic, guilty, discouraged, and unlovable." Even with these basically well-adjusted college students, a temporary mood-shift can dramatically influence their self-descriptions, their self-image, and their reported personality. It is as though they cannot discount or cancel out their current, temporary feelings: they err by taking their current feelings and thoughts as partial indicators of what they are really like most of the time (see Schwarz & Clore, 1983a,1983b). Incidentally, people are usually quite unaware of how much their temporary mood state is influencing the way they describe their personality.

These changes in self-descriptions can be explained again in terms of selective mood dependent retrieval. We may think of our self-concept as a unit in memory that has hundreds of associations attached to it—all kinds of demographic facts as well as trait labels, behavioral happenings, opinions about us gathered from acquaintances, as well as self-observations. Some of these are positive, some are negative, many are simply neutral. When we are in a positive mood, this positive activation will spread to the positive opinions and positive memories about ourselves. These highly available thoughts come flooding to mind and this biased evidence tricks us into believing that we are really a wonderfully competent person in all facets of our lives. Of course, the sadness of the depressed person works in the same exaggerated way but with just the opposite result.

These mood changes affect not only a person's self-described personality but also his or her overt behavior. Subjects we have induced to feel happy will have an upright expansive posture with their heads held high and their shoulders thrown back; our subjects induced to feel sad appear to be caved in, huddled over, pensive, and fatigued. Their expressive styles are also radically different. Happy people are bubbly, smiling, energetic, and outgoing; they speak loudly and quickly, and move quickly. Sad people are just the reverse: they are slow moving, speak slowly and softly, and appear depleted and downcast (see, e.g., Clark, 1983; or Goodman & Williams, 1982, for reviews).

Although these behaviors are quite familiar, I want to make two points that relate to multiple personality. First, different temporary emotional states can produce what appear to be quite different behavioral styles and personalities, even in normal individuals. And along with these personality differences, moods also create partial amnesia for memories acquired in different emotional states, as I noted before.

Second, I think these results may help us understand some phenomena of multiple personality disorders. As I read the literature on multiple personalities, I was struck by how often each alternate ego was characterized by a different dominant emotional state or different prevailing affective tone, often one surrounding its identification with another person who exemplified that emotional style. For example, one alter ego may exemplify hostile vengeance, with its basic script having been acquired in identification with someone who abused the patient as a child.

There is much support for this view that personality splitting usually occurs along affective lines, with each alter ego dealing with a related set of conflicts and feelings. At a speech a few years ago at the American Psychiatric Association, Dr. Cornelia Wilbur, who treated the famous patient Sybil, said, "In the analysis of the various alternate personalities of a multiple personality, we find individuals who deal with rage and hatred, individuals who deal with hypocrisy and dishonesty in others, alternates who deal with envy and jealousy in themselves and in others, and individuals who encapsulate intense affect and conflict of all kinds" (Institute of Noetic Sciences, 1985, p. 13). Dr. Bennett Braun published similar ideas in a theoretical paper in 1984. He wrote: "Multiple personalities . . . are created via repeated dissociation that occurs under extreme stress (most often child abuse). These dissociations often have similar affective states . . . that chain them together so that they can develop a history of facts and memories . . . and a set of response patterns (that are operantly learned and maintained)" (p. 173).

Eugene Bliss (1980) noted a similar tendency for alternate egos to fulfill different coping functions, to express specific emotions, and to deal with particular problems. He wrote, "The activation or emergence of an alter ego usually indicates that the subject herself experiences an intense emotion that has previously been delegated to a personality whose speciality it is—be it fear, anger, rejection, loneliness, or a sense of inadequacy" (p. 1390).

In a well-documented case reported by Ludwig, Brandsma, Wilbur, Bernfeldt, and Jameson (1972), a young man named Jonah had three alter egos. One ego state (King Young, the lover) came out when Jonah wanted to make sexual advances to women, another (Usoffa Abdulla, the warrior) came out when Jonah got into fights and brawls, and the third ego (Sammy, the slick con man and shyster) came out to help get the other two out of trouble. Jonah is a clear example of different sets of beliefs, values, and memories clustered around different motivational complexes and dominating themes.

I suggest that these different ego states may be intensely involving role enactments originally brought on as defenses in different emotional situations. With practice, these roles become completely suffused and bound up with these distinctly different emotions, so that they create separate memory compartments. Thus, when Jonah felt angry and aggressive, that state recruited a set of memories, beliefs, and behavioral scripts relevant to expressing aggression, and this configuration emerged as the character of Usoffa Abdulla. When Jonah got into a situation where he felt sexually aroused, that emotional state triggered a different set of memories, beliefs, and behavioral scripts that were manifested in the role of King Young, the lover.

Furthermore, I think that these parallels between mood-state dependent memory and multiple personality even extend to a few qualifiers of their features. First, the amnesia between personalities is often not symmetric; the alternate personalities typically know about events that happened when the host personality was in control, whereas the host is usually blacked out and amnesic regarding events that happened when the alternates were in control. But such asymmetric amnesia is often found too in laboratory studies with drugs and mood changes. For example, alcohol produces such asymmetries: events learned when people are drunk are state-bound in that the events are recalled best if they get drunk again. However, events learned when people are sober are about equally well recalled whether they are sober or drunk (see Eich, Weingartner, Stillman, & Gillin, 1975).

A second qualifier in our parallel is that the dissociations between the different mood states are *not* 100%, all-or-none; rather, they are graded or partial, showing more or less access to memories in the alternate states. Even in our best demonstrations of mood-dependency, subjects in an opposite mood could still recall about half of the material they recalled when in the original mood. Interestingly, a similarly *partial* amnesia also occurs with many multiple personalities. For instance, the objective studies of Jonah's memory by Ludwig and his associates demonstrated that most of Jonah's alter egos showed partial memory for neutral word lists learned by the other personalities.

A third qualifier to our parallel of mood dependency and dissociation is that memory from one mood or personality state to another varies dramatically according to which memory indicator we use. The memory index that shows the greatest loss, or amnesia, is what we call *free recall* or *unaided recall*. In free recall, we give almost no memory aids or cues at all to the subject except for the prompt, "Tell me what you were doing during such and so time" (such as during a blackout or during a mood shift). This open-ended question produces relatively poor recall inasmuch as the person is left to his or her own devices for reinstating the original context and generating his or her own internal cues or reminders. In contrast to this deficit with free recall tests, the amnesia appears far less severe if we test the person with more explicit cues, prompts, and reminders. For example, if we test our subjects' memory by forced recognition where they select which of two items they had learned before, then we rarely find a state-dependent memory loss from either drugs or emotional states (for a review, see Eich, 1980).

The point is that retrieval depends on the power of the cues, prompts, and reminders used to test for a certain memory; and I would expect that the amnesias shown clinically across multiple personalities would appear significantly less massive if the person were tested with stronger prompts or recognition reminders for events that had happened to them while they were in an alternate state.

The discrepancy between different memory indicators became salient for me recently while reviewing the evidence for dissociation produced by post-hypnotic amnesia. I mention the topic here because post-hypnotic amnesia is often viewed as a model of memory dissociation of the sort seen in multiple personality. In fact, Eugene Bliss' theory (Bliss, 1980) is that multiple personality arises when patients use frequent self-hypnosis to cope with their many traumatic abuses.

Now, post-hypnotic amnesia is surely a most dramatic display of dissociation in which subjects apparently are unable to retrieve certain target memories until the hypnotist gives a signal, releasing the amnesia. But upon close scrutiny, various qualifications begin to appear (see Coe, 1978). First, about two thirds of normal subjects do not show any post-hypnotic amnesia. Second, of those who do, about half can have their amnesia broken or breached by strong commands and social pressures to be honest and to try hard to recall. Third, many subjects who do not recall the target items appear to engage in active strategies to avoid searching memory, perhaps by simply thinking about other things. And fourth, a variety of indirect measures of memory, which by-pass consciously controlled forms of recollection, demonstrate that these subjects have perfectly good memory for the material they have supposedly forgotten.

Table 7.1
Memory Indices

Optional Controllable	Obligatory Uncontrollable
Free Recall	GSR
Narrative Reconstruction	Perceptual Fluency
Feeling of Knowing	Priming Fragments
	Practice Savings
	Interference

Table 7.1 lists these two different kinds of memory indicators. Those in the left column are called *controllable* or *optional* measures where subjects can consciously decide at their option to alter their performance (see Cofer, Chmielewski, & Brockway, 1976). These indicators reveal large forgetting and amnesia effects in mood-state and drug-state experiments, in multiple personality, and in post-hypnotic amnesia.

The measures in the right-hand column are labeled *uncontrollable* or *obligatory*, because these are often indirect, sneaky, outside the person's conscious control, and are difficult to fake. To briefly review these (see Bower, 1990), take the phenomenon of post-hypnotic amnesia. Subjects exhibiting post-hypnotic amnesia will nonetheless show a strong GSR (sweating of the palms) to target items which they've been told to forget. Also, when the allegedly amnesic items are quickflashed in a tachistoscope or spoken over noisy earphones, the subjects will still perceive those items more quickly than control items. Also, if a word has been presented and primed but covered with amnesia, the subject is still very likely to use that word to complete a word fragment. For example, if the word STEEL has been presented under hypnosis and then covered with amnesia, and subjects are later asked to complete a fragment S T _ _ L with the first word that comes to mind, they are very likely to spell STEEL rather than STILL, STOOL, or STALL.

Amnesic subjects also show big savings in practice on motor tasks such as target tracking in videogames—their improvement in such skills carries over from one practice session to the next, despite subjects professing that they have never seen the task before. Finally, material that is learned and then covered with an amnesia suggestion nonetheless continues to cause its normal amount of interference and forgetting when the person tries to remember some other material. To illustrate, suppose I first teach you to associate 10 women with the names of their first husbands; and then all 10 get divorced and remarry. I then teach you the names of their second husbands; but afterwards I cover this second learning with a hypnotic amnesia suggestion. When I later ask you to recall each woman's first husband, you will still show massive forgetting and interference due to the second learning. Moreover, the forgetting is just as great whether or not I tried to get you to wipe out that second learning with an amnesia suggestion. In other words, interference in memory is not something you can consciously turn on or off at your option; it is an obligatory feature of the human memory system.

I now return to the topic of dissociative disorders. As a memory theorist, these disorders are fascinating to me because they show a pattern of apparently massive forgetting across altered states. However, I think we need more objective memory studies carried out with such patients during their alternate states in order to get a clearer idea of what kinds of information transfers occur between the different states and how the transfer varies according to which memory indicators are used. I would expect that the uncontrollable, obligatory indicators will show large amounts of memory being transferred from one personality state to the other, whereas the controllable indicators (which clinicians mainly rely on) will show state-specific amnesia. But we clearly need some more systematic studies to reach such a conclusion and develop its implications for the understanding of multiple personality and its treatment.

To review my main points, I have discussed mood-dependent retrieval of memories and also indicated the impact of people's temporary emotions on their attitudes, opinions, judgments, forecasts, fantasies, self-image, expressive style, interpersonal behavior—in short, their personality. These studies involved normal, well-adjusted adults who simply were behaving under the spell of some temporary emotion. I view these changes as a mild form of the extreme kinds of personality shifts and memory dissociations that clinicians might see in their patients.

Although my results can provide us with such parallels in normal people, I must confess that I still approach the clinical phenomena of multiple personality and dissociation with a mixture of mystery, awe, and wonderment. It is a challenging task to try to explain any part of those puzzles, and I surely admire the courage and persistence of clinicians who are trying to understand and conduct therapy with such patients.

REFERENCES

Bliss, E. L. (1980). Multiple personalities. *Archives of General Psychiatry, 37*, 1388-1397.

Bower, G. H. (1981). Mood and memory. *American Psychologist, 36*, 129-148.

Bower, G. H. (1983). Affect and cognition. *Philosophical Transactions of the Royal Society of London, 302*, 387-402.

Bower, G. H. (1990). Awareness, the unconscious, and repression: An experimental psychologist's perspective. In J. Singer (Ed.), *Repression and dissociation* (pp. 209-232). Chicago, IL: University of Chicago Press.

Bower, G. H., & Mayer, J. D. (1985). Failure to replicate mood dependent retrieval. *Bulletin of the Psychonomic Society*, 39-42.

Bower, G. H., & Mayer, J. D. (1989). In search of mood-dependent retrieval. *Journal of Social Behavior and Personality, 1*, 121-156.

Bower, G. H., Monteiro, K. P., & Gilligan, S. G. (1978). Emotional mood as a context for learning and recall. *Journal of Verbal Learning and Verbal Behavior, 17*, 573-578.

Braun, B. G. (1984). Toward a theory of multiple personality and other dissociative phenomena. *Psychiatric Clinics of North America, 7*, 171-193.

Clark, D. M. (1983). On the induction of depressed mood in the laboratory: Evaluation and comparison of the Velten and musical procedures. *Advances in Behavior Research and Therapy, 5*, 27-49.

Coe, W. C. (1978). The credibility of posthypnotic amnesia: A contextualist's view. *International Journal of Clinical and Experimental Hypnosis, 26*, 218-245.

Cofer, C. N., Chmielewski, D. L., & Brockway, J. F. (1976). Constructive processes and structure of human memory. In C. N. Cofer (Ed.), *The structure of human memory* (pp. 190-203). San Francisco: W. H. Freeman,.

Eich, J. E. (1980). The cue-dependent nature of state-dependent retrieval. *Memory and Cognition, 8*, 157-173.

Eich, J. E., & Birnbaum, I. M. (1988). On the relationship between the dissociative and affective properties of drugs. In G. M. Davies & D. M. Thomson (Eds.), *Memory in context: Context in memory.* Amsterdam: North-Holland.

Eich, J. E., Weingartner, H., Stillman, R. C., & Gillin, J. C. (1975). State-dependent accessibility of retrieval cues in the retention of a categorized list. *Journal of Verbal Learning and Verbal Behavior, 14*, 408-417.

Forgas, J. P., Bower, G. H., & Krantz, S. E. (1984). The influence of mood on perceptions of social interactions. *Journal of Experimental Social Psychology, 20*, 497-513.

Goodman, A. M., & Williams, J. M. G. (1982). Mood induction research: Its implications for clinical depression. *Behavior Research and Therapy, 20*, 373-382.

Institute of Noetic Sciences (1985). Multiple personality. *Investigations: A Research Bulletin, 1*, 3-4.

Kavanagh, D.L., & Bower, G. H. (1985). Mood and self-efficacy: Impact of joy and sadness on perceived capabilities. *Cognitive Therapy and Research, 9,* 507-525.

Kluft, R. P. (1984). An introduction to multiple personality disorder. *Psychiatric Annals, 7,* 19-24.

Ludwig, A. M., Brandsma, J. M., Wilbur, C. B., Bernfeldt, F., & Jameson, D. (1972). The objective study of a multiple personality. *Archives of General Psychiatry, 26,* 298-310.

Osgood, C. E., & Luria, Z. (1954). A blind analysis of a case of multiple personality using the semantic differential. *Journal of Abnormal Social Psychology, 49,* 579-591.

Osgood, C. E., Luria, Z., Jeans, R. F., & Smith, S. W. (1976). The three faces of Evelyn: A case report. *Journal of Abnormal Psychology, 85,* 247-286.

Plutchik, R. (1980). A language for the emotions. *Psychology Today,* 68-78.

Schenk, L., & Bear, D. (1981). Multiple personality and related dissociative phenomena in patients with temporal lobe epilepsy. *American Journal of Psychiatry, 138,* 1311-1316.

Schwarz, N. & Clore, G. C. (1983a). Explaining the effects of mood on social judgment. Paper presented at the April meetings of the Midwestern Psychological Association, Chicago, IL.

Schwarz, N., & Clore, G. C. (1983b). Mood misattribution, and judgments of well-being. *Journal of Personality and Social Psychology, 45,* 513-523.

Snyder, M., & White, P. (1982). Moods and memories: Elation, depression and the remembering of the events of one's life. *Journal of Personality, 50,* 149-167.

Spanos, N. P., Weekes, J. P., & Bertrand, L. D. (1985). Multiple personality: A social psychological perspective. *Journal of Abnormal Psychology, 94,* 362-376.

Tversky, A., & Kahneman, D. (1973). Availability: A heuristic for judging frequency and probability. *Cognitive Psychology, 5,* 207-232.

Weingartner, H., Miller, H., & Murphy, D. L. (1977). Mood-dependent retrieval of verbal associations. *Journal of Abnormal Psychology, 86,* 276-284.

Weingartner, H., Murphy, D. L., & Stillman, R. C. (1978). Mood state dependent learning. In F. C. Colpaert & J. A. Rosencrans (Eds.), *Stimulus properties of drugs: Ten years of progress* (pp. 445-453). Amsterdam: Elsevier/North-Holland.

Wright, J., & Mischel, W. (1982). Influence of affect on cognitive social learning person variables. *Journal of Personality and Social Psychology, 43,* 901-914.

III
SCIENTIFIC
ANALYSIS

8
Cerebral Aspects of Hysteria and Multiple Personality

Pierre Flor-Henry
Alberta Hospital, Edmonton

In this chapter, the similarities and differences existing between hysteria and multiple personality are examined, from a clinical and a cerebral perspective. The underlying affinity linking schizophrenia and hysteria in females, and the evidence indicating that psychopathy in the male and hysteria in the female are corresponding syndromes of the dominant hemisphere modified in their expression by gender, is discussed. Finally, an attempt is made to explain why hysteria and multiple personality are characterized by opposite directionality of relative right/left hemisphere activation, as measured by alpha power suppression.

HYSTERIA

The annals of the history of medicine indicate that the first illness, for which there is written documentation, was the disease of the "wandering womb," the polysymptomatic disease of women which the Egyptians described in the Kahun Papyrus in 1900 B.C. Hysteria has a very long history and, in the light of some recent attempts to abolish the concept of hysteria (which, in fact, DSM-III has removed from the official terminology of the American Classification), Sir

Aubrey Lewis (1975) pointed out in a celebrated paper that hysteria in its long history has always outlived its obituarists.

The problem with hysteria is that it is heterogeneous and, in any studies of hysteria or hysterical manifestations, one has to differentiate fundamentally among three different but interrelated groups of diseases or states. The first is *hysterical personality*, which is neither a disease nor a psychopathological state. The second is *conversion hysteria* (Group 2 symptoms; see Table 8.1) in isolation from the other symptoms, of chronic pain, affecting various bodily systems. In general, as one now knows, conversion symptomatology is often the first sign of central nervous system disease which, in the initial stages, is neurologically silent and which, on follow up 10 years later, is eventually fatal in 12% of such cases, 16% becoming totally disabled and only 20% being symptom free (Slater, 1965). Finally, there is *chronic hysteria*, the disease of the ancient Egyptians, which was rediscovered in France in the 19th century by Briquet (1859). The American Classification has adopted Briquet's eponym to define chronic hysteria as a disease that remains static through time. Perley and Guze (1962) have shown empirically that, if one operationally defined hysteria as that disease which occurs before the age of 35 in people who have at least 25 symptoms which must come from at least 9 out the 10 functional systems, the illness is stable (Table 8.1).

Of people who satisfy this symptomatic checklist for hysteria, 90% are women. In Edmonton, a few years ago, we undertook a neuropsychological investigation of the stable syndrome of hysteria (Flor-Henry, Fromm-Auch, Tapper, & Schopflocher, 1981); out of the 10 subjects, 9 (or 90%) were female. We compared these systematically with 10 healthy controls, and 10 psychotic depressions, 10 schizophrenias (defined by the criteria of Taylor & Abrams, 1978—by far the most restrictive criteria in schizophrenia research available). All of these patients were unmedicated. The groups were matched with hysteria for age, education, full-scale IQ, handedness, and sex. Also, the subjects were given the Weschler Intelligence Scales. When compared with the healthy controls, women with hysteria

TABLE 8.1
Symptoms for Hysteria According to Perley and Guze (1962)

Group 1
Headaches
Sickly most of life

Group 2
Blindness
Paralysis
Anesthesia
Aphonia
Fits or convulsions
Unconsciousness
Amnesia
Deafness
Hallucinations
Urinary retention
Ataxia
Other conversion symptoms

Group 3
Fatigue
Lump in throat
Fainting spells
Visual blurring
Weakness
Dysuria

Group 4
Breathing difficulty
Palpitation
Anxiety attacks
Chest pain
Dizziness

Group 5
Anorexia
Weight loss
Marked fluctuations in weight
Nausea
Abdominal bloating
Food intolerances
Diarrhea
Constipation

Group 6
Abdominal pain
Vomiting

Group 7
Dysmenorrhea
Menstrual irregularity
Amenorrhea
Excessive bleeding

Group 8
Sexual indifference
Frigidity
Dyspareunia
Other sexual difficulties
Vomiting during 9 months pregnancy
or hospitalized for hypermesis
gravidarium

Group 9
Back pain
Joint pain
Extremity pain
Burning pains of sexual organs,
mouth or rectum
Other bodily pains

Group 10
Nervousness
Fears
Depressed feelings
Need to quit working or inability to
carry on regular duties because of
feeling sick
Crying easily
Feeling life was hopeless
Thinking a good deal about dying
Wanting to die
Thinking of suicide
Suicide attempts

Note: 25 symptoms or more for 9 of 10 groups, onset before age 35. For symptoms to qualify: (a) must interfere with patient's life, and/or (b) patient should have taken medication or drugs for symptoms in addition to aspirin, and/or (c) patient must have consulted a doctor for symptoms.

exhibited bilateral cerebral dysfunction (fronto-temporal), right hemisphere dysfunction greater than left. Further analysis indicated that patients with hysteria were more impaired relative to controls on Raven's Matrices, Finger Localization (Preferred Hand), and Verbal Learning, presumably because of disturbed left hemisphere functions. Hysteria patients, when compared to patients with depression, showed poorer performance for Finger Localization (Preferred Hand), Finger Tip Writing (Preferred Hand), and Delayed Recall (verbal), again implicating the left hemisphere. G-analysis (a type of cluster analysis) showed complete separation between the two groups in terms of neuropsychological configuration.

A cluster analysis, based on the scores derived from the neuropsychological test battery, was carried out on the four groups, consisting of the healthy controls, the hysterias, the psychotic depressions, and the schizophrenias. Three definite clusters emerged: the healthy controls, the psychotic depressives, and, fused together in the same cluster, schizophrenia and hysteria, with a similar underlying neuropsychological configuration. This would suggest a link between schizophrenia and hysteria. There is now abundant evidence that the fundamental deficit in schizophrenia is dominant hemispheric (See Flor-Henry, Fromm-Auch, & Schopflocher, 1983), suggesting (on the basis of the preceding neuropsychological data analysis) a similar deficit in hysteria.

MULTIPLE PERSONALITY

We have studied two cases of multiple personality (Flor-Henry, Tomer, Kumpula, Koles, & Yeudall, 1990) in detail using neuropsychological and quantitative EEG measures. The first, who was dextral, became asymptomatic in the remarkably short period of 3 months following intensive hypnotherapy with videotaped recordings, which the subject then saw the next day. Before treatment she (the basic personality) showed on neuropsychological testing impairment for Verbal Learning, Coloured Progressive Matrices,

Purdue Pegboard for the left hand and Tactual Performance for the left hand and both hands. This pattern of deficit indicates dominant, or left, temporal and bilateral frontal dysfunction, right > left. The presence of right frontal dysfunction further emerged on dynamometric hand strength with an 8 kg difference between the preferred and nonpreferred hands, the nonpreferred hand being the weaker one. In normals there is a difference of 1-3 kg at the most in the strength of the two hands. Retested on the extensive neuropsychological test battery when asymptomatic after treatment, the left hemisphere indices of dysfunction had become normal but the right frontal deficit remained in evidence. There were interesting changes also in the WAIS-R before and after treatment. Before treatment, when the patient showed symptoms of secondary depression, both the Performance and Verbal IQ were similar and in the normal range: Performance IQ = 102, Verbal IQ = 106. On retesting three months later, the Verbal IQ was unchanged but the Performance IQ increased to 126. Thus, from a psychometric point of view, her basic cerebral state is one of relative dominant hemisphere hypofunction in view of the striking Verbal/Performance discrepancy. The fact that the Performance IQ had dropped so considerably initially is related to the depression, which itself perturbed the efficiency of the nondominant hemisphere. On recovery, the underlying dominant hemisphere hypofunction, which had been masked by the depression, re-emerged. The fact that the neuropsychological test battery and the WAIS-R, considered here as a "mini" neuropsychological battery are not identical (as was also reported by Zillmer, Fowler, & Newman, 1988) is because neuropsychological systems and psychometric analysis reflect different aspects of underlying cerebral organization. Notably, psychometric scales monitor essentially posterior, higher order cognitive processing.

The second woman with multiple personality, who was sinistral, showed neuropsychological deficits on the following tests: Aphasia Screening test, Williams' Verbal Learning, Purdue Pegboard (Preferred, Nonpreferred and both hands), Halstead Category test,

Dynamometric test (Preferred and Nonpreferred hand). On the Dynamometric hand strength there was a difference of 12 kg between the preferred and nonpreferred hand (the weaker hand). Psychometrically, on the WAIS-R, Verbal IQ was 93, Performance IQ 122, and Full Scale IQ 104. Thus, neuropsychologically, the pattern of dysfunction was bilateral frontal, right > left and dominant temporal, since she was impaired on aphasia screening test and verbal learning, irrespective of whether her hemisphere dominant for speech was left or right. The psychometric pattern of the second case, as was true for the first patient, revealed hypofunction of dominant hemispheric systems. Because the patient was not cured at the time of discharge there is no knowledge of neuropsychological state after recovery.

In the quantitative EEG investigations, subjects are studied during rest (eyes open, eyes closed), during two conditions of verbal cognitive activation (Vocabulary subtest of the WAIS-R and Oral Word Fluency), and during spatial processing (Block Design subtest of the WAIS-R). The interested reader is referred to Koles and Flor-Henry (1981) for details of the technical aspects of the analysis. In normals, there are task-dependent changes in the log of the Right/ Left Power Ratios (8-13 Hz) which are significantly greater during verbal than during spatial tasks, this indicating relative left hemisphere activation during language and relative right activation during spatial cognition (Butler & Glass, 1985; Glass, 1984, Koles & Flor-Henry, 1981). Remarkably, in the two subjects with multiple personality, all personalities showed pronounced relative left hemisphere activation across all conditions (see Figs. 8.1 and 8.2 for eyes closed; the same pattern was seen in all other conditions). Fig. 8.1 shows that both before and after treatment the cerebral organization of the first patient was in a state of pronounced relative left brain overactivation in all the cerebral regions monitored: frontal, anterior and posterior temporal, and parietal. It is seen that a similar pattern of abnormal relative left brain activation is true for the second patient before treatment for three alternate personalities. Since she did not

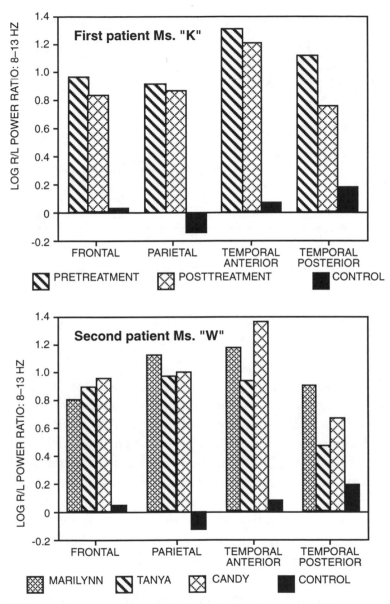

FIG. 8.1: Patterns of hemispheric activation in two multiple personality patients. (eyes closed condition). Top panel shows data from one patient before and after treatment. Bottm panel shows data from a second patient in different personalities.

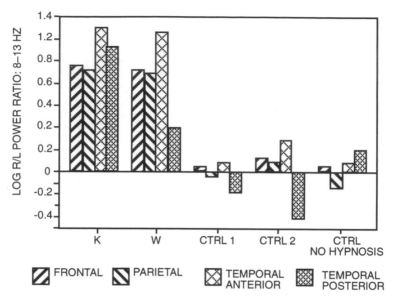

FIG. 8.2: Patterns of hemispheric activation (eyes closed) in multiple
personality patients and controls. CTRL1 = Dextral control under
hypnosis. CTRL2 = Sinistral control under hypnosis.

become asymptomatic there is no post treatment data. It is also clear
in these two figures that the controls are in a state of relatively
symmetrical hemispheric activation in the eyes closed condition. Fig.
8.2 which compares the log of the right/left power ratios (8-13 Hz)
of the two patients with MPD, one of whom was sinistral, the other
dextral, with two normal female controls matched for handedness,
under hypnosis, shows that the left brain activation patterns are not
a reflection of the hypnotized condition. On the other hand, 10
women with chronic hysteria (Briquet's syndrome), but without
multiple personality were in a state of relative right hemisphere
activation (Fig. 8.3). The 10 women with chronic hysteria were
compared with 10 age- and sex-matched healthy controls while the
two subjects with multiple personality were compared with 10
(different) healthy women in the same age range, who were tested
on six different occasions. This made it possible to investigate the

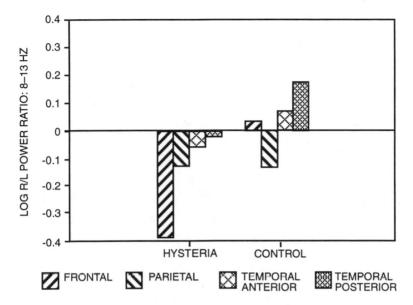

FIG. 8.3: Patterns of hemispheric activation in chronic hysteria (n = 10) and normal controls (n = 10), eyes closed condition.

variability of the EEG in the same subject on repeated occasions. The variance of the EEG between the alternate personalities was not significantly different than the variance of the healthy controls on different days. Thus, there does not seem to be a significant EEG signature to the various alternates in the multiple personality syndrome. Similar observations have been made by Putnam (personal communication, 1987). By studying two healthy subjects—both female, one dextral and one sinistral—during hypnosis, we were able to show that the left hemisphere activation characteristic of multiple personality cases was not a consequence of the hypnotic state.

CLINICAL ASPECTS OF HYSTERIA AND MULTIPLE PERSONALITY

Boor (1982) calculated the gender ratio for all the published American cases of multiple personality, which shows that in 80% of instances the syndrome occurs in women. Putnam, Post, Guroff, Silberman, and Barban (1983), in their statistical investigation, found that 92 of their 100 cases were women. The associated symptoms present during the initial evaluation are of interest. These are of depression (88%), suicidal mood (68%), headaches (66%), amnesic episodes (57%), fugue spells (55%), panic attacks (54%), depersonalization (53%), and psychogenic pain (46%). Auditory hallucinations are prominent in dissociative states (Bliss, Larson, & Nakashima, 1983; Farley, Woodruff, & Guze, 1968; Fitzgerald & Wells, 1977; Goodwin, Alderson, & Rosenthal, 1971; Modai, Sirota, Wijsenbeek, & Wijsenbeek, 1980). In spite of recent attempts to separate the multiple personality syndrome from hysteria, it is clear from the preceding enumeration that it is a disorder with profound and intimate links with hysteria. Sexual abuse in childhood was present in 83%, and physical abuse or extreme neglect in some 70% of instances. There were significant and positive correlations between the total number of types of childhood abuses and the number of alternate personalities and between the total number of psychopathological symptoms and the number of alternates, 65% of the series claimed to have been victims of incest, 48% victims of rape, and 83% to have suffered some other form of sexual molestation. Thirteen of the 14 cases of multiple personality reported by Bliss (1980) are characterized by a very large number of conversion symptoms and satisfy the criteria for the stable syndrome of hysteria; all were women. Most of these patients had been previously diagnosed as schizophrenic because of their auditory hallucinations, delusions, perceptual disturbances and strange behaviors. Specialists in multiple personality, such as Putnam and Bliss, emphasize that the foremost diagnostic indicator is "lost time." "Gaps" must be sought for, however, because the amnesic periods usually are not spontaneously revealed. The key to therapy, the fusion of the alternate personalities, and their re-integration into the basic personality also hinge on memory. As one of the patients, cited by Bliss (1980), expressed it: "The first step is to recover the memory

. . . if I lost time the personalities take over" (p. 1393). Remarkably, in 37 of the 100 patients reviewed by Putnam et al. (1983) the switch into a different personality was accompanied by a shift in handedness, thus demonstrating massive transient functional shifts in lateral hemispheric organization. Three (or 30%) of cases of multiple personality associated with temporal lobe epilepsy also have different hand preference in different personalities (Mesulam, 1981; Schenk & Bear, 1981). In one of our patients, the basic personality was strongly dextral, but in one of her alternate personalities she became sinistral. The various personalities had very different handwriting styles.

An association of multiple personality with temporal lobe epilepsy is indicated by Schenk and Bear (1981) and Mesulam (1981). The latter collected seven cases showing the above association over a one-year period, out of 61 patients with psychomotor epilepsy (i.e. 11%), not encountering a single case in 246 patients with other forms of epilepsy or other neurological problems seen in the same period. No history of sexual or physical torture in childhood is described in these patients, although the absence of such abuse is not explicitly stated. If abuse was indeed absent, the implication would be that epileptic disorganization of critical temporal lobe systems is, here, etiological. In non-epileptic cases of multiple personality, the interaction between extreme and prolonged stress in early childhood and consequent, affectively driven, perturbation of a developmentally vulnerable left hemisphere is presumably etiological. In the 10 cases of multiple personality dissociation associated with temporal lobe epilepsy reported by Mesulam (1981) and Schenk and Bear (1981), the average number of alternate personalities is three and the distribution of foci appears to be random with approximately equal numbers of unilateral right, unilateral left, and bilateral epilepsies. In this particular group the incidence of sinistrality is high, 40%; compensatory sinistrality is characteristic of left hemisphere lesions arising early in ontogeny.

Yakovlev and Rakic (1966) demonstrated, in the study of 130

fetal and neonatal autopsies, asymmetrical patterns of decussation of the cortico-pyramidal tracts and bulbar pyramids: the decussating bundles of the left pyramid are larger than those of the right pyramid, more fibers of the left pyramid cross to the right side than vice versa, and there are more ipsilateral corticospinal projections on the right side than on the left. Wyke (1967), in the investigation of the effects of right and left brain lesions on the rapidity of single and repetitive movements of the upper limbs, found that left hemisphere lesions produced both ipsilateral and contralateral abnormalities, whereas right brain lesions had only contralateral effects. Semmes (1968), in her studies of discriminative sensibility (passive movement, touch pressure threshold, two-points discrimination, and point localization), came to the important conclusion that sensorimotor representations were discrete and punctate in the left hemisphere whereas the pattern in the right hemisphere was of diffuse representation. In addition, she observed ipsilateral deficits with left, but not with right cerebral lesional groups where deficits were always contralateral. It is clear that, given these general principles of neural organization, if such a system is perturbed—other things being equal—there will be a higher probability of evoking either bilateral or left-sided motor weakness, motility abnormalities, or sensory disturbances. This will be particularly true in women, given the relative vulnerability of their right hemisphere systems, compared with men (Flor-Henry, 1983; Yeo, Turkheimer, & Bigler, 1984).

It has been appreciated in the last 10 to 15 years that in hysteria, if there is unilateral conversion, then significantly it is on the left side of the body. This has a contralateral right hemispheric implication. However, the fact that this statement is only true for women, and in males conversion symptomatology is as often present on the right side, is usually ignored. This was also the case in the material of the 19th century. Ley (1980) reviewed the classical cases described by Charcot, by Breuer, by Freud, by Dubois, and by Ferenczi. Choosing all the cases where enough clinical information was given, there was overall an excess of left-sided symptoms which outnumbered right-sided symptoms, but this was only statistically significant for women. Women, and only women, have an excess of left-sided symptomatology, conversion type, which emphasizes the special vulnerability of the right hemisphere in women.

Women with hysteria have chronic and constant pain which doctors can do nothing for—a conversion symptom more common on the left side. This predilection of the left side of the body for pain is more general and is true for both psychogenic, hypochondriacal, hysterical, and also organic pain. Studies in England in the 1930s, for example those of Halliday (1937) and Edmonds (1947), showed that patients with rheumatoid arthritis complained significantly more of pain on the left side of the body than on the right side. Similarly, in the United States, Morgenstern (1970), who studied in great detail bilateral amputations of the upper and lower limbs, controlling for factors such as the clinical state of the stump, noted that subjects reported greater pain on the left side. Thus, there is a lateralization in the right hemisphere for pain representation and pain perception in general (and, therefore, also in women with hysteria). There are familial relationships between chronic pain and depression in first degree relatives. Depression afflicts women much more frequently than men, and is also related to right hemisphere dysfunction.

The cluster analysis described in Table 8.1 suggested that, in terms of neuropsychological configurations, schizophrenia and hysteria are similar, with an underlying fundamental similarity. Is there any other kind of evidence suggesting that there are affinities between the syndromes of hysteria and schizophrenia? Returning to the Perley and Guze checklist for the stable syndrome of hysteria, it is striking that, according to these authors, there is only one psychiatric category that shows false positives and this is schizophrenia in women. Thus an underlying similarity between hysteria and schizophrenia in women is again suggested. Even though women with hysteria are often secondarily depressed, it is an odd fact that in all the long term follow-up studies of the fate of women with hysteria who later become psychotic, the consequent psychosis is not manic-depressive but is schizophrenic. Slater (1961), studied in the London series of monozygotic twins, those with hysterical reaction and found that there was zero concordance for hysteria; the twin with hysteria significantly had lower birth weight and was more often sinistral. This suggests left hemispheric damage, vulnerability, or perturbation: birth, perinatal, or intrauterine developmental anomalies with compensatory sinistrality.

Hysteria is a female disease and the corresponding illness in men is psychopathy. In the same way that it is rare for a man to have the definite syndrome of chronic hysteria, it is extremely rare for a woman to have the full blown syndrome of homicidal, sexual psychopathy. The familial investigations of the St. Louis school in the United States have documented that there are familial associations which link psychopathy in men and hysteria in women. If one starts with women with hysteria, there is a significant excess of psychopaths or alcoholics in the male first degree relatives and of hysteria in their female first degree relatives. Conversely, antisocial female criminals in jails are prone to conversion symptomatology and also have an excess of psychopathy and alcoholism in their first degree male relatives. This would suggest that psychopathy in men and hysteria in women are fundamentally the same syndrome, the expression of which is modified by gender: If it occurs on the male cerebral organization it is psychopathy, if it occurs on the female cerebral organization it is hysteria.

The association between hysteria in women and psychopathy in males is also true for non-clinical groups as Spalt (1980) has shown in a study of this relationship in university students, utilizing detailed personality inventories based on the Washington University/Feighner et al. diagnostic criteria for psychiatric research.

MODEL FOR THE CEREBRAL ORGANIZATION IN HYSTERIA AND MULTIPLE PERSONALITY

The argument is that, in the neuropsychological comparison of hysteria versus controls, even though there is a greater degree of dysfunction in the right hemisphere, the important locus of cerebral dysfunction is, in fact, in the left hemisphere. We recall the relationships briefly described between hysteria and schizophrenia, itself a syndrome of the dominant hemisphere. Psychopathy, in the male, on independent evidence, is associated with dominant hemisphere dysfunction. The studies of psychopathic criminals, undertaken in Edmonton by Yeudall (1977), who has now accumulated a series of more than 200 such patients tested with an extensive neuropsychological test battery (Yeudall, Reddon, Gill, & Stefanyk, 1987), have shown that criminal psychopaths have bilateral frontal dysfunction, left > right, and left temporal dysfunction. A variety of other experimental approaches have also demonstrated the subtle but very constant disturbance of left hemisphere function in psychopathy: tachistoscopic (Hare & Jutai, 1988), event related brain potentials (Jutai, Hare, & Connolly, 1987), and verbal dichotic listening (Hare & McPherson, 1984). Nachshon (1983), reviewing the evidence relating to hemisphere dysfunction in psychopathy came to the same conclusion, as did Miller (1987), in an integrative review of the neuropsychology of the aggressive psychopath. A disturbance of left hemisphere function is also implied by the curious finding that criminality and sinistrality are associated, as was shown in a prospective study by Gabrielli and Mednick (1980). A check of Danish police registers 6 years later demonstrated that 65% of the sinistral boys had been arrested at least once, compared with only 30% of the dextral group. The evidence from epilepsy is persuasive: English and American observations (Serafetinides, 1965; Sherwin, 1977; Taylor, 1969) find that psychopathic personality disorder associated with temporal lobe epilepsy is the result of very early onset epilepsy of the left hemisphere in the male. The peculiar vulnerability of the left hemisphere of the male to cerebral insult is dramatically illustrated by the study of Taylor and Ounsted (1971) of temporal lobe epilepsy occurring as a result of convulsive hypoxia. Convulsive hypoxia leading to mesial temporal sclerosis is one of the major neuropathological causes for temporal lobe epilepsy. The left hemisphere is significantly more often affected in boys than in girls on account of the slower developmental pace of the left hemisphere in boys.

The evidence suggests that, in hysteria and in psychopathy, the fundamental locus of disorganization is in the dominant hemisphere, even though in hysteria there is a greater degree of right hemisphere neuropsychological disorganization—the result of a disruption of left brain inhibitory stabilization of right brain systems producing abnormal contralateral activation of the right hemisphere from a left brain locus of origin.

The characteristic verbal imprecisions in the discourse of women with hysteria and the affective incongruity traditionally called *la belle indifférence* are immediately derivative. Similarly, the conversion symptomatology complex and the chronic pain can be understood as resulting from defective processing of sensory motor integration and of endogenous somatosensory signals, respectively. The dysphoric mood, affective lability, anorgasmic state, and the left-sided preponderance of unilateral conversion symptoms follow from the disruption of normal left brain inhibitory regulation of emotionality, aggression and sexual arousal which, in the mammalian brain, are all related to right hemispheric systems (Denenberg, 1981); hence, this relative right hemisphere activation in chronic hysteria (see Fig. 8.4).

It is a curious paradox that at the level of EEG analysis the state of relative hemispheric activation is opposite in chronic hysteria and multiple personality dissociation: relative right brain activation in hysteria, relative left brain activation in multiple personality. The following model is proposed, perhaps provocatively, in an attempt to explain this unexpected state of affairs, with the obvious caveat that the samples are very small. Multiple personality, which may occur with hysteria or independently of hysteria, is probably best understood as a peculiar form of affectively driven amnesia occurring in women with preexisting left hemispheric vulnerability. This is reflected in their state of relative left hemisphere activation.

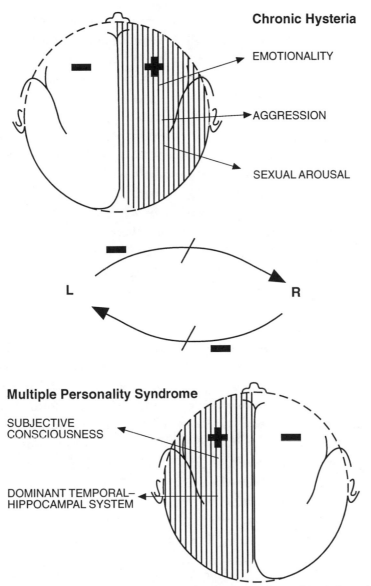

FIG. 8.4: Directionality of altered interhemispheric relationships in hysteria
and multiple personality. In chronic hysteria, lack of left hemisphere
inhibition results in right hemisphere overactivation, whereas in
multiple personality, the lack of right hemisphere inhibition brings
about the pathological left hemisphere activation.

Interestingly, in a SPECT imaging study of a woman with multiple personality, Saxe, Vasile, Hill, Bloomingdale and van der Kolk (1992) report a selective increase in left temporal blood flow occuring in each of four (alternative) personality states. There are curious analogies between the existence of alternate personalities with amnesia and state dependent learning. The only drugs that can induce state-dependent learning are drugs that have an influence on mood, that is, alcohol, amphetamines, marijuana, diazepam, phenobarbital or opiates (see Bower, this volume). Thus, the multiple personality syndrome might be viewed as a special case of state-dependent learning in which the encapsulated amnesia is determined not by drugs but by particular affective states (mediated by the right hemisphere) impinging on the neural substrates of subjective *consciousness* (mediated by the left hemisphere). A prior, developmental instability of these left hemispheric systems has to be postulated. Subjective *consciousness* appears to be a function of critical neural systems linking the brain stem reticular formation to the left mesial frontal cingulate axis since "consciousness" is lost after surgical ligation of the left, but not the right anterior cerebral artery (Dandy, 1931). Similarly, mental confusion is characteristic of right but not left sided hemiplegias (Alford, 1933). Serafetinides, Hoare, and Driver (1965) found loss of consciousness followed intracarotid amytal injection of the dominant, but not the non-dominant hemisphere. In experimental animals, prolonged stress leads to hippocampal necrosis as a result of the toxic effects of excess adrenal glucocorticosteroids (Sapolsky, 1988). Thus the extreme sexual and physical torture characteristically found in the antecedents of women with multiple personality syndrome might lead (through intolerable stress) to a disruption of hippocampal inhibition, disrupting the organization of the dominant hemisphere, triggered later in life by right hemisphere modulated affective states. In contrast to chronic hysteria without multiple personality, the directionality of the abnormal interaction between the hemispheres, in this case, would be right to left (Fig. 8.4).

REFERENCES

Alford, L. B. (1933). Localization of consciousness and emotion. *American Journal of Psychiatry, 89,* 789-799.

Bliss, E. L. (1980). Multiple personalities. *Archives of General Psychiatry, 37,* 1388-1397.

Bliss, E. L., Larson, E. M., & Nakashima, S. R. (1983). Auditory hallucinations and schizophrenia. *Journal of Nervous and Mental Disease, 171,* 30-33.

Boor, M. (1982). The multiple personality epidemic. *Journal of Nervous and Mental Disease, 170,* 302-304.

Briquet, P. (1859). *Traite clinique et therapetic de l'hysterie* [Clinical and Therapeutic Aspects of Hysteria]. Paris: J. B. Balliere.

Butler, S. R., & Glass, A. (1985). The validity of EEG alpha asymmetry as an index of the lateralization of human cerebral function (pp. 370-394). In D. Papakostopoulos, S. Butler, I. Martini (Eds.) *Brain, Clinical and Experimental Neuropsychopharmacology.* Croom Helm: London.

Dandy, W. E. (1931). The brain. In D. Lewis (Ed.), *Practice of surgery* (pp. 53-54). Hagerstown, MD: W.F. Prior.

Denenberg, V. H. (1981). Hemispheric laterality in animals and the effects of early experience. *Behavioral and Brain Sciences, 4,* 1-49.

Edmonds, E. P. (1947). Psychosomatic non-articular rheumatism. *Annals of the Rheumatic Diseases, 6,* 36-49.

Farley, J., Woodruff, R., & Guze, S. (1968). The prevalence of hysteria and conversion symptoms. *British Journal of Psychiatry, 114,* 1121-1125.

Fitzgerald, B. A., & Wells, C. E. (1977). Hallucinations as a conversion reaction. *Diseases of the Nervous System, 38,* 381-383.

Flor-Henry, P. (1983). *Cerebral basis of psychopathology.* Boston: John Wright,.

Flor-Henry, P., Fromm-Auch, D., & Schopflocher, D. (1983). Neuropsychological dimensions in psychopathology. In P. Flor-Henry & J. Gruzelier (Eds.), *Laterality and psychopathology* (pp. 59-82). Amsterdam: Elsevier Science.

Flor-Henry, P., Fromm-Auch, D., Tapper, M., & Schopflocher, D. (1981). A neuropsychological study of the stable syndrome of hysteria. *Biological Psychiatry, 16,* 601-626.

Flor-Henry, P., Tomer, R., Kumpula, I., Koles, Z. J., & Yeudall, L. T. (1990). Neurophysiological and neuropsychological study of two cases of multiple personality syndrome and comparison with chronic hysteria, *International Journal of Psychophysiology, 10,* 151-161.

Gabrielli, W. F., & Mednick, S. A. (1980). Sinistrality and delinquency. *Journal of Abnormal Psychology, 89,* 654-661.

Glass, A. (1984). Cognitive and EEG asymmetry. *Biological Psychology, 19,* 213-217.

Goodwin, D. W., Alderson, P., & Rosenthal, R. (1971). Clinical significance of hallucinations in psychiatric disorders: A study of 116 hallucinatory patients. *Archives of General Psychiatry, 24,* 76-80.

Halliday, J. L. (1937). Psychological factors in rheumatism. *British Medical Journal, Jan. 30,* 213-217.

Hare, R. D., & Jutai, J. W. (1988). Psychopathy and cerebral asymmetry in semantic processing. *Personality and Individual Differences, 9,* 329-337.

Hare R. D., & McPherson, L.M. (1984). Psychopathy and perceptual asymmetry during verbal dichotic listening. *Journal of Abnormal Psychology,* 93, 141-149.

Jutai, J. W., Hare, R. D., & Connolly, J. F. (1987). Psychopathy and event-related brain potentials (ERPs) associated with attention to speech stimuli. *Personality and Individual Differences, 8,* 175-184.

Koles, Z. J., & Flor-Henry, P. (1981). Mental activity and the EEG: task and workload related effects. *Medical and Biological Engineering and Computing, 19,* 185-194.

Lewis, A. (1975). The survival of hysteria. *Psychological Medicine, 5,* 9-12.

Ley, R. G. (1980). An archival examination of an asymmetry of hysterical conversion symptoms. *Journal of Clinical Neuropsychological, 2,* 61-70.

Mesulam, M. M. (1981). Dissociative states with abnormal temporal lobe EEG: Multiple personality and the illusion of possession. *Archives of Neurology, 38,* 176-181.

Miller, L. (1987). Neuropsychology of the aggressive psychopath: An integrative review. *Aggressive Behavior, 13,* 119-140.

Modai, I., Sirota, G., Wijsenbeek, C., & Wijsenbeek, H. (1980). Single case study. *Journal of Nervous and Mental Disease, 168,* 564-565.

Morgenstern, F. S. (1970). A study of some general features which play a role in maintaining a state of chronic pain after amputation. *Modern Trends in Psychosomatic Medicine, 2,* 225-245.

Nachshon, I. (1983). Hemisphere dysfunction in psychopathy and behavior disorders. In M. Myslobodsky (Ed.), *Hemisyndromes: Psychobiology, neurology and psychiatry* (pp.389-414). New York: Academic Press.

Perley, M. G., & Guze, S. (1962). Hysteria – the stability and usefulness of clinical criteria. *New England Journal of Medicine, 266,* 421-426.

Putnam, F. W., Post, R., Guroff, J., Silberman, E., & Barban, I. (1983). *100 cases of multiple personality disorder.* Paper presented at the annual meeting of the American Psychiatry Association, May, New York .

Sapolsky, R. M. (1988). Lessons of the Serengeti. Why some of us are susceptible to stress. *The Sciences, May/June,* 38-42.

Saxe, G. N., Vasile, R. G., Hill, T. C., Bloomingdale, K., & van der Kolk, B.A. (1992). SPECT imaging and multiple personality disorder. *The Journal of*

Nervous and Mental Disease, 180#10, 662-663.

Schenk, L., & Bear, D. (1981). Multiple personality and related dissociative phenomena in patients with temporal lobe epilepsy. *American Journal of Psychiatry, 138,* 1311-1316.

Semmes, J. (1968). Hemispheric specialization: A possible clue to mechanism. *Neuropsychologia, 6,* 11-26.

Serafetinides, E. A. (1965). Aggressiveness in temporal lobe epileptics and its relation to cerebral dysfunction and environmental factors. *Epilepsia* (Amst) *6,* 33-42.

Serafetinides, E. A., Hoare, R. D., & Driver, M. V. (1965). Intracarotid sodium amylobarbitone and cerebral dominance for speech and consciousness. *Brain, 88,* 107-130.

Sherwin, I. (1977). Clinical and EEG aspects of temporal lobe epilepsy with behaviour disorder: The role of cerebral dominance. *McLean Hospital Journal* (special issue) *June,* 40-50.

Slater, E. (1961). The thirty-fifth Maudsley lecture "Hysteria 311." *Journal of Mental Sciences, 107,* 359-371.

Slater, E. (1965). Diagnosis of hysteria. *British Medical Journal, 1,* 1395-1399.

Spalt, L. (1980). Hysteria and antisocial personality. *Journal of Nervous and Mental Disease, 168,* 456-464.

Taylor, D. C., & Ounsted, C. (1971). Biological mechanisms influencing the outcome of seizures in response to fever. *Epilepsia , 12,* 33-45.

Taylor, D. C. (1969). Aggression and epilepsy. *Journal of Psychosomatic Research, 13,* 229-236.

Taylor, M. A., & Abrams, R. (1978). The prevalence of schizophrenia: A reassessment using modern diagnostic criteria. *American Journal of Psychiatry, 135,* 945-948.

Wyke, M. (1967). Effect of brain lesions on the rapidity of arm movement. *Neurology, 17,* 1113-1120.

Yakovlev, P. I., & Rakic, P. (1966). Patterns of decussation of bulbar pyramids and distribution of pyramidal tracts on two sides of the spinal cord. *Transactions of the American Neurological Association, 91,* 366-367.

Yeo, R. S., Turkheimer, E., & Bigler, E. D. (1984, February). The influence of sex and age on unilateral cerebral lesion sequelae. Paper presented at the 12th annual meeting of the International Neuropsychology Society, Houston, TX.

Yeudall, L. T. (1977). Neuropsychological assessment of forensic disorders. *Canada's Mental Health, 25*(2), 7-15.

Yeudall, L. T., Reddon, J. R., Gill, D. M., & Stefanyk, W. O. (1987). Normative data for the Halstead-Reitan neuropsychological tests stratified by age and sex. *Journal of Clinical Psychology, 43,* 346-367.

Zillmer, E. A., Fowler, P. C., & Newman, A. C. (1988). Relationships between the WAIS and neuropsychological measures for neuropsychiatric inpatients. *Archives of Clinical Neuropsychology, 3,* 33-45.

9
Evaluating Amnesia in Multiple Personality Disorder

Mary Jo Nissen
James L. Ross
University of Minnesota

Daniel B. Willingham
University of Virginia

Thomas B. Mackenzie
University of Minnesota

Daniel L. Schacter
Harvard University

The focus of this chapter is interpersonality amnesia, a phenomenon that typically accompanies multiple personality disorder (MPD). In instances of interpersonality amnesia, one personality has no direct awareness of the existence of another personality. Even though such personalities are able to recall events that happened to *them*, they appear unable to consciously remember the experiences of other personalities or events occurring during alternate personality states.

Although amnesia is not a DSM-III criterion for the diagnosis of MPD, it is one of its hallmarks. In a survey of 100 cases of MPD (Putnam, Guroff, Silberman, Barban, & Post, 1986), episodes of amnesia were reported in 98% of the cases. In the view of some, interpersonality amnesia is central to multiple personality disorder. For example, Kenny (1986) argued that it is only the amnesic separation between personalities that makes MPD a distinctive disorder at all. He referred to the view of the 17th-century philosopher John Locke that it is memory that gives us a continuous sense of personal identity (Locke, 1959). In MPD, where an individual's unified personal identity is lost, a consideration of the changes that occur in memory processes may approach the core of the disorder.

There are many questions about interpersonality amnesia that are as yet unanswered. Perhaps the most salient one, and the one that most of this chapter addresses, is this: Is knowledge that is acquired by one personality completely compartmentalized and unavailable to another personality, or can it be shown that acquired knowledge can exert an influence across personalities? A second general issue involves the extent of interpersonality amnesia. Are all memories effectively compartmentalized, or only some? If only some, which ones, or which types? Alternate personalities typically share some abilities that require memory, such as reading and calculation, and they typically share general world knowledge, such as the names of cities and the customs of daily life. Is this knowledge represented separately and redundantly for each personality, or does it have a single representation in memory, but one that all personalities can access? In either case, why is this knowledge not functionally compartmentalized? One possibility is that it is available across personalities because it is emotionally neutral; another is that it does not involve memories of particular episodes in the past; yet another hypothesis is that this knowledge is not compartmentalized because it was acquired before the dissociation of personalities. This last possibility raises another issue: Is the amnesia observed in MPD only anterograde amnesia, affecting information learned after the dissociation, or does it also have a retrograde component, affecting memory for information learned before the dissociation? The idea that dissociation occurs in order to provide protection against having to remember traumatic events assumes that there is a retrograde component. Mary Reynolds, the first case of MPD to be described in detail (S.L. Mitchell, 1816; S.W. Mitchell, 1889) apparently *was* amnesic for all knowledge acquired prior to dissociation, including the skills of reading, calculation, and writing, but it is more typical that not all knowledge acquired before the dissociation is compartmentalized.

Each of these issues is complex. It seems likely, however, that the search for answers to them will be facilitated by advances made recently in the study of organic amnesia, and particularly by the development of new methods for studying memory and amnesia that this work has stimulated. One of the themes of this work is that memory can be expressed with neither the intention to remember nor the awareness that one is remembering. The performance of a task can be affected by prior experience even in the absence of the ability to recall that experience, a phenomenon that has been referred to as implicit memory. (See Richardson-Klavehn & Bjork, 1988, and, Schacter, 1987, for reviews of implicit memory, and Schacter & Kihlstrom, 1989, for a discussion of implicit memory in functional amnesia.) The availability of implicit or indirect tests of memory allows the investigation of whether one personality has access to knowledge acquired by another, without having to ask that personality to explicitly recollect the experiences of the other.

The remainder of this chapter illustrates how these methods can be used to study interpersonality amnesia by presenting an investigation of memory and awareness in a patient with MPD. It is not clear how representative our findings on interpersonality amnesia in this single case will be of most patients with MPD. It would not be especially surprising if there proved to be greater variability among patients with functional amnesia than among those with organic amnesia of a particular etiology. We present the case here as a vehicle for showing the range of tasks that can be applied to the study of interpersonality amnesia and as an example of the form that the phenomenon can take. A complete report of this research can be found in Nissen, Ross, Willingham, Mackenzie, and Schacter (1988). A brief description of the case is presented next, followed by an outline of the types of methods used to assess the patient's interpersonality amnesia and some of the results that were obtained. Finally, more general methodological issues that arise in evaluating amnesia in MPD are discussed.

CASE DESCRIPTION

The patient is a 45-year-old woman who has been divorced five times, is unemployed, and lives alone. She is the mother of two daughters, and was hospitalized on the psychiatry service at the University of Minnesota on five occasions between 1983 and 1987. She meets DSM-III criteria for the diagnosis of multiple personality disorder.

According to family members, the patient's behavior before the age of 5 was quiet and compliant. The family noted the onset of episodes of violent and aggressive behavior when she was 5 or 6 years old, and they recall that she would refer to herself by different names when such behavior occurred. The patient has no history of head trauma or neurological problems. Neurological evaluations, including EEG and CAT scans, were normal. Neuropsychological testing indicated a prorated verbal IQ of 81, a prorated performance IQ of 100, and an estimated Full Scale IQ of 89.

The patient has shown 22 different personalities ranging in age from 5 to 45 years. Three identify themselves as being male, and three maintain that they are left-handed. Most of the personalities have no direct awareness of the others and are amnesic for the experiences of the others. However, three of the younger personalities (ages 5, 12, and 13) report that they hear advice and instructions from several of the older personalities. Furthermore, one personality claims to have direct awareness of all of the others; she reports being capable of "listening to" and "observing" the others. Hypnotism has not been used to induce the patient to reveal alternate personalities.

Our testing focused on eight adult personalities who were all amnesic for each other. The main aim of the research was to determine whether knowledge acquired by one personality would be accessible by some means to another personality. Thus, most of our experiments involved presenting information to one personality and then, after a delay of 5 to 10 minutes, giving another personality a task that would normally be sensitive to the prior presentation of the information. Changes between personalities were made at the request of the patient's psychiatrist (JLR), who would ask if he could speak with an alternate personality, referring to the alternate by name. The transition between personalities took less than 1 min. On three occasions during testing sessions, a switch occurred spontaneously.

CATEGORIZATION OF METHODS

If information is initially presented to Personality 1, then a task can be given to Personality 2 to determine whether she has access to that same information. The various methods for investigating interpersonality amnesia differ in the nature of the task that is given to Personality 2 (see Table 9.1).

Direct Methods

The task given to Personality 2 can employ a direct method of memory assessment, in which Personality 2 is asked to explicitly remember what Personality 1 learned. For example, we taught one personality a set of word pairs. Some of the pairs were easy, such as NORTH-SOUTH; and some were difficult, such as SCHOOL-GROCERY. After she had learned all of the pairs, we gave a second personality the first word of each pair and asked her to recall the word that the other personality had learned with that item. We found that

TABLE 9.1
Characteristics of Tasks Given to Personality 2

DIRECT METHOD
EXPLICIT REMEMBERING OF EXPERIENCES OF
PERSONALITY 1
    Example: Cued Recall

INDIRECT METHODS
EXPLICIT REMEMBERING OF EXPERIENCES OF
PERSONALITY 2
•   EVALUATION OF FACILITATION EFFECTS
    Examples: Forced-Choice Recognition
                  Successive Story Recall
•   EVALUATION OF INTERFERENCE EFFECTS
    Example: Proactive Interference in Paired-Associate
                 Learning

NO EXPLICIT REMEMBERING
•   EVALUATION OF FACILITATION EFFECTS
    Examples: Repetition Priming of Perceptual Identification
                  Sequential Learning Effects on Reaction Time
                  Interpretation of Ambiguous Paragraph
•   EVALUATION OF INTERFERENCE EFFECTS
    Example: Stroop paradigm

the second personality got all but one of the easy items correct, perhaps by being able to correctly guess these high associates, but she got none of the difficult pairs correct. This result is typical of the results we obtained when we asked one personality to remember the experiences of another. The patient was unable or unwilling to consciously recall or recognize stimuli presented to an alternate personality. This failure is, of course, the essence of the phenomenon of interpersonality amnesia.

Indirect Methods

The rest of the methods to be described assess interpersonality memory indirectly. In contrast to direct methods, indirect methods do not require one personality to recollect explicitly the experiences of another personality.

Methods Requiring Explicit Remembering Within a Personality.
     In one type of indirect method, a personality is not required to explicitly remember events that happened to another personality, but she is required to explicitly remember her own prior experiences. The rationale behind this method is to determine whether the prior experiences of Personality 1 affect the ability of Personality 2 to learn and remember her *own* experiences.
     Evaluation of Facilitation Effects. In one example of this procedure, Personality 1 listens to a short story and then tries to recall it immediately. Then Personality 2 listens to the same story and is also asked to recall it. The question of interest is whether Personality 2 is better able to recall the story as a result of the prior experience of Personality 1 with the story. This is an indirect method of assessing interpersonality memory because one personality is not asked to recall what happened to another. Note, however, that Personality 2 is called upon to recall her own experience. This method was used in a previous study of a patient with MPD (Ludwig, Brandsma, Wilbur, Bendfeldt, & Jameson, 1972).
     When we used this technique, we found no evidence of facilitation of performance across personalities. We presented the same story to five personalities in turn, asking each to recall it. Table 9.2 presents the number of story segments that each of the five personalities recalled. The left panel shows results when the story was first read to Alice, then Bonnie, and so on. The right panel shows results from a later session when we used a different story and tested the same personalities but in the opposite order. In neither case was there evidence for systematic improvement in recall with the number

of times the story had been presented. Despite the fact that this task did not require one personality to explicitly remember the experience of another — only her own — it did not reveal access to knowledge across personalities.

TABLE 9.2
Number of Segments Recalled from
Wechsler Memory Scale Stories

| | Story A | | Story B | |
| | *Presentation* | *Number* | *Presentation* | *Number* |
Personality	*Order*	*Recalled*	*Order*	*Recalled*
Alice	1	11.5	5	6
Bonnie	2	4	4	12.5
Donna	3	6.5	3	6
Charles	4	8.5	2	10
Harriet	5	4	1	4

Another test of this type that we used involved the forced-choice recognition of faces. Personality 1 (Alice) was shown a set of 54 faces, and then Personality 2 (Bonnie) was shown a different set of 54 faces. Immediately after this, Bonnie was given a four-alternative forced-choice recognition test. On each trial she saw four faces and was asked to indicate which one she had seen before or seemed most familiar to her. Three types of test trials were included:

1. On some trials, the alternatives included one face that Bonnie had seen previously and three new faces that neither personality had seen. Bonnie selected the face that she had seen 52% of the time.

2. The alternatives on other trials included one face that Alice had seen previously and three new faces. Bonnie selected the face that Alice had seen 42% of the time. If Bonnie had had no knowledge of Alice's experience, she should have selected the face Alice had seen

only 25% of the time.

3. In the third type of trial, one of the faces was one Bonnie had seen, one was a face Alice had seen, and two were new faces. Bonnie selected the face she had seen 33% of the time. Her accuracy at selecting the face she had seen was thus somewhat lower when that face appeared with one Alice had seen than when it did not, as in the first type of trial. Results also showed that when Bonnie did *not* choose the face she had seen, she selected the face Alice had seen 63% of the time. The chance rate would have been 33%.

In short, the results of this forced-choice recognition test indicated that there was interpersonality access to information about the stimuli used in this experiment.

Evaluation of Interference Effects. The two experiments just described assessed facilitative effects on performance across personalities. There are also indirect methods requiring one personality to explicitly recollect her own experience that might be sensitive to interference effects from the experience of another personality. One example, which was used previously in a study of multiple personality disorder (Silberman, Putnam, Weingartner, Braun, & Post, 1985), investigates proactive interference effects in learning. We used an A-B, A-Br paradigm to assess this negative transfer effect in a paired-associate learning task (Bower & Hilgard, 1981).

We first taught Bonnie a set of 10 pairs of unrelated words. Table 9.3 shows the number of correct responses she obtained on each of 10 learning trials. Alice was then given a different set of 10 word pairs that was constructed by re-pairing the words from Bonnie's list. Individuals who do not have MPD find it very difficult to learn a set of word pairs if they have previously learned the same items in different combinations. We found that the same was true in this case: Alice had great difficulty learning a set of word pairs comprised of recombinations of word pairs that Bonnie had learned. As Table 9.3 shows, Alice never got more than two items correct during her four learning trials. This negative transfer effect was evident in Alice's affect as well as her accuracy. She became increasingly frustrated and agitated during testing until the patient's aggressive male personality appeared suddenly and spontaneously, swore at the experimenter, and stormed out of the room. In order to document that Alice was capable of paired-associate learning, we gave her an entirely new set of word pairs 1 week later and found, as Table 9.3 shows, that her accuracy was nearly as good as Bonnie's initial performance. In short, this procedure produced evidence of interpersonality access to information.

TABLE 9.3
Number of Correct Responses (out of 10) on
Paired-Associate Learning Test

	Personality and Stimuli			
	Bonnie A-B	Alice A-Br	Bonnie A-B (retest)	Alice C-D (1 week later)
Trial				
1	5	1	10	4
2	5	0		5
3	6	2		
4	6	1		
5	7			
6	9			
7	10			
8	10			
9	10			
10	10			

Methods Not Requiring Explicit Remembering.
    Another category of indirect methods to be considered has been used extensively in studies of organic amnesia. What sets the

techniques in this category apart is that, although they are designed to assess memory, the tests themselves do not appear to be tests of memory at all from the subject's point of view. The individual is not asked to try to recall, recognize, or otherwise recollect anything. Instead, it seems to the subject that what is being tested is problem-solving ability, perceptual ability, comprehension, or speed of response, depending on which particular test is used. (See Dick-Barnes, Nelson, & Aine, 1987, for an application of a method in this category to the study of MPD.)

Evaluation of Facilitation Effects. One of the methods from this category that we used involved a perceptual identification task. On each trial the patient first saw a visual masking stimulus consisting of a pattern of lines of different orientations, then a word, and then the masking stimulus again. The patient was simply asked to read each word aloud. This would have been trivially easy except for the fact that the word was presented for only 50 msec. We determined how accurately the patient could identify the words.

Some words appeared several times within a set of trials (repeated words); others were not repeated across trials (nonrepeated words). Control subjects become more accurate at identifying the repeated words than the nonrepeated words, and this advantage increases with additional training (Jacoby & Dallas, 1981). This repetition priming effect, or the advantage for repeated words, occurs even in patients with organic amnesia who cannot recall or recognize the set of repeated words (Nissen, Cohen, & Corkin, 1981).

We asked whether training given to one personality would cause an increase in the repetition priming effect when a different personality was tested. We gave Donna four blocks of trials, then Charles completed four blocks, and finally Donna completed another two blocks. Of the 30 trials in each block, 15 involved the presentation of words that appeared in every block, and 15 involved nonrepeated words.

Both personalities demonstrated a repetition priming effect (RPE): They responded more accurately to repeated than nonrepeated words (Fig. 9.1). What is of interest is that the size of the RPE demonstrated by Donna increased as a result of the experience Charles had on the task. Donna showed an average RPE of 10% during her first set of blocks, but following the training that Charles received, Donna's RPE increased to 34%. This increase is even more striking if one compares only the last block of Donna's first set of four (an RPE of 0%) to the first block of her second set (an RPE of 53%).

Thus, using this method, we found evidence for shared access of knowledge between personalities.

A second technique in this category that we have used in several studies of organic amnesia involves measuring reaction time (RT) to visual stimuli (Nissen & Bullemer, 1987; Nissen, Knopman, & Schacter, 1987; Nissen, Willingham, & Hartman, 1989; Knopman & Nissen, 1987). The patient sits in front of a video monitor and rests her fingers on four buttons. On each trial a light appears in one of four positions arranged horizontally on the monitor, and the patient is asked to press the button directly below the stimulus as fast as possible. As soon as she responds to one light, it disappears and another one appears after 500 msec. The patient receives 100 such trials in each block. Short rest periods separate successive blocks.

The condition of most interest in this procedure is a repeating sequence condition, in which the position of the stimulus follows a particular 10-trial sequence of the four possible positions. Each block of 100 trials comprises 10 repetitions of this sequence, but the end of one sequence and the beginning of the next is not marked in any way. Thus, in the absence of knowledge of the sequence, this would appear to be a random series of light positions. The fact that there is a repeating sequence is never mentioned to the patient. Responses of control subjects and patients with organic amnesia become progressively faster in this condition as they learn the sequence. We know that this improvement reflects the acquisition of the specific sequence rather than a more general skill, because when subjects are switched to a random sequence their responses become substantially

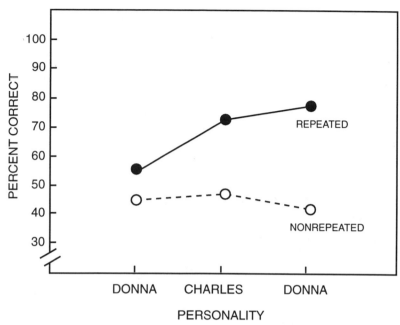

FIG. 9.1. Percentage correct responses in perceptual identification task.

slower. This learning occurs even in individuals who are unaware that a repeating sequence was present and, thus, is an example of implicit learning, or learning without awareness.

We first gave several blocks of a random sequence to Bonnie in order to determine her baseline reaction time. This was an important first step because we had found that different personalities had different average reaction times on this task, ranging from approximately 340 msec to 1000 msec. Following the determination of Bonnie's baseline RT, we gave Alice training on the repeating sequence to allow her to learn it. Finally, we gave Bonnie the same repeating sequence that Alice had learned. We wanted to know whether Bonnie's RT would reveal that she had also learned it. It appeared from the results (Fig. 9.2) that she did: She responded faster to this repeating sequence, which Alice had learned, than she had to a random sequence. This was, thus, another assessment of memory

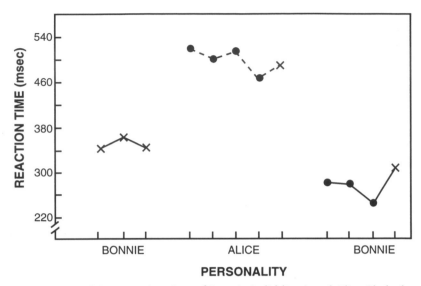

FIG. 9.2. Mean reaction time of Bonnie (solid lines) and Alice (dashed
lines) in four-choice visual reaction time task. Filled circles represent
results on repeating sequence; X's represent results on random
sequence.

not requiring explicit remembering that revealed that the
compartmentalization of knowledge in this patient was incomplete.

It is not the case, however, that all methods within this category
yield evidence of access to knowledge across personalities. Another
task that we used involved assessing the patient's ability to interpret
an ambiguous paragraph. The paragraph began in the following way:

*If the balloons popped, the sound wouldn't be able to carry, since
everything would be too far away from the correct floor. A closed window
would also prevent the sound from carrying, since most buildings tend
to be well insulated. Since the whole operation depends on a steady flow
of electricity, a break in the middle of the wire would also cause
problems.... (Bransford & Johnson, 1973, p. 392).*

In the absence of any context, it is difficult to comprehend the
meaning of this paragraph. If, however, subjects are shown the

drawing that is reproduced in Fig. 9.3 before reading the paragraph, they find the paragraph much more comprehensible (Bransford & Johnson, 1973).

Our goal was to determine whether contextual information given to one personality would facilitate comprehension by another personality. Thus, we showed the drawing to Donna and asked her to describe the situation it depicted. After about 75 minutes, Charles was given the ambiguous paragraph and was asked to interpret it. He failed to provide an interpretation that was consistent with the drawing, saying instead that he thought the paragraph had "something to do with Marconi and electricity." It would appear that Donna's familiarity with the drawing did not affect Charles's interpretation of the passage. In a later session, we showed Charles the drawing and after a delay of 90 minutes asked him again to interpret the passage. In this case he provided an interpretation that corresponded to the drawing.

Evaluation of Interference Effects. It is theoretically possible that previous experience might interfere with the performance of a task not requiring explicit memory, and that this method might also be useful in evaluating interpersonality amnesia. Our project did not use any methods in this category. There are some indications in the literature that implicit memory tasks are not as susceptible to proactive interference effects as are explicit memory tasks (e.g., Graf & Schacter, 1987), so this category of methods may turn out to be relatively empty.

Nevertheless, one possibility for developing an implicit memory test that would be sensitive to interference effects might involve the Stroop task (Stroop, 1935), in which subjects are shown words printed in colored ink and are asked to name the ink color as quickly as possible. Responses are slow when the word is a color name that is different from the ink color (e.g., the word "red" written in blue ink). One interpretation of this effect is that accessing the representation of a familiar word in memory occurs automatically, such that, even though the task requires access only to the name of

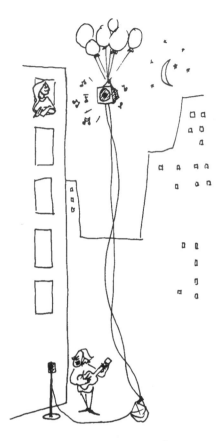

FIG. 9.3. Drawing corresponding to the ambiguous paragraph. (From Bransford & Johnson, 1973, reprinted by permission of the authors and Academic Press.)

the ink color, two different responses may become available, producing response competition (Posner & Snyder, 1975).

MacLeod and Dunbar (1988) used the Stroop task to investigate the development of automaticity in accessing a name in memory. They used novel shapes printed in colored ink and instructed subjects that each of the shapes had a particular color name. When subjects were asked to name the ink color, they initially showed no Stroop interference from conflicting shape names—that is, they were not slow to respond "red" when the shape that was called "BLUE" was printed in red ink. After they had completed substantial practice in naming the shapes, however, they did demonstrate such interference, presumably because the pairing of each shape with its color name was learned so well that the color name assigned to the shape was accessed automatically and produced response competition with the name of the ink color.

This method could be used to investigate interpersonality amnesia by giving one personality extensive training in naming the shapes and then determining whether another personality shows Stroop-like interference.

INTERPRETATION OF RESULTS

Having outlined the range of methods that are available to investigate interpersonality amnesia in MPD and having described a few of the findings from our patient, we now turn to a more complete summary and interpretation of our results. Our work indicates, first of all, that in order to uncover evidence that one personality has access to knowledge acquired by another, it is necessary to use indirect methods. Our work also shows, however, that indirect methods are not sufficient for identifying interpersonality access. Some of the experiments in which we used indirect methods did not provide evidence of access between personalities.

The pattern of results we obtained from this patient suggests that the accessibility of knowledge across personalities depends on the nature of the knowledge being considered. When the material being learned was rather simple, semantically empty, and not likely to invite much cognitive embellishment, we found that the experience of one personality did indeed affect the performance of another. For example, in the subset of our experiments described in this chapter, we found that there was interpersonality access in the following situations: when the stimuli were individual, isolated faces; when pairs of unrelated words were presented and we assessed proactive interference; when single words were presented briefly for identification; and when the task required pressing buttons in response to simple visual stimuli. In contrast, when the material was more complex and was likely to be interpreted differently by different personalities, then it was as if each personality was experiencing the material for the first time. In the experiments described here, we found evidence of compartmentalization when we presented different personalities with a story that could have induced different affective interpretations, and when the task involved interpreting a paragraph that, because of its ambiguity, invited a variety of interpretations.

This pattern of results can be considered within the framework of state-dependent learning discussed by Bower (1981; this volume) and Szostak, Lister, Eckart, & Weingartner (this volume). Material that allows a variety of interpretations and whose interpretation might be expected to depend on one's mood or other characteristics of one's state is relatively inaccessible across personalities. This may be because the way information is interpreted determines how it is represented in memory. The way it is represented, in turn, determines what search cues will be effective in retrieving it from memory (Tulving & Thompson, 1973). In contrast, when the material that is presented does not induce a level of embellishment at which personality-specific factors might operate, its representation in memory may be more personality-neutral, allowing greater access to it by alternate personalities.

METHODOLOGICAL ISSUES

There are some general methodological concerns that arise in studying interpersonality amnesia. We have described a variety of methods that can be used. We wish to stress that no one of these is inherently better than the others in investigating interpersonality amnesia. It is important to use a variety of methods when possible. This point should be clear from the results we have described. Had we used only one of these methods, we might have concluded incorrectly that all information is fully available across personalities; if we had used another method, we might have concluded (also incorrectly) that all knowledge is compartmentalized. We would not have uncovered the interesting pattern of results that we did if we had not used a range of methods. Another reason for using a broad selection whenever possible relates to the likelihood that there will be greater variability among patients with functional amnesia than among patients with organic amnesic of a particular etiology, as mentioned earlier in this chapter. If only a single test is used to study each patient, one could obtain what appears to be a puzzling lack of consistency. In contrast, if each patient is studied more thoroughly with a range of methods, each may present an interpretable and meaningful, if not identical, pattern of results.

A question that arises in investigating interpersonality amnesia involves what the appropriate control is. One solution would be to test a group of healthy control subjects matched on important variables to the patient and compare their average results to those of the patient. An alternative is to use the patient as his or her own control. When possible, the latter solution is more attractive. One would compare, for example, the amount of proactive interference in learning a set of word pairs when a different set of words was presented previously to the same personality versus another personality. This procedure is particularly important if one wants to determine not only whether there is interpersonality access but also whether it is as effective as intrapersonality access.

A methodological issue that is unavoidable in studying amnesia in MPD is malingering. There are several reasons we think it is unlikely that the patient we studied was malingering. Among them are that if she had been feigning interpersonality amnesia, one might have expected her to *avoid* responses corresponding to material that had been presented previously to an alternate personality. But her performance on several tests gave no evidence of such a tendency. Additionally, the purpose of the experiments in which results indicated a failure of access to knowledge across personalities was, overall, no more transparent than that of the experiments in which there was interpersonality access. Finally, the authenticity of MPD has been most questioned when the patient has been implicated in a crime (Orne, Dinges, & Orne, 1984; Schacter, 1986a) and is considered to be highly creative and brilliant. None of those characteristics applies to this patient.

We believe there are ways to reduce the possibility of malingering. For instance, it would seem to be harder to feign amnesia when indirect methods of assessing memory are used, especially those in which no explicit remembering is required. Also, situations in which one looks for interference effects on performance as a result of the experience of an alternate personality should generally be less susceptible to malingering than those methods that detect facilitatory effects, for the following reason. On tests designed to detect interference effects, malingerers (who actually experienced interference from the prior stimulus presentation but who wanted to demonstrate no interference) would have to perform *better* than they were able to. In contrast, on tests designed to detect facilitatory effects, malingerers (who experienced facilitation from the prior stimulus presentation but who wanted to demonstrate no facilitation) could simply perform below their ability. It would seem to be easier to perform worse than one could than to perform better than one is able to.

Schacter (1986a, 1986b) addressed the problem of distinguishing between genuine and simulated amnesia. He identified differences in performance between nonamnesic subjects who were simulating amnesia for a previous episode and those who truly did not remember the episode. These two groups were asked to make feeling-of-knowing ratings regarding the likelihood that they could remember the forgotten event if they were given more time to try to remember it, or if they were given various clues. Schacter found that the simulators, as a group, were less likely to indicate that hints would help them remember the event. In contrast, subjects who were not simulating amnesia for the event felt that hints would help them to remember it.

This research represents the type of empirical approach that is needed to address the issue of malingering. It should be noted, however, that what Schacter found was a difference between a group of simulators and a group whose lack of memory for the episode was genuine. What is needed in clinical and legal settings, and in the study of patients such as the one described in this chapter, is a way to determine whether an individual is or is not simulating amnesia. In Schacter's experiment, there was substantial overlap between the two groups, so that it would be impossible, as Schacter acknowledged, to use this technique to claim with certainty whether a particular subject was genuinely amnesic or was simulating amnesia.

For one of the experiments conducted on our patient, we compared her results to the results of a group of subjects who were asked to simulate amnesia. This was the successive story recall test, in which the same story was presented to several personalities in turn in order to determine whether the accuracy of recalling the story increased with the number of times it was presented. The group of control subjects heard the story once and tried to recall it. They were then told to pretend that they had not heard the story before. That instruction was elaborated upon, and then the subjects heard the same story a second time and tried to recall it again. This group of 45 individuals showed an improvement of 50% on the second recall attempt as compared to the first. However, there was one control subject who showed no improvement. The fact that only one out of the group of 45 subjects produced this "amnesic" pattern of results suggests that it is either not obvious to most individuals, difficult to produce, or both. Nevertheless, if it can be assumed that the lack of improvement in recall by that one subject was a consequence of an intention to simulate, the results indicate that it is possible to simulate the amnesic pattern on this test.

In short, there simply is no way to claim with certainty that an individual patient is or is not simulating amnesia. In studying patients with MPD, the best course would seem to be to accept the fact that these individuals have dramatic changes in state — whether those changes are or are not under their control — and determine what effects those changes have on memory. We believe that the reward of such efforts will be a better understanding of the phenomenon of dissociation, possibly new ideas for integrating dissociated personalities, and new hypotheses regarding normal memory processes as well.

ACKNOWLEDGMENTS

This project was supported in part by the Center for Research in Learning, Perception, and Cognition of the University of Minnesota and by ONR contract N00014-86-K-0277. We thank P. W. Fox for many helpful suggestions. All the figures, and a small portion of the text, are from "Memory and Awareness in a Patient with Multiple Personality Disorder" by M. J. Nissen *et al., Brain and Cognition,* 1988, *8,* 117-134. Copyright 1988 by Academic Press, Inc.. Reprinted by permission of the publisher.

REFERENCES

Bower, G. H. (1981). Mood and memory. *American Psychologist, 36,* 129-148.
Bower, G. H. (1994). Temporary emotional states act like multiple personalities. In R. M. Klein & B. K. Doane (Eds.), *Psychological concepts and dissociative disorders.* Hillsdale, NJ: Lawrence Erlbaum Associates.
Bower, G. H., & Hilgard, E. R. (1981). *Theories of learning* (5th ed.). Englewood Cliffs, NJ: Prentice-Hall.
Bransford, J. D., & Johnson, M. K. (1973). Considerations of some problems of comprehension. In W. G. Chase (Ed.), *Visual information processing* (pp. 383-438). New York: Academic Press.
Dick-Barnes, M., Nelson, R. O., & Aine, C. J. (1987). Behavioral measures of multiple personality: The case of Margaret. *Journal of Behavior Therapy and Experimental Psychiatry, 18,* 229-239.
Graf, P., & Schacter, D. L. (1987). Selective effects of interference on implicit and

explicit memory for new associations. *Journal of Experimental Psychology: Learning, Memory, and Cognition, 13,* 45-53.

Jacoby, L. L., & Dallas, M. (1981). On the relationship between autobiographical memory and perceptual learning. *Journal of Experimental Psychology: General, 3,* 306-340.

Kenny, M. G. (1986). *The passion of Ansel Bourne: Multiple personality in American culture.* Washington, DC: Smithsonian Institution Press.

Knopman, D. S., & Nissen, M. J. (1987). Implicit learning in patients with probable Alzheimer's disease. *Neurology, 37,* 784-788.

Locke, J. (1959). *An essay concerning human understanding.* New York: Dover.

Ludwig, A.M., Brandsma, J.M., Wilbur, C.B., Bendfeldt, F., & Jameson, D.H. (1972). The objective study of a multiple personality. *Archives of General Psychiatry, 26,* 298-310.

MacLeod, C. M., & Dunbar, K. (1988). Training and Stroop-like interference: Evidence for a continuum of automaticity. *Journal of Experimental Psychology: Learning, Memory, and Cognition, 14,* 126-135.

Mitchell, S. L. (1816). A double consciousness, or a duality of person in the same individual. *Medical Repository, 3,* 185-186.

Mitchell, S. W. (1889). *Mary Reynolds: A case of double consciousness.* Philadelphia: William J. Dorman.

Nissen, M. J., & Bullemer, P. (1987). Attentional requirements of learning: Evidence from performance measures. *Cognitive Psychology, 19,* 1-32.

Nissen, M. J., Cohen, N. J., & Corkin, S. (1981). The amnesic patient H.M.: Learning and retention of perceptual skills. *Society for Neuroscience Abstracts, 7,* 235.

Nissen, M. J., Knopman, D. S., & Schacter, D. L. (1987). Neurochemical dissociation of memory systems. *Neurology, 37,* 789-794.

Nissen, M. J., Ross, J. L., Willingham, D. B., Mackenzie, T. B., & Schacter, D. L. (1988). Memory and awareness in a patient with multiple personality disorder. *Brain and Cognition., 8,* 117-134.

Nissen, M. J., Willingham, D., & Hartman, M. (1989). Explicit and implicit remembering: When is learning preserved in amnesia?, *Neuropsychologia, 27,* 341-352.

Orne, M. T., Dinges, D. F., & Orne, E. C. (1984). On the differential diagnosis of multiple personality in the forensic context. *International Journal of Clinical and Experimental Hypnosis, 32,* 118-169.

Posner, M. I., & Snyder, C. R. (1975). Attention and cognitive control. In R. L. Solso (Ed.), *Information processing and cognition.* Hillsdale, NJ: Lawrence Erlbaum Associates.

Putnam, F. W., Guroff, J. J., Silberman, E. K., Barban, L., & Post, R. M. (1986).

The clinical phenomenology of multiple personality disorder: 100 recent cases. *Journal of Clinical Psychiatry, 47*, 285-293.

Richardson-Klavehn, A., & Bjork, R. A. (1988). Measures of memory. *Annual Review of Psychology, 39*, 475-543.

Schacter, D. L. (1986a). Amnesia and crime. How much do we really know? *American Psychologist, 41*, 286-295.

Schacter, D. L. (1986b). Feeling-of-knowing ratings distinguish between genuine and simulated forgetting. *Journal of Experimental Psychology: Learning, Memory, and Cognition, 12*, 30-41.

Schacter, D. L. (1987). Implicit memory: History and current status. *Journal of Experimental Psychology: Learning, Memory, and Cognition, 13*, 501-518.

Schacter, D. L., & Kihlstrom, J. F. (1989). Functional amnesia. In F. Boller & J. Grafman (Eds.), *Handbook of neuropsychology*, (Vol. 3, pp. 209-231). New York: Elsevier.

Silberman, E. K., Putnam, F. W., Weingartner, H., Braun, B. G., & Post, R. M. (1985). Dissociative states in multiple personality disorder: A quantitative study. *Psychiatry Research, 15*, 253-260.

Stroop, J. R. (1935). Studies of interference in serial verbal reactions. *Journal of Experimental Psychology, 18*, 643-662.

Szostak, C., Lister, R., Eckart, M., & Weingartner, H. (1994). Dissociative effects of mood memory. In R. M. Klein & B. K. Doane (Eds.), *Psychological concepts and dissociative disorders*. Hillsdale, NJ: Lawrence Erlbaum Associates.

Tulving, E., & Thompson, D. M. (1973). Encoding specificity and retrieval processes in episodic memory. *Psychological Review, 80*, 352-373.

10

The Switch Process in Multiple Personality Disorder and Other State-Change Disorders

Frank W. Putnam
National Institute of Mental Health

I was honored to participate in *Psychological Concepts and Dissociative Disorders*, a symposium stimulated by the contributions of D. O. Hebb. When I received my invitation, the image of a blue-bound college textbook flashed into my head, Hebb's *Textbook of Psychology*. Later that evening, I was able to find it easily although it had been more than 20 years since I had last opened it. The underlined passages remained fresh, original, and yet contemporary. It has traveled well and remained with me long after I shed the accretion of musty books accumulated from years of college, graduate, and medical schools. The same is true for the ideas of D. O. Hebb. They have remained with us and have traveled well.

It should come as no surprise to the students of D. O. Hebb that, in his last years, he seized upon the phenomena inherent in dissociation to probe the structure and function of the mind. In most respects, he had already anticipated the issues raised by the Hilgards' discoveries in hypnosis and the recent resurgence of clinical material from cases of multiple personal disorder (MPD). Hebb had long recognized the multiplicity of attention, the importance of set in determining response, the role of a central organizing process in guiding goal-directed thought and behavior, and the role of experience in building up discrete structural units that affect subsequent behavior. The convergence of his cell assembly model with the phenomena embodied in the discrete alter personality states of MPD must have indeed been exciting for him.

It remains for us to continue the process of applying his legacy to the understanding of dissociation and thereby to the larger understanding of the mind. In MPD, with its dissection of the stream of consciousness into alter personality states, one can begin to glimpse structural units that may approximate blocks of cell assemblies. The issues inherent in Hebb's cell assembly model (e.g., the differential activation of specific assemblies, the influence of latent assemblies on an active assembly, and the switching between assemblies) can be experimentally traced in the laboratory by studying the alter personality states of MPD patients.

In this chapter, I use the terminology of *states of consciousness* to describe our work in these areas. I leave it for the reader to translate our observations into D. O. Hebb's model. This chapter presents a model of MPD and other psychiatric disorders that are conceptualized for the purposes of this chapter as "state-change" disorders. We first discuss the concept of states of consciousness, focusing on the properties of states that are relevant to state-change psychopathology. Next, we explore the phenomenology and physiology of the state-change or switch process. Finally, we discuss implications of the model for clinical interventions and further research.

STATES OF CONSCIOUSNESS

Definitions. The concept of state, mental state, or state of consciousness, originally derived from the Latin *status*, meaning "condition of being," has a long and complex history beyond the scope of this chapter. The concept of states of consciousness came into its present usage by the end of the 18th century, was central to the early descriptions of hypnotic phenomena, and remains a pivotal idea in modern psychology. Today, the term is widely used in the psychological and psychiatric literature and represents an unquestioned assumption in clinical formulations and psychological theories. The supposition of a dichotomy between state and trait properties is, for example, central to much of the current research in biological psychiatry.

Although there is no single definition of *state* that covers the range of clinical uses, the one proposed by Emde, Gaensbauer, and Harmon (1976), drawing on earlier work by Prechtl and his colleagues (Prechtl, Theorell, & Blair 1968), is a good place to begin. They defined *state* as: "a constellation of certain patterns of physiological variables and/or patterns of behaviors which seem to repeat themselves and which appear to be relatively stable" (p. 29). Wolff (1987), also citing Prechtl's contributions, further added that states are "ensembles of self-organizing variables" and noted that "state transitions [switches] are discontinuous relationships among ensembles of state variables rather than linear changes along a quantitative continuum of levels of arousal or excitation" (p. 19).

PROPERTIES OF STATES OF CONSCIOUSNESS

There is a large and diverse literature on states of consciousness, including: (a) work on a variety of pathological states of consciousness such as affective, anxiety, psychotic, catatonic, and dissociative states; (b) sleep/wake alterations in state of consciousness; (c) hypnotic and meditational states of consciousness; (d) drug-induced states of consciousness; (e) psychoanalytic work on ego states; and (f) states of consciousness during infancy. A number of central properties of states emerge from a review of this literature. The first is the idea that states are discrete and discontinuous. Tart (1977) and others have, in fact, argued that it is more precise to speak of a "discrete state of consciousness" than the more commonly used "state of consciousness." The discontinuous nature of different states of consciousness is best demonstrated by the work on infant consciousness (Wolff, 1987), bipolar disorders (Bunney, Wehr, Gillin, Post, Goodwin, & van Kammen, 1977), and state-dependent psychophysiology (Lydic, 1987).

A second general property of states of consciousness is that they are self-organizing and self-stablizing structures of behavior. When a transition (switch) from one state of consciousness to another state of consciousness occurs, the new state acts to impose a quantitatively and qualitatively different structure on the variables that define the state of consciousness and that new structure acts to reorganize behavior and resist changes to other states.

A good illustration of this property comes from the work on infant states of consciousness. Wolff (1987) has shown, for example, that transitions from waking to Sleep State I in infants (infant sleep is classified by "states" rather than the "stages" used in adults) follow a predictable sequence and that entry into Sleep State I results in a rapid reorganization of a number of state variables. Once the infant has stablized in Sleep State I, he or she is resistant to destablization caused by attempts to wake the infant. A nudge, tickle, or loud noise may briefly disorganize the sleep state and wake the infant, who rapidly reorganizes back to Sleep State I. The stability of a given state and its resistance to disorganization vary from state to state; for example, infant Sleep State I is more resistant to experimental disruptions than infant Sleep State II (Wolff, 1987). Resistance to destabilization declines over time in a given state; for example, Sleep State I is more resistant to destablization early on than after it has been present for 20 minutes.

A third general principle is that switches between states are manifest by nonlinear changes in a number of variables (Wolff, 1987). These variables include: (a) affect; (b) access to memory, that is state-dependent memory; (c) attention and cognition; (d) regulatory physiology; and (e) sense of self. For reasons discussed later, changes of state are difficult to discern in normal adults. Changes in affect and mood are, however, probably the single best marker of state switches in normal adults. The most important marker of state-dependency of learning and memory in normal adults is mood (Blaney, 1986; Bower, 1981; Weingartner, Miller, & Murphy, 1977). State-dependent access to memory and state-dependent learning, while most robustly demonstrated with drug-induced manipulations of state (Overton, 1984), can be observed in a variety of psychiatric and neurologic state-change disorders (Eich, 1986; Nissen, Ross, Willingham, MacKenzie, & Schacter, 1988; Silberman, Putnam, Weingarter, Braun, & Post, 1985; Weingartner, 1978). with hypnotic manipulations of state (Blaney, 1986), and with mood manipulations of state (Bower, 1981). Attention and cognition vary with state; examples range from the extreme shifts across sleeping versus waking states to more subtle manifestations seen in state-dependent learning studies and found in state-change disorders such as bipolar illness (Reus, Weingartner, & Post, 1979).

There is an extensive experimental literature on state-dependent or state-specific physiology (Lydic, 1987). It is likely that state-specific physiology has been an unrecognized contaminant in the current search for biological traits that differentiate specific psychiatric disorders. State-dependent differences in sense of self, such as self-esteem and body image, are commonly noted in clinical alterations of state (Horowitz & Zilberg, 1983; Putnam, 1990). As an illustration, one need only recall the dramatic transformation of sense of self from worthless to grandiose that accompanies switches from depressive to manic states in bipolar patients.

DEVELOPMENT OF STATES OF CONSCIOUSNESS

States appear to be the fundamental unit of organization of consciousness and are detectable from the first moments following birth. Wolff (1966, 1978) and others have used a standard taxonomy of states to describe neonatal behavior up to about age 1. As Emde,

Gaensbauer, and Harmon (1976) observed, "the amount of scientific literature dealing with state-related variables drops off precipitiously after the newborn period" (p. 30). This is due in large part to the fact that behavioral states become increasingly difficult to differentiate with maturation and are less likely to show obvious physiological correlates. Reseachers therefore discuss differences in subjects' readiness to respond in terms such as: attitudes, set, cognitive style, and psychological structures (Emde et al., 1976). A few investigators, such as Horowitz (1979), however, continue to focus on states as clinically important determinants of cognition and behavior.

In part, the increasing difficulty in specifying state is probably a reflection of a normal developmental process that smooths out the transitions across states of consciousness in normal individuals. We speak of this developmental task in infants as learning to achieve homeostasis, that is, the ability of the infant/child to modulate state so that he or she is in a context-appropriate state and to recover from disruptions of state. This developmental task is significantly influenced by input from caretakers who help the infant/child achieve appropriate state transitions, such as waking up and alerting at feeding time and relaxing at nap time.

Nowhere is caretaker-faciliated state change more apparent than with premature infants, who require extensive modulating input from caretakers before they can achieve the state of alertness and motor organization necessary for successful feeding. With experience and maturation of the nervous system, the infant/child becomes increasingly able to self-regulate state. This developmental task represents another arena in which aberrant caretaker behavior may play a role in the dysregulation of state seen in psychiatric conditions such as MPD.

A second reason that discrete states of consciousness become more difficult to discriminate as children grow older is that there are an increasing number of states, differentiated by more subtle changes in state variables. Neonatal researchers agree on a constellation of five to seven discrete states shown by normal infants. By age 1, a child may well have added dozens of states and by adulthood may have hundreds of discrete states and is able to make transitions among them almost seamlessly. It is only in certain disorders where there are pathological states (e.g., depression, anxiety, catatonia) that the role of states of consciousness in the patterning and organization of behavior can again be appreciated.

Certain psychiatric disorders can be conceptualized as "state-change" disorders, in that a major pathophysiological component of the disorder comes from a dysregulation of the state transition process. Depression can be used as an example. Everyone becomes depressed periodically, but we typically cycle out of the depressed state spontaneously or with a little deliberate self-induced state manipulation (e.g., a shopping spree makes some individuals feel better). Depression only becomes a clinical condition when the person becomes "stuck" in the depressed state for a specified length of time—for example, a minimum of 2 weeks by DSM-III-R criteria (American Psychological Association, 1987). It is the failure to switch out of this universally experienced state that defines it as a pathological condition. Other disorders, such as panic attacks, are characterized by precipitous shifts in state from normal states to pathological states without obvious cause. In some cases, such as "specific" phobic disorders or posttraumatic flashbacks, the precipitous shift in state of consciousness is triggered by an environmental stimulus.

MULTIPLE PERSONALITY DISORDER AS A STATE-CHANGE DISORDER

MPD can be thought of as a disorder in which the individual's consciousness is organized into a series of discrete dissociative states (alter personalities) centered around specific affects, body images, modes of cognition and perception, state-dependent memories, and behaviors. By and large the transitions between these rarified states are abrupt and discontinuous, compared to the smoother transitions between normal states of consciousness. These highly segregated dissociative states are developed during childhood in the context of severe trauma, generally repetitive child abuse (Bliss, 1980,1986; Putnam, Guroff, Silberman, Barban, & Post, 1986).

At least two processes probably converge to enhance the distinctness and separation of these alter personality states. First, the data suggest that the trauma must occur relatively early in development and almost always before puberty (Bliss, 1980; Greaves, 1980; Putnam et al., 1986). This suggests that the trauma may be interrupting the normal developmental process of smoothing out transitions between states, thereby leaving the individual with abrupt state transitions that resemble those of infants and small children.

Second, it is thought that it is adaptive for the traumatized child to enter into dissociative states of consciousness that appear to heighten the state-dependentness of variables such as affect, memory retrieval, and behavior (Braun & Sachs, 1985; Kluft, 1984). By binding these variables to discrete, circumscribed dissociative states, the child protects himself or herself against being overwhelmed by a flood of painful affects and memories during times when he or she is not being traumatized. This enables the child to successfully function in other areas of his or her life. Over time, and in a way that is not yet understood, the repeated entry into these heightened dissociative states of consciousness builds up alter personalities with an elaborated sense-of-self, who personify specific affects, behaviors, and developmental ages and who often become invested in their own separateness and in conflict with other alter personality states.

THE PHENOMENOLOGY OF THE SWITCH PROCESS

For the purposes of this chapter, I will define a state-change or switch as the psychobiological events associated with shifts in state of consciousness as manifest by changes in state-related variables such affect. Access to memories, sense of self, and cognitive and perceptual style are often reflected in alterations in facial expression, speech and motor activity and interpersonal relatedness. In working with nonmultiple patients, Mardi Horowitz (1979) has observed that state changes are ". . . commonly recognized during a clinical interview because of changes in facial expression, intonation and inflection of speech, focus and content of verbal reports, in degree and nature of empathy, and other communicative qualities" (p. 31).

SUBJECTIVE EXPERIENCE OF THE SWITCH PROCESS

One might expect that there would be a large introspective literature on switching. What does it feel like to switch? Yet there is almost nothing. Researchers of altered states of consciousness in particular, have tried to study the subjective state-change experience with little success. Zinberg (1977) described a Zen sect that attempted to introspectively observe the exact moment of transition between waking and sleep without success. Tart (1977) tried to study the moment of getting "high" on marijunia, with equally poor results. The vast majority of users only became aware of "being stoned" sometime after they felt that they had become stoned. Gil and Brenman (1959) found the same problem with hypnotic state transitions. Deikman (1977) has labeled this phenomena "the problem of the missing center." It is as if the "self" that observes and remembers is state-dependent and is suspended during the moment of transition between states of consciousness. Studies of memory performance during alcohol-induced changes in state indicate that impairment of memory is most sensitive to the rate of change rather than the absolute blood level of alcohol (Jones,1973). Taken together, these subjective and experimental observations suggest that, during periods of rapid transition between states, individuals do not observe, learn, or store information well.

SWITCH SPEED

How rapidly do switches occur? Several factors influence the precision with which we can determine the rate of a state transition. The first is the sampling rate of the measurement device. The ability to determine the rate of change is a function of how often one tests for a change. For example, the same behavioral rating scale will yield different results if it is applied every 5 minutes or every 8 hours. The second limitation is identification of clear endpoints that signify that a state change has been completed. For example, if one requires a certain amount of change in a nurse-administered rating scale, such as four points over a previous baseline, it may take several hours or days before the subject behaviorally manifests this degree of change in the presence of the nursing staff. If you are testing for a significant change in motor activity, speech, or facial expression, a switch may become apparent within minutes or hours. The obvious problem is that with so many levels of temporal resolution across different measures it is difficult to cross-validate any given measure.

Figure 10.1 shows the mean duration of switching for nine MPD patients measured across six or more alter personality changes. In this case, the behavioral endpoints for determining that a new stable state (i.e., alter personality) had emerged was based on continuous observation and verbal interaction with the subject until it was established from the individual's facial expression, behavior and verbal report that a new alter personality was present and stabilized. These data are in agreement with reports by the vast majority of therapists that alter personality switches typically occur within 5 minutes (Putnam et al., 1986). Similar observational data have been collected on state transitions in infants yielding switch times of the same magnitude (Wolff, 1987). Drug-induced flashbacks and panic attacks, likewise, have onset/offset times of the same order of magnitude (Rainey et al., 1987).

If one studies videotapes of alter personality switches in MPD patients using facial changes as endpoint markers, some switches

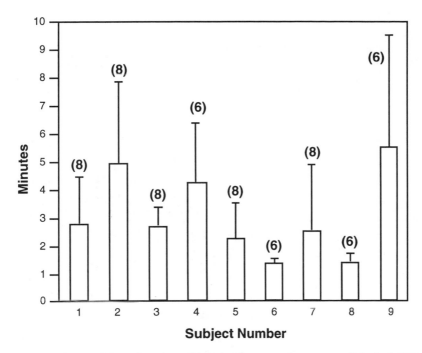

FIG. 10.1 Mean duration of switches between alter personalities in MPD subjects. Number in parentheses is number of switches studied.

appear to occur within a few seconds. Similar results have been noted in bipolar patients undergoing sleep-deprivation induced switches into mania and then back into depression (Rubinow, unpublished data). Switch speed data on bipolar patients from studies conducted during the mid-1970s using nursing ratings administered every 8 hours, suggest a greater variability of switch speed, ranging from 5 minutes to several days to complete the transition between retarded depression and mania (Bunney & Murphy, 1974; Bunney et al., 1977). The majority of these switches were completed with an hour, however, and a review of the nursing notes on these patients (Bunney, Murphy, Goodwin, & Borge, 1972) reveals comments describing these switches as "rapid, sudden, striking, marked change," implying a much faster process than reflected by the infrequent behavioral ratings.

Triggers for Switching. Switches can be triggered by a wide range of stimuli. Cognitive stimuli, such as depressive trains of thought (Seligman, 1975; Beck, 1976), anniversary reactions (Hilgard & Newman, 1969), social situations or expectations, and volitional self-induced state changes probably occur in most individuals. Bunney et al. (1972) found that discussions of passes or discharge planning often appeared to trigger switches into mania. Sensory stimuli are powerful triggers of state change, particularly for evoking dissociative or anxiety states. Researchers studying dissociative and anxiety reactions in posttraumatic stress disorder make use of auditory and/ or visual stimuli that are similar to combat sights and sounds to evoke abreactions and anxiety reactions (Dobbs & Wilson, 1960; Kolb, 1987), though cognitive imagery techniques can be equally effective (Pitman , Orr, Forgue, de Jong, & Claiborn, 1987). Olfactory (Kline & Rausch, 1985) and tactile stimuli can likewise be powerful cues for triggering a switch into a dissociative or anxiety state.

Forced motor activity in depressed adults (Post & Goodwin, 1973) and postural changes in infants (Wolff, 1987) appear to induce changes in state of consciousness. Young children appear to make use of postural and motor changes such as twirling and hanging upside down to alter their state of consciousness (Weil, 1972). Drugs and alcohol are well-documented triggers for state changes, even when actual blood levels are very low, suggesting a cueing effect. In cocaine and opiate addictions, drug-craving or drug-withdrawal states can be produced in abstinent abusers by idiosyncratic environmental cues linked to past drug use (Gawin & Kleber, 1986). Pain, fatigue, and sleep deprivation (Wehr , Sack, & Rosenthal, 1987) are common physiological triggers of state change.

OBSERVATIONS ON THE SWITCH PROCESS IN MPD PATIENTS

During our studies of hundreds of alter personality state switches in MPD patients using various combinations of slow-motion videotapes, EEG, and autonomic physiological measures, a number of common features have emerged. The first is that the majority of alter personality switches occur relatively rapidly, typically in under 5 minutes, though determination of switch speed is subject to all of the methodological limitations discussed previously. Secondly, most, but not all, patients exhibit either a burst of rapid blinking or one or more upward eye rolls at the beginning of the switch. This may be followed by a transient "blank" or vacant gaze. Thirdly, there is a disturbance of ongoing autonomic regulatory rhythms, particularly heart rate and respiration, together with a burst of diffuse motor discharge. On videotape, one can see a rearrangement of facial musculature that coincides with the motor discharge. The facial rearrangement often occurs in a stepwise fashion as a series of grimaces. As the new alter personality state stabilizes, there are often postural shifts.

The newly emerged alter personality state differs from the preceding one along a number of dimensions. Typically, there is a shift in affect. Voice and speech differences, long noted by clinicians working with MPD (e.g., Cory, 1919; Goddard, 1926, Mason, 1893; Peck, 1922; Prince, 1917), are common and are not merely secondary to changes in pitch but also involve shifts in format frequency (Ludlow & Putnam, unpublished data) as well as rate and volume. Baseline motor activity and muscle tension are usually altered. Perceptual and cognitive changes may be manifest by the newly emerged alter personality state's responses to the environment. Not infrequently, the current alter personality state takes great pains to differentiate itself from the preceding state, reflecting a significant shift in the person's sense of self.

Although all of these changes are clinically striking, similar changes have long been reported with state changes in other psychiatric disorders. For example, switches between depression and mania in bipolar affective patients are characterized by a dramatic shift in affect, together with changes in rate and volume of speech (Bunney et al., 1972), motor activity (Wolff, Putnam, & Post, 1985), and cognitive function (Bunney et al., 1972). And, of course, there is a significant shift in sense of self from the worthlessness and hopelessness of depression to the grandiosity of full-blown mania. Periodic catatonia, likewise, is characterized by precipitous shifts in affect, speech, motor activity, and state-specific physiology (Gjessing, 1974).

ORDER EFFECTS

Clinical observation and research on state changes in psychiatric disorders suggests that there are a number of order effects. The first is a directional or pathway effect, that is to say that transitions from State A to State B may follow a different pathway than transitions from State B to State A. This is apparent in bipolar illness, where switches from depression to mania typically pass through a transient intervening euthymic state, whereas switches from mania into depression progress through an "unstable period" characterized by rapid alternation between the symptoms of depression and mania until the individual finally stablizes in a state of retarded depression (Bunney et al., 1972).

In working with MPD patients we have observed that access to a specific alter personality state may require traversing an idiosyncratic pathway passing through an ordered succession of intervening alter personality states; for example, Alter A may only be accessible through Alter D who is only accessible through Alter C so that one may have to pass from C to D to reach Alter A. These observations suggest the existence of an underlying hierarchical organization of states or a set of different switch pathways dependent on the direction of the switch. Wolff (1987) endorsed the latter position, noting from his work on infant sleep/wake transitions that ". . . the presumed neurological processes which effect a transition for waking to sleep may thus differ qualitatively from mechanisms required for the transition from sleep to waking" (p. 54).

A second type of order effect appears to be that certain alter personality states are likely to be preceded or followed by specific other alter personality states. While this apparent increased probability of one alter personality state following another currently remains a clinical observation, the experiential sampling methodology used by Lowenstein, Hamilton, Alagna, Reid, and DeVries, (1987) to study a single MPD patient's naturalistic switching pattern can be applied to the question of alter personality state sequences in MPD. The increased likelihood of specific state sequences occurring in relation to feeding has, however, been well documented by Wolff (1987) and others in infants.

Based on preliminary results from our study of switching in MPD patients, it appears as if the order in which one studies a group of alter personalities will affect the psychophysiology of any given alter personality state. It is as if each alter personality state, while tending towards a state-specific baseline on a given measure, such as heart rate, is also influenced to some extent by the alter personality states that preceded it. For example, Alter A may show heart rate acceleration when preceded by Alter B and deceleration when preceded by Alter C. This order effect appears to extend retrogradely through several preceding personality states, though the number of permutations rapidly makes this a difficult issue to study.

MIXED STATES

The issue of mixed states is one that is going to have to be addressed if we are to understand the interactional role of states in normal and psychopathological processes. Clinicians have reported the existence of mixed or "co-conscious" alter personality states in MPD patients since the earliest cases (e.g., Prince, 1917), and this phenomena continues to be important therapeutically (Braun, 1987) and experimentally (Loewenstein et al., 1987). Phenomenologically, mixed states appear to be present at times in bipolar mood disorders and are dramatically manifest by the duality of consciousness seen with hypnotically induced conditions such as the "hidden observer" phenomenon and in some age-regressed individuals (Hilgard, 1977). Mixed states may also contribute to "passive influence" symptoms such as thought insertion, thought withdrawal, and "made impulses" commonly noted in MPD patients (Kluft, 1987).

IMPLICATIONS OF STATE-CHANGE MODEL FOR PSYCHOPATHOLOGY TREATMENT

This model would predict that there are three levels of psychopathology involved in state-change disorders. The first is at the level of the states per se; that is, the individual enters into a state of consciousness, (e.g., anxiety) that is dysfunctional and/or dysphoric. The second level is a disturbance in the switch mechanism, which may malfunction in a number of ways. It may become "stuck" so that the individual does not normally cycle out of a commonly experienced dysphoric state; it may exhibit a "lability" so the individual can not stabilize in a state, such as occurs with rapid switching in MPD (Kluft, 1983, Putnam et al., 1984); or it may be highly susceptible to activation by environmental triggers leading to stimulus-induced activation of states (e.g., flashbacks). The third level of psychopathology arises from the individual's responses to the first two levels. For example, the person may attempt to modulate state by using drugs or alcohol. Loss of control over state modulation may lead to secondary depressions (Himmelhoch, 1987), generalized anxiety, or phobic avoidance of environmental triggers.

Therapeutic interventions based on this model would have to take into account the level(s) of psychopathology. For example, treatment of substance abuse that is an attempt at self-modulation of state would be expected to have a poor outcome unless the primary problem with modulation of state is addressed. It is well known that the treatment of secondary symptoms, such as depression and anxiety, commonly seen in MPD have little impact on the patient's psychopathology (Putnam, Loewenstein, Silberman, & Post, 1984). Conversely, when the dissociative alter personality states are worked with directly in therapy, many of the secondary affective, anxiety and somatic symptoms disappear (Braun, 1987; Putnam, 1989).

This model suggests several levels of therapeutic intervention in state-change disorders. The first is that of changing state. This may be accomplished in a variety of ways. Medications, such as antidepressants and anxiolytics, may act by biologically changing state. Psychotherapy may work by enabling the patient to cognitively change his or her state of consciousness. Chronobiologic manipulations; for example, sleep deprivation, may alter state by interfering with circadian state sequences (Campbell & Gillin, 1987). Interestingly, many of these therapeutic interventions can, in susceptible individuals, induce rapid perturbations of state such as the rapid cycling in bipolar patients (Campbell & Gillin, 1987; Wehr & Goodwin, 1987). There is also evidence of cross-reactivity between state-change modalities; for example, certain antidepressant medications interfere with circadian rhythms (Zetin, Ptkin, & Urbanchek, 1987).

It is apparent that merely changing state is usually not enough; one must stabilize the individual in more functional states and prevent reentry into dysfunctional states. Some medications, particularly Lithium, may act by stabilizing state (Wehr & Goodwin, 1987). Psychotherapy may help patients stabilize or modulate their state by enabling them to identify state-change triggers (e.g., depressive trains of thoughts, anniversary reactions, etc.) and provide them with alternative outcomes for these triggers. Psychotherapy may also act to disrupt the discreteness of some types of states, such as dissociative states, by bringing emotionally charged state-dependent material into nondissociative states of consciousness to be worked through and integrated. Behavioral desensitization techniques, often used with phobic-stimulus induced panic disorders, may provide a quasi-state stabilization effect by reducing vulnerability to environmentally triggered state-change (e.g., phobic object-induced panic attacks).

RESEARCH

The states of consciousness/state-change model provides a unique isomorphic concept that cuts across the many domains of psychiatric knowledge. Conceivably, the specification of a state of consciousness can span the current chasm from the receptor level to the "ego." It is also a model well-rooted in the new discoveries of developmental psychology with its recent emphasis on the integration of "self" (Stern, 1985). MPD provides a unique example of a traumatically induced state-change disorder with a profound disturbance in sense of self.

Studies of the psychology and biology of the alter personality states permit us a powerful look at the variables that define states of consciousness and at the psychophysiological processes by which states of consciousness are created, maintained, and exchanged.

REFERENCES

American Psychiatric Association (1987). *Diagnostic and statistical manual of mental disorders*, (3rd ed., rev.). Washington DC: American Psychiatric Press.

Beck, A. T. (1976). *Cognitive therapy and emotional disorders*. New York: International Universities Press.

Blaney, P. H. (1986). Affect and memory: A review. *Psychological Bulletin, 99*, 229-246.

Bliss, E. L. (1980). Multiple personalities: A report of 14 cases with implications for schizophrenia and hysteria. *Archive of General Psychiatry, 37*, 1388-1397.

Bliss, E. L. (1986). *Multiple personality, allied disorders and hypnosis*. New York: Oxford University Press.

Bower, G. H. (1981). Mood and memory. *American Psychologist, 36*, 129-148.

Braun, B. G., & Sachs, R. G. (1985). The development of multiple personality disorders, Predisposing, percipitating, and perpetuating factors. In R.P. Kluft (Ed.), *Childhood antecedents of multiple personality* (pp.37-64). Washington DC: American Psychiatric Press.

Braun, B. G. (1987). Issues in the psychotherapy of multiple personality disorders. In B.G. Braun (Ed.), *Treatment of multiple personality disorders* (pp.1-28).

Washington DC: American Psychiatric Press.

Bunney, W. E., & Murphy, D. L. (1974). Switch process in psychiatric illness. In N.S. Kline, (Ed.), *Factors in depression* (pp. 139-158). New York: Raven Press.

Bunney, W. E., Murphy, D. L., Goodwin, F. K., & Borge, G. F. (1972). The "switch process" in manic-depressive illness. *Archive of General Psychiatry, 27,* 295-302.

Bunney, W. E., Wehr, T. P., Gillin, J. C., Post, R. M., Goodwin, F. K., & van Kammen, D. P. (1977). The switch process in manic-depressive psychosis. *Annals of Internal Medicine. 87,* 319-355.

Campbell, S. S., Gillin, J. C. (1987). Sleep disruption: A treatment for depression and a cause of mania. *Psychiatric Annals, 17,* 654-663.

Cory, C. E. (1919). A divided self. *Journal of Abnormal Psychology, 14,* 281-291.

Deikman, A. (1977). The missing centre. In N. E. Zinberg (Ed.), *Alternate states of consciousness* (pp. 230-241). New York: The Free Press.

Dobbs, D., & Wilson, W. P. (1960). Observations on the persistence of war neurosis. *Diseases of the Nervous System, 21,* 40-46.

Eich, J. E. (1986). Epilepsy and state specific memory. *Acta Neurologica Scandanavia, 74,* 1-21.

Emde, R. N., Gaensbauer, T. J., & Harmon, R. J. (1976). Emotional expression in infancy: A biobehavioral study. *Psychological Issues. 10,* (Monograph 37). New York: International Universities Press.

Gawin, F. H., & Kleber, H. D. (1986). Abstinence symptomatology and psychiatric diagnosis in cocaine abusers. *Archives of General Psychiatry, 43,* 107-113.

Gil, M., & Brenman, M. (1959). *Hypnosis and related states: Psychoanalytic studies in regression.* New York: International Universities Press.

Gjessing, L. R. (1974). A review of periodic catatonia. In N. S. Kline (Ed.), *Factors in depression* (pp. 227-249). New York: Raven Press.

Goddard, H. H. (1926). A case of dual personality. *Journal of Abnormal and Social Psychology, 21,* 170-191.

Greaves, G. B. (1980). Multiple personality: 165 years after Mary Reynolds. *Journal of Nervous and Mental Disease, 168,* 577-596.

Hilgard, E. R. (1977). *Divided consciousness: Multiple controls in human thought and action.* New York: Wiley.

Hilgard, E. R., & Newman, M. F. (1969). Depressive and psychotic states as anniversaries to sibling death in childhood. *International Psychiatry Clinics, 6,* 197-211.

Himmelhoch, J. M. (1987). Cerebral dysrhythmia, substance abuse, and the nature of secondary affective illness. *Psychiatric Annals, 17,* 710-727.

Horowitz, M. J. (1979). *States of mind.* New York: Plenum.

Horowitz, M. J., & Zilberg, N. (1983). Regressive alterations in self concept. *American Journal of Psychiatry, 140*, 284-289.

Jones, B. M. (1973). Memory impairment on the ascending and descending limbs of the blood alcohol curve. *Journal of Abnormal Psychology, 82*, 24-32.

Kline, N. A., & Rausch, J. L. (1985). Olfactory precipitants of flashbacks in posttraumatic stress disorder: Case reports. *Journal of Clinical Psychiatry, 46*, 383-384.

Kluft, R. P. (1983). Hypnotherapeutic crisis intervention in multiple personality. *American Journal of Clinical Hypnosis, 26*, 73-83.

Kluft, R. P. (1984). Treatment of multiple personality disorder. *Psychiatric Clinics of North American, 7*, 9-30.

Kluft, R. P. (1987). First-rank symptoms as a diagnostic clue to multiple personality disorder. *American Journal of Psychiatry, 144*, 293-298.

Kolb, L. C. (1987). A neuropsychological hypothesis explaining posttraumatic stress disorder. *American Journal of Psychiatry, 144*, 989-995.

Loewenstein, R. J., Hamilton, J., Alagna, S., Reid, N., & deVries, M. (1987). Experimental sampling in the study of multiple personality disorder. *American Journal of Psychiatry, 144*, 19-24.

Lydic, R. (1987). State-dependent aspects of regulatory physiology. *Journal of the Federation of the American Society of Experimental Biology, 1*, 6-15.

Mason, R. O. (1893). Duplex personality. *Journal of Nervous and Mental Disease, 18*, 593-598.

Nissen, M. J., Ross, J. L., Willingham, D. B., Mackenzie, T. B., & Schacter, D. L. (1988). Memory and awareness in a patient with multiple personality disorder. *Brain and Cognition 8*,117-134.

Overton, D. A. (1984). State dependent learning and drug discrimination. Iverdrn, L. L., Iverson, S. D., & Snyder, S. H. (eds.). *Handbook of Psychopharmacology*, (Vol. 18, pp. 60-127). New York: Plenum.

Peck, M. W. (1922). A case of multiple personality: Hysteria or dementia praecox? *Journal of Abnormal and Social Psychology, 17*, 274-291.

Pitman, R. K., Orr, S. P., Forgue, D. F., de Jong, J. B., & Claiborn, J. M. (1987). Psychophysiologic assessment of posttraumatic stress disorder imagery in Vietnam combat veterans. *Archives of General Psychiatry, 44*, 970-975.

Post, R. M., & Goodwin, F. K. (1973). Simulated behavioral states: An approach to specifity in psychobiological research. *Biological Psychiatry, 7*, 237-254.

Prechtl, H. F. R., Theorell, K., & Blair, A. W. (1968). Behavioral state cycles in abnormal infants. *Developmental Medicine and Child Neurology, 15*, 606-615.

Prince, W. F. (1917). The Doris case of quintuple personality. *Journal of Abnormal Psychology, 11*, 73-122.

Putnam, F. W., Loewenstein, R. J., Silberman, E. K., & Post, R. M. (1984). Multiple personality disorder in a hospital setting. *Journal of Clinical Psychiatry, 45*, 172-175.

Putnam, F. W., Guroff, J. J., Silberman, E. K., Barban, L., & Post, R. M. (1986). The clinical phenomenology of multiple personality disorder: A review of 100 recent cases. *Journal of Clinical Psychiatry, 47*, 285-293.

Putnam, F. W. (1989). *Diagnosis and treatment of multiple personality disorder.* New York: Guilford.

Putnam, F.W. (1990). The disturbance of "self" in victims of childhood sexual abuse. In R.P. Kluft (Ed.), *Incest-related syndromes of adult psychopathology* (pp. 113-132). Washington DC: American Psychiatric Press.

Rainey, J., Aleem, A., Ortiz, A., Yeragani, V., Pohl, R., & Berchou, R. (1987). A laboratory procedure for the induction of flashbacks. *American Journal of Psychiatry, 144*, 1317-1319.

Reus, V. I., Weingartner, H., & Post, R. M. (1979). Clinical implications of state-dependent learning. *American Journal of Psychiatry, 136*, 927-931.

Seligman, M. E. (1975). *Helplessness: On depression, development and death.* San Francisco: W.H. Freeman & Co.

Silberman, E. K., Putnam, F. W., Weingartner, H., Braun, B. G., & Post, R. M. (1985). Dissociative states in multiple personality disorder: A quantitative study. *Psychiatry Research, 15*, 253-260.

Stern, D. N. (1985). *The interpersonal world of the infant: A view from psychoanalysis and developmental psychology.* New York: Basic Books.

Tart, C. T. (1977). Putting the pieces together: A conceptual framework for understanding discrete states of consciousness. In N. E. Zinberg (Ed.), *Alternate states of consciousness* (pp. 158-219). New York: The Free Press.

Wehr, T. A., & Goodwin, F. K. (1987). Can antidepressants cause mania and worsen the course of affective illness? *American Journal of Psychiatry, 144*, 1403-1411.

Wehr, T. A., Sack, D. A., & Rosenthal, N. E. (1987). Sleep reduction as a final common pathway in the genesis of mania. *American Journal of Psychiatry, 144*, 201-203.

Weil, A. T. (1972). *The Natural Mind: A new way of looking at drugs and the higher consciousness.* Boston: Houghton Mifflin.

Weingartner, H. (1978). Human state dependent learning. In B. T. Ho, D. W. Richards, & D. C. Chute (Eds.), *Drug discrimination and state dependent learning* (pp. 361-382). New York: Academic Press.

Weingartner, H., Miller, H., & Murphy, D. L. (1977). Mood-state-dependent retrieval of verbal associations. *Journal of Abnormal Psychology, 86*, 276-284.

Wolff, E. A., Putnam, F. W., & Post, R. M. (1985). Motor activity and affective illness. *Archives of General Psychiatry, 42,* 288-294.

Wolff, P. H. (1966). The causes, controls and organization of behavior in the neonate. *Psychological Issues, 5,* (Monograph 17). New York: International Universities Press.

Wolff, P. H. (1987). *The development of behavioral stess and the expression of emotions in early infancy.* Chicago: University of Chicago Press.

Zetin, M., Ptkin, S., & Urbanchek, M. (1987). Effects of psychactive drugs on circadian rhythms. *Psychiatric Annals, 17,* 682-694.

Zinberg, N.E. (1977). The study of consciousness states: Problems and progress. In N. E. Zinberg (Ed.), *Alternate states of consciousness* (pp. 1-36). New York: The Free Press.

IV
ROUND TABLE
DISCUSSION

11
Prospects for a Psychology of Dissociation:
A Round-Table Discussion

At the end of the symposium there was a 3-hour round-table discussion that was taped and subsequently transcribed. The discussion was animated, if not heated, in places. It reveals excitement about the prospects for understanding dissociative phenomena, as well as skepticism. Needless to say, the discussion was also free-ranging and somewhat disjointed. To present the reader with an intelligible summary, in this final chapter we have distilled, edited, and organized the discussion around several distinct themes.

Klein: We have brought scholars who do both clinical work and research in the area of dissociative disorders together with those who do research in the brain and cognitive sciences. We have had individual opportunities to present our work as it relates to understanding dissociative disorders. In this round table forum, we can more freely exchange ideas, challenge one anothers' conceptions, and generate ideas for interdisciplinary research and theory. To get us started, let me begin by posing some questions: Is the enthusiasm Hebb had for research on dissassociative disorders justified? Have we made progress towards understanding them? Where do we go from here?

Doane: Hebb saw the whole multiple personality issue as one that might fit in well with an updated version of his cell-assembly framework. He was very enthusiastic about Hilgard's work, in which rigorous scientific methodology had been brought to bear on the controversial area of hypnosis. He was calling for a similar effort in the area of dissociative disorders. He was bothered by the lack of precise definitions of terms such as *hypnosis, dissociation, trance,* and so forth. He was bothered by the apparent contradictions of classification in this field. What does one mean by *personality,* for example, when a patient is said to have over 100 of them?

TOWARD AN EXPLICIT MODEL OF DISSOCIATION

Hebb thought that dissociative disorders would remain mysterious and on the fringes of psychology until plausible and testable models were developed. He felt that a neural network model, like his cell-assembly theory, would be a fruitful starting point. In this discussion, Gordon Bower presents an explanation of network modeling, and shows how such a model can explain why recall, but not recognition memory or repetition priming, is affected by context. He then goes on to show how normal memory dissociations (as, for example, in mood state-dependent memory) can be accommodated within an associative network. Klein wonders what kind of adjustments to the model would be needed to achieve dissociations of a pathological severity, and Barresi feels that what is missing is the fact that a normal individual remains one person during his mood swings, whereas each mood seems to have its own "personhood" in MPD. Bower suggests that the network model might be able to account for the major phenomenon of MPD if it is assumed that not only episodes, but also different interpretive rules for processing and producing behavior, become powerfully associated to different moods.

Klein: Hebb would have been pleased with Nissen's talk, because it conforms to his suggested strategy: application of rigorous experimental thinking to a clinical phenomenon. He would also be pleased with large-scale studies like that of Putnam, Guroff, Silberman, Barban, and Post (1986) because they demystify the phenomenon. However, in Hebb's view, it was not just gathering the data that might help demystify the phenomenon and get it more readily acceptable amongst the scientific community, but the development of a materialistic explanation for it. When you have a phenomenon like hypnosis or MPD, you often see a sort of ostrich strategy: "I can't understand it so I won't pay any attention to it." When Hebb held forward the possibility of accounting for MPD in the context of cell-assembly theory, he was not suggesting that we pin our hopes on this specific theory. He felt that we needed to develop an explanation in terms of the underlying cognitive and/or neural machinery.

Is there a current framework from which we can jump, using Hebb as a launching point, to get a better understanding of dissociative phenomena?

Bower: I've been working on a neural network theory. Under the guise of *connectionism* or *associative networks* such theories are becoming very popular in cognitive science. They are made up of layers of little computing units (figurative neurons) that are connected together and can be trained to produce any given output given almost any input by adjusting the weights on the connections. Within such a framework, you can produce state dependency or context dependency, so that in the presence of context A, when I give you X you say Y, in context B when I give you X you say W, in the context of C when I give you X you say Z. You can program these things easily enough and so these neural nets can learn, just by adjustment.

Let's talk about free recall versus recognition memory to illustrate how such a network accounts for one sort of dissociation. Free recall shows mood-context effects: When you change the mood, you change recall. Recognition memory, however, is not so sensitive to context effects. In the network theory, what you are assuming is happening is that when the person is in a particular mood state, say sad, at a time when the person is reading these items, or being exposed to a set of items in short-term memory, he also has a representation of the list context in his mind. So he is saying, "This is List 1 that he is teaching me now," and that is in his mind at the time he is also feeling sad, and at the same time the word "dog" appears on the input list. [See Fig.11.1] At that moment these three elements are simultaneously active in STM or in memory and so, because of that simultaneous activity, they get associated. So you have associations from sadness to "dog", from list context to "dog" and likewise for all the other words from the input list. In a free recall test, the person is asked to give everything that was on the input list, and so you activate the node for the particular list context and all the associations to that context become active as well. With so many activated alternatives you have a lot of competition. But if I put you back in the same emotional state, you also have connections from that emotional state to the words that were on the list (e.g., dog) and you get enough activation to exceed threshold and reduce competition. So what the mood is doing, in part, is providing you with an additional retrieval cue. That's free recall.

In recognition memory what you have to do is retrieve the fact that the word "dog" was presented to you in a certain context. So suppose you present the word "dog", you access that node in memory and you ask, does it have an association to context? However, you don't have the same kind of overloading and competition of associations that the list cue [produced] when I asked you to tell me everything that is connected to the list cue. In recognition, we are asking, "Is there an association between 'dog' and the list?" So you're basically doing a pair recognition, and there is less competition or interference and so performance is better. Because there is so little competition involved in the recognition judgment, providing the original mood state as an additional retrieval cue provides little or no benefit. Reinstating the original mood was important when you had a search problem on your hands, and when I give you list context and say, "search for things attached to it," it helps to have the emotional state.

Now, let's talk about repetition priming. In tasks such as

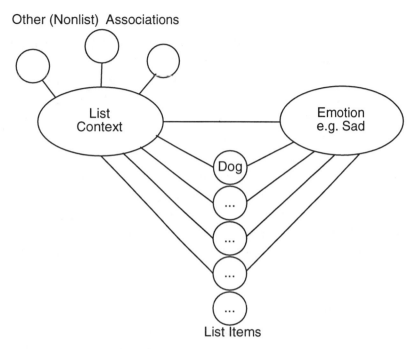

FIG. 11.1 See text for explanantion

completing a word fragment (_TE_L), or recognizing a briefly presented word, performance is improved if you have seen the target stimulus recently (even up to 1 week earlier). Network theories usually distinguish between a concept node and a word node and also the stimulus patterns that activate that word node. For example, for the word "steel" there will be a word node, as well as another node naming the concept and, off of that, you have attached all the associations to everything you know about steel. You conceive the process of reading or perception of the word as activating the features, visual features if it is a visual word, like "s" in the first position, "t" in the second position, "e" in the third position, and so on, and these visual features simultaneously send associative activation up to the word node STEEL. This is exactly the way models of word reading work (McClelland & Rumelhart, 1981), and those associations of a letter in a certain position can be strengthened by the presentation of the word STEEL. So the more often you see STEEL, the stronger the association of "s" in the first position to the word node. So you get repetition priming in such a theory because letters in certain positions get associated with words with letters in those positions. So when you present STEEL, it automatically strengthens a preexisting association from the letters to the word. And that is the basic process involved in priming because, if I show you that word degraded or very fast on a T-scope, you [need] only a little bit of sensory evidence to trigger off these associations. Or, in fragment completion, if I give you _TE_L, that's enough to activate the association . . . Because what you're really doing is making use of this part of the associative structure, reinstating the mood doesn't really help much here. This theory integrates three things. You get big context mood effects on free recall, you don't get any on recognition memory, and you don't get any on priming.

Now what Mary Jo (Nissen) was able to show was that this [mood] does start to have an impact on you when the words have multiple meanings. When what you have to remember is the meaning of the words, then mood changes and personality changes have an impact. So you get different interpretations of a word like "lead"(to "lead" someone or the metal "lead") depending upon the mood you're in . . .

Klein: Gordon. I want to try to apply this "protomodel." It is easy to see how mood can relate to a state in a MP patient. What would "list context" correspond to?

Bower: Oh, the time of day in which you present it, where you were.

Klein: But if one were to apply this framework to MPD, it's really the mood swings that are going to be attaching the *amnestic barriers* (if you accept that term). What I'm saying is that it's the fact that there is a mood swing that makes some of these pathways accessible from some moods and not others (or personalities). If we accept your network framework and use it to explain amnesia between personalities, is mood-state dependent memory *quantitatively* different from, but maybe not *qualitatively* different from, the "normal" dissociations you've explained using it?

Bower: I haven't thought it all the way through, obviously. I was just thinking, what differences are there in the memories you get out of a person, depending on the personality state they are in? If you say, "Tell me what's happened to you in the last couple of weeks, or what's been going on in your life or what do you think of Ronald Reagan?" There, the notion is you've [stored] away lots of different memories in association with different emotional states or personality states. The basic idea is the same notion of free association . . . where you have a whole bunch of words, like *joy, freedom, wonderment,* et cetera and *death, struggle* and *toil,* et cetera. And [some of] these are hooked up to negative moods—fear, sadness—and these are hooked up to positive moods, and a lot of words like *life* or *magazine* are not hooked up to anything for me. What happens when I say, "Free associate to this word" when you are in one mood state [e.g., happy] is you get summation of activation at nodes associated to that state, and so some words get a greater sum than others. If your mood state changes [e.g., to sad], this will alter the set of most highly activated nodes, and different words will be reported. It is the same when you get a MP who is very angry and I say, "Tell me about your mother or father," and then I get him very sad or very happy and I say, "Tell me about your father," or "Tell me what's been happening to you the last couple of weeks." If you're here [in a particular emotional state], you get these memories, if you are here [another state] you get these memories. Now that's a kind of dissociation; we call it *context-dependent retrieval.* What you retrieve by [a particular] stimulus depends on what state you are in. This all comes out of the notion of summation of activation-summation of spreading activation.

The following interjection demonstrates how the notion of spreading activation in the network model strikes a chord with experiences in the clinic.

Fraser: With the patient that Ben [Doane] brought me to see, when I used the word *memory*, it triggered off a switch to the fetal [position]. With another patient, who I saw last week, a person walked in who she must have seen before and started to trigger off a switch. She didn't know what happened, but I knew from one or two signals that she somehow knew that person and that person's presence started to trigger her off, her eyes rolled, she said "My eyes were rolling up and I was trying to switch and I was fighting it so." There is some "association" there.

Bower: What I've described is a general framework that people in artificial intelligence and language processing have been using for some time to talk about how context picks out the meaning of certain ambiguous words. Once you start to study language, how people understand language, the first thing you have to deal with is how to pick out the meaning of ambiguous words appropriate to context, and this notion of spreading activation has been around for years in that literature. Mary Jo's results show that when the material permits different interpretations of certain words [or other materials], then you don't get much interpersonality transfer of memory. This is like saying that "life" means one thing when you're happy, and "life" means another thing when you're sad, and that is why you don't get any transfer. I'm not sure that it can deal with all your results, I'm sure it doesn't. It's tentative, but it's better than nothing.

Barresi: To pursue it a little bit, I think from the point of view of MPD, the crucial question is, "How do moods become systems themselves and not temporary states?"

Bower: I have not been distinguishing between prolonged, pervasive, long-acting things as opposed to the spasmodic, episodic things.

Barresi: And how do "words" become those kinds of organized systems that are called MP and that could just change this picture entirely?

Bower: I think each mood state has attached to it a set of rules of interpretation of reality. That is, how do you decide if someone is being insulting or someone is attending to you or doesn't like you? I think you have rules of interpretation that you apply to social stimuli, other people's behavior, what they say in context. And you switch in different sets of rules for interpreting reality depending on your mood state, and what that does is to change the nature of that reality.

Barresi: But what changes that nature of the mood state as the same reality?

Bower: Sometimes it is and it's a circular process.

Barresi: Yes, but part of the circle you're looking at here is the part of the circle that applies to all of us. But the model we need to build must create a distinction between the kind of mood variations that we, as normal individuals, have and the kinds of mood changes in observed in MPD (i.e., that they're relatively static in one mood irrelevant of stimulus and then there are sharp transitions to another mood state which is another personality).

Bower: But Frank was telling us of a switch process in which there are certain stimuli that you can give to people which frighten them or call up certain memories.

Klein: On a sort of mechanical level, if you imagine a system that has mutually inhibitory moods with a lot of hysteresis in it, then once a particular stimulus pushes you into a particular mood state you will have a lot of trouble getting out of it until you develop the skills for switching, which, I guess, some patients either have or develop in therapy. You're not happy with that?

Barresi: No. What was I was thinking was that one of the things that Hebb found interesting was to think of the mood state as a cell assembly: When it became an MP it was sort of like an operating unit that maintained itself and inhibited alternative other "self" units (or whatever you want to call them). These switch with each other, and I think Dr. Putnam's work is very interesting in this regard. Hebb's notion of a cell-assembly would include what you have. But he was particularly interested in studying MP because it raises the question of phenomena that go beyond the model as applied to the average individual and into this sort of large, whatever you want to call it, cell-assembly, or system, or whatever it is, that is centered on a particular kind of mood system, determines and organizes the experiences in the period of time, biases all the experiences to their mood, and switches off only once in a while.

Bower: But what you want to have, again, is different interpretive rules for experience dependent on the mood state, or depending on the "personality state" you are in. It is as though similar to asking you to role-play a son of a bitch in a meeting, such as when interviewing a new job candidate; or role-play the friendly dutch uncle counselor to the job candidate; or role-play the childish playmate to the person. I think when you take on these roles they have particular interpretive rules attached to them, rules which determine what you say and how you interpret what they say.

Barresi: Allowing this interpretation to dovetail very nicely with what you were speculating on at the end of your presentation this morning.

Bower's extension of contemporary network models—as developed to explain normal memory phenomena—to pathological dissociations, is a step in the right direction. At a purely behavioral level, it should be possible to mimic even the dramatic shifts in behavior and the often complete interpersonality amnesias that characterize dissociative MPD and other dissociative disorders. It might be possible to achieve this with only quantitative adjustments of parameters within the network model. Moreover, such a model should be able to accommodate the treatment outcomes with multiple personality disorder that often result in successful reintegration. Indeed, the relative efficacy of different treatments can probably be used to discriminate among alternative models.

But something will be missing from a network, or cell-assembly model if it cannot explain the impression each dissociated state usually has, that it is a separate agent with its own identity, experiences, and goals: a separate, conscious self. Of course, it is a challenge for psychological theory to explain such notions as consciousness and personal identity in normal individuals, let alone in those who seem to house more than one. But this is not a "cart before the horse" problem. Here there is an opportunity for symbiosis. It was Hebb's view that the effort to understand, and precisely model, how the development of normal personal identity goes awry under some forms of severe stress will reap rewards both for clinical practice and for normal psychological theory.

SKEPTICISM

Gordon Bower suggests that there is a widespread skepticism about the genuineness of the phenomenon of MPD, and wonders if there are some "knock down" demonstrations. Kluft responds that it is not his style to "convince" the skeptic, but rather to amass data on the disorder. (To appreciate one thrust of Kluft's tropical fish metaphor it is useful to know that in many of Spanos' experiments the behavior of individuals who have been asked to simulate a hypnotic state is compared to that of subjects who have undergone hypnosis.) Kluft feels that much of the skepticism is born of ignorance. Ken Bowers raises the historical parallel between hypnosis and MPD, and asks if we are debating the genuineness of the phenomenon or the explanations for it.

Bower: I wonder whether these basic questions of "What is a personality? What is amnesia? How is it all to be defined?" sort of underlies what is, I think for all of us, a real undertoe skepticism about MP, functional amnesia, dissociation generally, and even hypnosis (and there are skeptical attitudes toward hypnosis). Just as some scientists are skeptical about the existence of separate "states" in hypnosis, some people think that MPD is all a figment of the imagination of the therapist who is imposing these kinds of views upon the patient et cetera. On the other side are the clinicians who are actively working with dissociative disorders. They would say, "We aren't doing that at all; these are the presenting symptoms of the patient; we are just reporting them." And somehow or other, this field is not going to become "respectable" in psychiatry or probably even in academic psychology until there are some knock down arguments or demonstrations that it is really there and not a figment of the imagination of the therapist. Now, I know, Rick [Kluft], you've probably had to fight this battle 88 times over, with everybody giving you the skeptical argument, "that these don't exist and how come you're seeing these 'fairies dancing on pinheads' and no one else does?" Rick, what do you say to convince a skeptic, let's say, Spanos?

Kluft: I think that one of the important things to understand is that I really don't try to convince anyone, least of all myself, because I think you have to be as dispassionate and objective as you can in a controversial area. I don't try to convert the disbeliever (I don't think that's a useful frame of reference against an adversarial stance). What I try to do is amass an amount of information and let people form their own conclusions from it. One of the things that has been most troubling to me is the willingness of many folk to make widespread conclusions about these phenomena in the total absence of data. Many people in the field, for example, are not familiar with clinical MP, they attempt to extrapolate from known bodies of knowledge to what they assume clinical MP is, and that's a very dangerous, although occasionally very productive point of view. I think that, very often, you get a very nice cogent line of reasoning developed, and there is only one problem, it doesn't resemble anything I've seen in a clinic. There is another problem, there's been a considerable expansion of the database available about this condition in a short period of time, and relatively few people outside the field have absorbed it (some who have tried have dismissed it saying that it doesn't satisfy their criterion for scientific data).

One of the speakers this morning, I think it was you Herb [Weingartner], made a very important point that at a certain stage in the development of a concept you're going through a phase of demonstration of what is there to be further understood. And then you move to find out what "drives" the phenomenon. As a clinician, Dr. Nissen's work was particularly impressive to me because, to my mind, it was an excellent attempt to learn from the phenomena, rather than apply a preconceived body of theories and notions to it. I was most impressed; it seemed to be a very objective way to go about the beginnings of the objective study of this condition. I think that some of the theorists you alluded to in passing—some of the skeptical school of hypnosis analysts—are also jumping on the skepticism bandwagon about MPD with very little connection to the clinical phenomena.

To use a silly analogy, I raised tropical fish as a boy, and I got used to all these bright-colored fresh water fish that were largely from Central America and the Yukatan, and then I went down there and put on a mask and snorkle, and I went into the water and I recognized the species by their configuration very easily, but they didn't have those nice bright colors, those were breeder's artifacts. The real fish in nature over those sand flats would be instantly picked up by a bird of prey if they had that coloration. Well, MP as a clinical phenomenon—according to what to Frank [Putnam] has shown, I think convincingly, and [Bennett] Buddy Braun has documented— is not this wonderfully florid picture all the time. If it were, there wouldn't be that 6.8 year delay between first seeking help and diagnosis. So I'm encouraged when someone takes an actual patient and studies that patient to see what's there and I get alarmed, perhaps unnecessarily, perhaps overly alarmed, when someone walks up to what they think this phenomenon is and slaps on a body of theory and says, "thus and so, and thus and so, and thus and so." I find that pseudo-science.

Bowers: I am wondering what is the level of agreement or disagreement between people who are more or less experimentally oriented, on the one hand, and people who are clinically oriented, on the other. It might be helpful to put this in the historical context of the study of hypnosis with which the study of dissociative disorders shares similar characteristics. When hypnosis began to surface again in the early 1960s, discussion was characterized by two polarities, represented by Hillgard and Borne, on the one hand and Ted Barber on the other. The skeptical view, as spearheaded by Barber, was that hypnosis wasn't a genuine phenomena. To designate this condition, he always put hypnosis in quotation marks in the titles of all his articles. There was a clear attempt to discredit this phenomena as a genuine one, including saying when hypnotic analgesia is induced, the person feels the pain alright —he just doesn't feel like alarming the physician by acknowledging the pain that he feels. That was the level of the debate at that time. Now, what is interesting and what has happened in the last 20 years is that the nature of the debate has shifted very subtly because Spanos, who is the current *bette noire*, has acknowledged on many occasions (although people wonder how serious he is about it) that hypnotic analgesia is genuine, there is a genuine reduction in pain and that hypnotic amnesia is genuine, there is a genuine forgetting that occurs as a result of hypnotic suggestion . . . . As far as hypnosis is concerned, today's skepticism is not about the genuineness of the phenomena, be it analgesia or amnesia or what have you, but how do we explain it? The explanation, from Spanos's point of view, is some kind of expectational effect or some kind of interpretation of the instructions, social compliance or what have you; whereas the more traditional view is that there is some kind of dissociative mechanism involved. So you see, we have progressed from putting hypnosis in quotation marks where the phenomena was the issue, to a point of arguing about what the proper explanation is.

What I would like us to address is the following issue: Is there a debate about whether or not MP are genuine in the same sense that hypnotic analgesia or hypnotic amnesia is genuine? Are we agreeing that there is a genuine phenomena there and we can understand it in different ways and those different ways of understanding or explaining it are the point of issue? Or are we arguing about the genuineness of the phenomena? Whether the phenomena exists, or it's malingering, or it's some sort of simulation, or it's some kind of dissociation that may be a kind of temporary imaginal product that has no developmental implications. I would like to get some kind of handle on how people are conceptualizing the phenomenon and whether we are agreeing that it is a phenomenon to account for in different ways, or whether we are arguing about if the phenomenon even exists. It is not clear to me that there is a consensus about the genuineness of the phenomenon in the same way that there is now a consensus (almost a consensus) about hypnosis.

Bowers' question wasn't explicitly answered by the participants. There was an implicit consensus that there is something interesting here, something worth studying. There was disagreement, however, as to the underlying nature of dissociative phenomena. At this point the discussion shifted to "What is a personality?"

PERSONALITIES, ALTERS, AND FRAGMENTS

Just what does it mean when a therapist refers to her or his patient as having 120 personalities? John Curtis begins this discussion by presenting a descriptive model that he and George Fraser have been using. Gordon

Bower's probing questions seek the underlying rules governing the operation of the system, and it is clear that he regards the framework as descriptive rather than explanatory.

Curtis: Could I draw on the board how one of my multiples explained her 120? Dr. George Fraser and I have a framework for looking at the personalities. We tend to look at the multiples as having the following: We believe they have a social component of their personality, a more logical component, and emotional components [see Fig. 11.2.]

With most multiples I work with, the emotional part can usually be subdivided into anger, sadness, fear and fun and joy, just like you [G. Bower] were talking about; consciousness usually resides in the social part; and the central part tends to be divided into a passive memory part and a more active rescuer part.

Bower: Where is your knowledge of mathematics, or the French language; where is long-term memory?

Curtis: A common pool somewhere. Not everything gets divided up. But the social memory and concern for social things that go on are in this segment. Memory for the whole person is in the "observing adult" section. The "action adult" aspect of the person often plays a "rescuer" role. I don't know, in the U.S., they don't find the inner self-helper as much as we do here [in Canada] and I think its a matter of technique. George [Fraser] and I have it in all of ours. The "observer" part often says it is not a part like all the other parts and is the memory for the person. [Memories associated with strong mood states would be attached to the corresponding emotional section. Memory for the angry, abusive events would be located in the "anger" section of the emotional component.]

Bower: Who has access to these things? You haven't told us the rules of operation in this field. Is it when I'm in a certain personality that

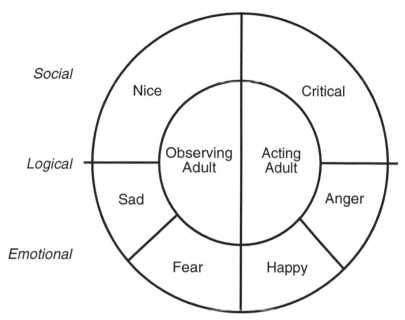

FIG. 11.2 See text for explanation.

I have access to this and not these things?

Curtis: The social part is the main personality of the person; each of the other components is another personality. [Basically] this is a subpersonality theory.

Bower: Does that mean when I'm feeling sociable I can't be sad?

Curtis: What I'm talking about is, yes, you can have a certain degree of sadness within the social aspect of the person; but sadness in a profound sense and the experiences of sadness that come with abuse, et cetera, come from this aspect. So the person would then switch into that because of environmental cues. I don't want to get bogged down too much on this.

Bower: Well, it looks like you only have seven[personalities].

Curtis: I think Terry does a really nice job [describing] how all of her personalities are grouped around the main personalities (see Fig. 11.3). She said, "It is like a spider's web," that attaches to these main personalities other personalities or special purpose fragments or memory fragments. By the way, this drawing only shows 6 personalities, but she has a lot of other personalities. Lets say this [angry component] is the assertive personality which is called Herb. [One of these satellite fragments] is her experience that she had one day being in the park and being stung by a bee. This component [points to neighboring larger circle] was the main personality that helped her deal with that experience but it is this one [small satellite] that has the memory for what was really only a half-hour in her life. So it's not like a personality.

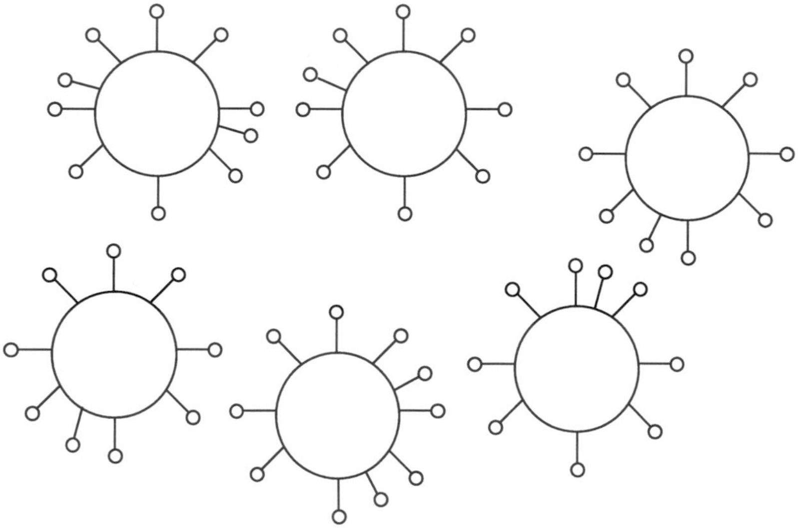

FIG. 11.3 See text for explanation.

Bower: So when she is sad, she can't remember that event.

Curtis: That is correct. It is remembered through the "angry" personality in her situation.

Ray: These little satellites are like episodes?

Curtis: Yes, these are episodes.

Bower: That was consistent with the way I was thinking about it, except I would say that everything was much more interconnected than this because she is obviously using the same language to talk about all these things.

Curtis: I can't draw it as nice as she [Terry] says, but she says what happens is that these intersect and they cross.

Bower: That is right, there is a character in this episode that is also in that episode.

Curtis: What she said was that they don't all intersect and cross. Just some of them.

Bower: That is the whole idea of memory being an associative network.

Barresi: But the issue is rather of self as an associative network.

Bower: I have gone on that assumption that your self is like your concept of mother and dog. You have a lot of associations to it, an awful lot, things your parents told you, things your first grade teacher, girlfriend, wife told you, et cetera, and all the episodes in which you have appeared.

Bowers: The issue here seems to be, what should one judge to count as real, as [sort of] an independent reality? You know, the model that Gordon [Bower] is suggesting is a kind of underlying mechanism for understanding Terry and her associations and how activations occur and so forth. He is sort of attributing reality to an underlying mechanism by which memories surface, fade, are amnesic from one another, et cetera. You're [Curtis] attributing reality [it appears to me that people who are really into this MPD thing, are attributing reality] to the specific embodiments of Terry. Each specific memory [that a person has] has an independent reality that can be quite convincing in a clinical context when it surfaces with a lot of affect and moral associations and so forth. I think the temptation, as a clinician, is to look at each of these emphatic surfacings as somehow having a boundary around it that defines a reality that is separate from the reality that happens on another occasion when another 'eruption' occurs. All of a sudden, you have these multiplicities that become mind-boggling to anybody who has an aesthetic need for simplicity to understand all that complexity. As a matter of fact, the entire history of early dissociation theory, in the hands of Janet, was aimed at figuring out what kind of invariance could be the basis for the plethora of symptomatology, whether they came out in terms of hallucinations, in or through actions and so forth. Janet had this scientific need to find invariance throughout the multiplicity and variety that confronted the clinician. I have a great deal of sympathy with that. The scientific spirit, in a sense, is to search out these invariances—what remains constant, what is there throughout the various manifestations of that constancy. What I find difficult to take as a clinician, as well a scientist, is the attribution of reality to every little thing that surfaces, every little blib, every little satellite or what have you. I need something that has more cohesion, something that has an invariant status, whether it is a mechanism or some kind of process or what have you.

In his choice of language to represent the appearance of separate selves, K. Bowers is trying to depict in neutral terms the phenomena that must be dealt with when a single person, Terry, appears as multiple "emphatic surfacing," or even as a "blib," or "satellite" of other root personalities (with similar affect but different specific memories). How do boundaries form to determine invariant "constant" things that may bridge across some but not all episodes of a particular kind of mood-state, and how is the scientist/therapist to decide what is real here? G. Bower's model postulates a relatively straightforward associative mechanism to determine what gets recalled or experienced in a given context. The reality of such a mechanism is quite different from the reality attributed by Janet to his postulated invariant-dissociative-states, some of which are selves. The question of boundaries and realities of mechanisms and selves has recently been discussed by Humphrey and Dennett (1991). They opt for a kind of pseudo-reality of "executive" selves who, acting like a president of a country, are neither true independent selves nor merely the sum total of excitations and inhibitions of neurons or cell assemblies.

Bower: Why don't you get Rick [Kluft] or George [Fraser] to say why they came up with the notion of fragments for the personalities?

Kluft: First, although I'm sympathetic with the aesthetic need for simplicity, I don't think the phenomena will allow it at this point of our understanding. Attempts to prematurely simplify, to bring this into a more acceptable and academic purview, have been understandable but perhaps detrimental. I don't think we know what we are trying to understand yet. To make my point I'll quote, not a notable scientist or a medical colleague, but Conan Doyle, whose character, Sherlock Holmes said: "It is a capital offense, Watson, to hypothesize in advance of the facts." The fact of the matter is there are many attempts to classify these structures (which I personally only call "personalities" because that is what the literature decided to call them). I think it is misleading; I think it takes us very far afield and activates associative networks that are counterproductive.

If you go to Georgia, to the Richview Institute Special Program for MPD, you'll find that when people talk to patients with MPD about the separate parts of the mind they use either the term *personality* or the term *element*. You'll find North of the border, where we are now, often the term *subpersonality* used in communication among colleagues. You'll find that used almost nowhere else. If you are involved with Bennet Braun's Dissociative Disorder Program there is an attempt to quantify the degree of definition of the different structures that one encounters and some sort of pecking order, ranging from a fully elaborated personality to less elaborated fragments, special purpose fragments, and special memory fragments. I don't like any of those terms. I talk to patients in terms of personalities because it is less of a problem to talk that way; because as T.S. Eliot says, "I got to use words when I talk to you," and for me to introduce any technical terms into a discussion with a patient seems pointless. The term *personality* works quite well in talking with them, so I use it. Empirically, I use the term *alter*, simply because at the time [that] I was searching for a neutral term that is the term I came up with.

This theme was revisited later in the discussion.

Kluft: Let me just elaborate on this a bit because I want to speak to that "so many personalities" thing . . . . When you deal with these entities clinically, you would refer to these as personalities because you don't want to bring in a bunch of technical language and it works with the patients. But surely it is almost impossible for a patient to have more than a half a dozen classically developed full personalities, just on a time-sharing basis. The problem is that many of them [entities; fragments; alters] have a lot more separateness than that. I've seen cases that have spontaneously walked in that are well over the several hundred mark. The point is to realize the myriad forms that the dissociative process can take and to recognize that the classical expression of MP is only one of them. Now suppose you have someone who has dissociated so many times that they are too multiple to be a classic multiple. Do we not call them multiple? We really have to contend with the child who develops idiosyncratic rules for how these structures are developed and how these painful experiences are kept from one another. I'm dealing with a patient now, just to give you an example, who has fragmented many times over and, as I've gotten to know her, what I've found out is that every day that she came home from school and was abused again she disassociated again. That means that she was abused 3 or 4 times a week from a young age until she was 18 and thus her particular rules for keeping it hidden and keeping the pain at abeyance led to a fragmentation of staggering proportions. Now is each one of those entities developed enough to be a classic personality? No. A couple are. But that doesn't mean that I don't have to deal with every one of those several hundred. And as they aggregate more and more, she becomes a more classic multiple because there are fewer entities and they've got more in each. Now it looks like (and this is what Bennett Braun has found with very complex cases too) you end up creating a more classic multiple [before] you wind up getting [them] well.

Doan: Richard, I'd like to understand this a little better. I have difficulty with the over 100 multiples, and this is why: I have no idea how to count them. I'm a practicing clinician and I know what it is like to sit and watch them come up. This woman's case, you just mentioned dissociating every day, each of those dissociations you're counting as a distinct separate fragment?

Kluft: If it was a separate memory alone I wouldn't call it as anything. If I have to speak to it because it has a sense of self, if I have to deal with it in that way, I enumerate it as another separate entity. [What do we call such an entity, when we] have to deal with it on a personal basis in therapy? If I'm talking to George Greaves in Georgia, I call it a minor element. If I'm talking to Bennett Braun in Chicago, I say a memory fragment. If I talk to George Fraser or John Curtis, I say this is certainly a fragment, it is not big enough to be a subpersonality. And if we're in my shop, we say it is another thing we've got to deal with. We used 'alters' for many years, but many people decided we were closet Jungians; so now we are looking for another term.

Nissen: I'm not sure I have any more trouble believing 120 as 2. Partly because a PDP [parallel distributed processing] model could generate 120 different states as well as 2. So, from the point of view of modeling it, 120 is fine. My trouble is deciding if I believe in 2. In studying the patient [I reported on earlier], when I began I wasn't sure it was real and I'm still not positive that I believe it was real. But the way I resolved it in my own mind was that she was undoubtedly undergoing changes in state, most of which I could see; changes which also appeared in her performance . . . .

Curtis: Just to bring up another small point, with all of my multiples I video tape these shifts and show them to other family members, and look for what I call the yawn factor, that is they sit there and say, "Well, so what? We've seen all that before." That is another form of acknowledging.

Fraser: With the multiple, if you think of it, this is very diagrammatic, if you think of the person as a piece of pie, if the first division works, you are going to end up with two pieces, or two personalities, but often the abuse is so significant, as in the case Rick described, that these people have to divide up many times, but it is the same piece of pie that is being divided up, and I guess when you get very small pieces you get crumbs, or fragments. The point is that is one piece of pie being divided up, and whether it is divided up into 120 or 2 you still have to deal with it. If you just take the big pieces and don't deal with the little pieces, you don't get the pie together again. We have to deal with all. We don't invent the personalities. They say there is another part that you are going to have to deal with because I don't have that person's memory. We are forced and perhaps you might want to think about them as 120 ego states making up one ego. That may make more sense . . . (in any event) They are *not* fully developed. They are ego-fragments . . . We don't have a better word for it at the moment; it's just not a "personality."

How does a clinician make the deduction that a patient has multiple personalities? Sometimes, the clinician experiences a switch serendipitously. But sometimes, information from the family history gives the therapist a clue.

Bower: How do you detect that a new alter has appeared?

Kluft: I will give a clinical example and see if it is understood. I was dealing with a lady who I thought had integrated . . . . I reread her entire chart to ask her and myself, what have we missed? You are basically still miserable in a certain area. What have we not encountered together; what have we not looked at? I looked through 5 years of notes, and found there was not a single reference to her older brother except when I took the initial family history and found there was an older brother. So, two weeks ago, when sitting with that patient, I said, "I've been concerned with why you seemed a little bogged down, and we've talked about this for a number of months and reviewing your chart it seemed to me that we have not discussed your older brother and on reflection I'm not sure I even know his full name," at which point the patient's face changed, she showed a configuration of facial muscle tension, an openness I was not familiar with, had not seen previously. The voice was somewhat different, not markedly, but somewhat different. She looked a little bit dazed, kind of equivocated a little, said a couple of words I could not make much of, and then suddenly the patient closed her eyes and resumed being the patient I usually encountered, but she looked kind of dazed and said she had a mild headache. As we talked about this and I talked about the brother, there was another of these spontaneous changes, and the third time I asked what's going on? In the normal clinical situation, unless someone comes out and declares oneself, one is very much in the position of those astronomers who induced that there had to be Pluto from the way Neptune's orbit was being perturbed.

You recognize that there is some factor in the equation that you can't understand . . . . If you are doing a compulsive history, a compulsive work-up, you usually find areas that the patient cannot account for, time gaps in their life history.

Bower: But, see, what that illustrates to me is an example of conditioned emotional response.

Kluft: I don't think those terms are mutually exclusive.

Bower: No, it's like I can sit here and you can get me frightened by saying, "Gordon, you're going to be audited by the IRS," or I can switch personalities. This isn't enough evidence to say she's switched personalities.

Kluft: That's only the top of a large collage. Generally, the way I find out what's going on is to simply start work with the patient, and as I take a very compulsive and old fashioned 1930s type of associative anamnesis, I see a good bit of spontaneous change as sometimes an individual, whatever you would like to call them—introduce themselves to me—(very often it is a while before they declare themselves as different) and I take pains to simply sit back and wait and see. Again I emphasize, the stereotype of a "Mouseketeers Role-Call" of personalities leaping out and saying, "I'm Jimmy; I'm Joan; . . . ." This you encounter sometimes, but basically there would not be such a difficulty making the diagnosis if it were that overt and florid a psychopathology all the time. So one simply proceeds and sees what one is dealing with. And there's another thing that one does, one really takes a much more compulsive history than is customary these days. I think it's important to note that, and this is a point I made in a recent clinical article, that if you really take a good history from these patients and you also ask them about their interviews by prior clinicians, it is very rare, almost vanishingly rare, for them to have had a good old-fashioned work-up . . . [But] if you are doing a compulsive history, a compulsive work-up, you usually find areas that the patient cannot account for, times in their life. And all you do as a clinician is simply ask about the unknown areas.

The importance of taking a thorough family history <u>cannot</u> be overemphasized. This is not only important from the point of view of good clinical practice; it also provides invaluable empirical data for developing models of the nature and etiology of the disorder.

As in Kluft's example, when the therapist accidentally hits upon a trauma related event, the patient may undergo a "switch" —it will appear involuntary and be accompanied by eye-rolling or other unusual behaviors; the emerging personality will usually talk about the earlier one in the third person, and might tell the therapist to "leave her alone."

Bower: What an experimentalist would want to do would be to bite that point, freeze the patient, and ask: "Now start telling me everything about yourself."

It is pointed out that that is precisely what the therapist does; although often not all at once.

Barresi: . . . In a sense each "multiple personality" is a list and, if you put all those lists together, you get a life history.

Bower: It's a list of episodes, a list of opinions . . . .

Barresi: No, I mean a serial-temporal list. An autobiographical list structure of episodes. If you put all those episodic-autobiographical lists together you get a life history of the person. Sometimes they are in parallel, sometimes they are alternating, but each one has its own list structure, which is a serial ordering of its own experiences. That is to me the fundamental difference between mood changes of "a" self and switches to alternative selves.

ROLE-PLAYING AND MPD:
A DISSOCIATIVE CONTINUUM?

A discussion occurs in which the multiplicity of a normal personality is described—we play different roles and exhibit quite different behavior patterns depending on the context. But, in spite of this duplicity, the normal individual is organized or integrated by a self that continues its existence in spite of the roles and moods that are dominant. Putnam suggests that dissociation and sense-of-self are not all-or-none phenomena, but instead may exist along continua.

Bower: Let me try this one on Ken [Bowers]: How about saying there are roles you can play . . . .

Fraser: That implies faking.

Bower: No, no . . . .

Bowers: Role enacting.

Bower: When Lawrence Olivier does Hamlet or when he does Richard the 3rd or something—he's not faking.

Fraser: But he has an awareness of it.

Bowers: But he's in charge.

Bower: He's in charge. It is presumably controllable.

Fraser: So there's not the same thing in these people—disconnection.

Bower: Now Lawrence Olivier has 193 fragments of roles presumably, that he can play. How does he differ from these fragments?

Fraser: He has connection with the memory, feeling . . . ."that is me playing this role."

Kluft: He has a sense of ownership of those experiences that is absent in the person with a more disaggregated sense of self.

Curtis: That is a nice way of saying it. Just keep in mind that the play is only an hour-and-a-half or two hours long and for the other twenty-some hours a day . . .

Bower: But he tries to get into the whole life (of the character) and tries to imagine what the whole life must have been like.

Doan: There's two issues in what you've raised, Gordon. One of them is the whole issue of co-consciousness . . . ongoing existence of a personality. If Lawrence Olivier is playing Richard the 3rd and finishes Act 1 and switches into King Lear (or something), as far as I'm concerned, Richard the 3rd goes away and doesn't exist anymore until he starts playing him again.

Fraser: That's what happens in a multiple.

Doan: Well, yeah. Except when you ask Richard the 3rd what's been going on the past 3 years or so, Richard may well be able to provide you with a history, a partial history, a history that even differs from King Lear's history. And I think the possible mistake that's made is that we reify that; we attribute some ongoing existence to Richard the 3rd, that really doesn't exist beyond the time that you are talking to him. And he has access to some memories that Lawrence has.

Curtis: I guess where I learned about the thing you are talking about was my first multiple when she came together—and the main assertive part of her personality—it turns out she was 31 years old and didn't know what Christmas was. She had never been around for Christmas; she had no experience of Christmas.

Putnam: You know—one of the issues—I mean everybody's trying to separate this—and I still say it's an issue of degree. Just as depression is an issue of degree; anxiety is an issue of degree; paranoia is a issue of degree. It's not as if we all have this phenomena. It's a matter of our being able to keep them within certain boundaries. And when they exceed those boundaries, then the phenomena becomes a problem of pathology. And these people—whatever . . . we all have different selves, we enact roles and it's not as if actors always have control over this. Actors can get stuck, there are accounts of that. One of the things I was consulted about . . . the CIA has people who go deep undercover and they get stuck in their cover personalities and they can't get out of those cover personalities. It is a problem for those agencies. When someone goes deep undercover people assume the cover and they can't get out. Well, I think it has something to do with the stress, and as you know with multiples, you enter an altered state under stress, its somehow gets encoded in a way that it becomes a "more than dream" sort of entity. I think there are some analogues of those sorts of phenomena. It is not as if we are ever going to be able to cleave this separately off. We have to, at some point, draw a line, where below this level is a pathological behavior and below this level is some sort of middle ground, where we are not sure. The issue is, do we make it worse or do we acknowledge it? The evidence is [that] these people, by not acknowledging it, are perpetuating all sorts of self-destructive behavior. We know the clinical history of these people [when they are not] treated as multiples. The evidence is emerging that treating them as multiples is really doing them a favor (the fascination notwithstanding).

Putnam's last point highlights what is sure to be a most fruitful research strategy: Analysis of the comparative effectiveness of different therapeutic interventions.

IATROGENESIS AND THE IMPORTANCE
OF DEVELOPMENTAL EVIDENCE

The possibility of iatrogenesis (therapist-induced dissociations) and the value of developmental evidence in countering this charge is discussed. It is very important to note that the very fact that dissociated "selves" can be produced iatrogenically or experimentally through hypnosis lends credence to the notion that splitting can occur naturally.

Bowers: It has an immediate and adverse impact when I hear about 123 personalities. Several personalities makes more sense to me; but—because it is so easy to produce them iatrogenically—it is essential to have a clear-cut developmental evidence for them. It is not enough to engender these kind of alternates in a consulting room. There are just too many things going on; there is an implicit kind of contract that is easy to enter into about the interest values of multiples; there is an imaginative person here, very highly hypnotizable. These things [personalities] can get engendered, not purposefully, not maliciously, or anything like that ... From my own clinical work I know how fascinating a patient can be in the consulting room, and the amazing things that can come out unexpectedly, "off the wall" so to speak. It is tempting to see these things with the spectacle of a possible multiple, and to explore that possibility, and suddenly under your very eyes you see this "creation" emerge. Just because you are trying honestly to investigate the situation, you kind of promote the very things that you seek. I'm not saying this is the only thing that happens, but I think it is something that anybody who wants to take this MP disorder seriously just has to contend with it, in an intellectually honest way. You just can't dismiss it, I've seen it happen. I've seen it happen in film and in an actual consulting situation. Unless there are ways of discriminating between this kind of creation, a creation of the clinician with a sort of cooperation of a willing patient, from a kind of developmentally rooted personality that has dependence and amnestic boundaries and so forth, we're just not going to get anywhere.

Kluft: It is incredibly unfair for you and anyone who takes this stance, to assume that because you find these ideas unpalatable, aesthetically unacceptable, and difficult to contend with, and because you may have seen some misadventures, to paint with a very broad brush . . .
Bowers: That is not the case. I am acknowledging that there are MPD, I am not dismissing that. On the basis of my reading of history going back at least 200 years there is very good documentation for MPD; I have no quarrel with the fact that this is a disorder. I may be wrong about that, but my present stance is that there is a real disorder here. I am not arguing that. What I am arguing is that all of a sudden we can see them everywhere. It has become an "in" thing to see them. I think that one is on very shaky grounds unless you have at least fairly convincing developmental evidence (that can be very hard to get, I grant) for the emergence of a personality as an alternate ego, that has some kind of independent status and internal coherence, and that splits off between the ages of, say, 5 and 12. That kind of evidence is the one thing that can secure the clinician against the possibility that these separable personalities or entities are creations of the therapeutic process. I really think that one of the problems of people who are really invested in this phenomenon is that the fascination of the clinical phenomena, of sort of seeing these things emerge, is not balanced against this need for developmental evidence that these things, these entities, or alter egos [had pre-existed] . . .

Kluft: What exactly do you mean by developmental evidence? The patient's own account?

Bowers: Look, its not easy . . . siblings, parents, teachers, social workers, case conference, child clinic evidence, that sort of thing.

That's the kind of research that has to be done, archival research, social worker and longitudinal. I'm sure that it is done and I'm sure that these kind of genuine multiples exist. I am questioning that you have 122 of them (personalities) in one patient or that every apparent dissociative entity is a genuine MP.

Putnam: Let me reply to this issue. First of all, I think that no one has addressed this; from the whole conference this has been missing: there is good data on the issue of continual disassociation. There is relatively good data showing that dissociation exists along a continuum, and some of these people are at one end of the continuum, and there are all sorts of intermediate forms of dissociation where people are evolving a sense of self, an intransient [?] form of personality, et cetera. The people at this end of the continuum are MP. Let's go back to sort out two issues. One issue is the developmental history. Now I actually did that in 1980, after I'd seen about 10 of these people. What bothered me at the time was the fact that they all told me of this history of child abuse which was, at that time, known to clinicians but not generally known in the literature, and I said, there is a pattern here, they all tell me that they've been this way since some time in their childhood; so I went and very systematically got their nutrition records and their school records, I got everything I could and I sat down with them and pored over them. What emerged was a profile of the behaviors that allowed me to generate a list of predictors of what children looked like, but they weren't behaviors that would say "multiplicity"; they would say "this is a spacy child." I then generated a list of predictors from this list and began to visit protective service agencies and said, "Have you ever seen a child that looks like this?" Then I began to generate a trickle of children in to see me. In what we alluded to earlier, in the first day, the child formed a very marked thing, where it looks differently at different times, it is like kids are more sharply illuminated at 10 and other kids are at 15 and 16. So there are a lot of variables here, I mean you can't get a good, clean developmental history for some of those issues. What you can get is a history of what is now called learning disabilities, there is now a comparable list generated very independently by clinicians that have a high degree of overlap. You have to know the history of these lists, but essentially I generated a list, Rick generated a list, the complete backing for my list, John Vaughan down in Georgia, and Nick Powell, if you lay these lists side by side, you'd be amazed at the degree of overlap. We all found developmental . . .

Bower: What are some examples of the things on the list?

Putnam: Well, the single highest predictor of all three lists was that the child has translex states. The teachers in the school report things like the child is very spacy, this child is in a world of its own.

Bower: Another one or two?

Putnam : The child shows perplexive forgetfulness. The child forgets ownership of possessions, forgets names of friends. One of the classic behaviors is that the child forgets to hand in the homework that they have done. There is no secondary gain in that. They have had the experience of getting back tests that they don't remember having taken. They have perplexive forgetting, they lose possessions. One of the classic stories you hear from foster parents is that the child comes home without his shoes or shirt and doesn't know where they are. We've got these kids in the children's hospital in wards, and one of the things you classically find is that they get lost changing classes on the ward. They only have to go down two rooms. The teachers will see them as being purposefully late and they really are having too many views there on the ward and are confused as to where they are to go. There is a whole series of those sorts of behavior that we see in these kids. These are a objective behaviors you can get information about from outside individuals.

Bowers: One of the problems we have with that kind of issue is that we don't know how that fits in with the normal population. I mean heaven forbid that you see my child forgetting a name, or shoes.

Putnam: What I think everybody is saying is that there is a normatively high dissociative potential in children and when does this break above threshold. That is why I feel it is important to embark on a prospective study to follow normal kids and abused kids. To see what are the normal behaviors, and when do they abate in normal development as opposed to abused kids? Are these dissociative behaviors perpetuated in the abused kids beyond some cutoff time in normals?

STRATEGIES FOR SCIENTIFIC ANALYSIS

The general theme of how to best achieve an understanding of dissociation was revisited several times, from quite different perspectives. Putnam suggested that perhaps we had too many models, and that there wasn't enough data to constrain our theories. Bowers points out that theories are always incorrect in some respects, but still useful guides for research.

Bowers: The thing about science, whether its in psychology or physics, is that its the first thing that comes along thrives on being wrong. I mean "self-correcting" . . . The thing that science provides is a way of making a phenomenon corrigible. I mean hypnosis was in big trouble for years and years and years until the Hilgards and Orne and other people came along and began to establish ways of investigating it on a replicable basis; and to sort of throw out as spurious certain kind of claims that had been made for it; to find new boundary conditions; its not that there's no controversies, for God's sake, or . . . there's a kind of consensus view—but, you know, compared to the kind of thing you could read 25 years ago and what you can read now—in terms of what's secure [knowledge/fact] and what's not. There's a kind of an evolution that goes along and it thrives on being wrong and having to correct itself; and for all the bad-mouthing that I can claim for Barber and Spanos and so forth (and have on occasion) they have served a useful corrective [purpose]. You think a little harder and better about alternatives and you try to steer your research to address the issues and so forth—without that it's just voodoo . . . . What I said this morning in my paper was I think every theory is wrong. Every theory is subject to error, whether it is a theory of the cosmos or a theory of behavior, and one just has to live in that kind of uncertainty . . . .

Later, Bowers points to the importance of measurement (e.g., good scales of hypnotizability) in the history of hypnosis research. Some of the necessary research on dissociation will require similar measures. It is pointed out that valid and reliable measures of dissociability have already been developed and used profitability .

Bowers: One of the overriding advantages of the research on hypnosis is that you have standardized scales. I cannot stress enough how critical that's been to the advance of fortunes in hypnosis research. Those individual differences are like a rock—they are so reliable and so replicable . . . The correlations are really very good. That kind of ability to scale people in hypnotic ability and demonstrate those kinds of consistencies has just been critical. And the problem is, with multiple personality, you don't have that kind of antecedent...

Bower: Can you get a scale for dissociability?

Putnam: Yes . . . . We have a scale, the DES, dissociative experiences scale . . . We usually refer to it as the "some people sometimes find scale." It's reliable and valid (we have data on that and people have replicated our work with large numbers of normals) . . . There's a cutoff where you can say, hey, above 40 on this scale you have a very high chance of having a diagnosis of multiple personality or a different dissociative disorder; we've done it in a blind fashion. Its not a bad instrument. But the way it's set up it's good for age 18 and up; it's not too useful for kids. So much of it has to do with people noticing discontinuities, in behavior and experiences. Children don't notice discontinuity the way adults notice it; they don't follow clock time. They don't have all of the kinds of issues that make them pay attention to linearity of time. Looking for discontinuity in children is not the way to go. With children you have to look externally. That's why we're generating a checklist of behaviors that caretakers could fill out about children in terms of dissociative behaviors. I think you have to go a different route with kids ...

In response to Bowers' suggestion that cumulative evidence is necessary to secure the phenomenon against the skeptic, Putnam and Kluft present a litany of studies.

Putnam: You [can] say there's replications. First Prince did this study ... and then Ludwig did the studies, and then Silberman; Herb, and I did this study and Mary Jo's done this study; others are interested in Mary Jo's technique. And we're redoing our study—we have 6 or 7 multiples now. And its starting to build this little pattern ...

Bowers: That's the only way to go, as far as I'm concerned. That kind of systematic inquiry—very often the evidence that establishes the justification of the knowledge claim is quite different from the evidence that establishes a reasonable hypothesis. It's a reasonable hypothesis that there are multiple personalities—on the basis of clinical evidence. But the kind of evidence that really secures that claim is not just more of the same. It's evidence of the kind that Mary Jo is collecting, it's the kind of replicative evidence where you cross-tabulate and get longitudinal studies where you get all sorts of multiple and converging lines of evidence that is impossible for any single clinician to find in his lifetime in his consulting room. That sort of inquiry is exactly what is needed; and it doesn't all have to be experimental laboratory research. It can be this kind of hard slogging archival research; longitudinal sort of stuff.

Kluft: A lot of longitudinal, followup studies have been done and are underway.

Bowers: That's terrific.

Kluft: Just to put that in context. Phillip Coons is following a cohort of 20 at some levels and 50 at other levels over time ... I'm following up a cohort that is well over 200—ranges between 5 days and 18 years, and have published the first 15 years of that followup. I think there is an unsystematic, roughshod body of followup literature that's developed. I'm most impressed with the stuff I see as a journal reviewer coming along about childhood multiplicity being found, more and more. We've got a natural history of this condition developing. Unfortunately, the therapy followup studies have some problems with them, but they do indicate that untreated patients stay sick and treated patients, whether its a shared convenient fiction or not, do a hell of a lot better. And that's come out of a couple of centers now—and are sorting their way through the refereeing process. So I think there is a coming together of many streams of knowledge, but I hasten to say that probably none of them are at the level of hard-core sophistication that even the clinicians in the field would like to see in the near future. But to pat this kind of research on the back a bit, none of it has ever been funded! Its important to realize that the people who have done this kind of work have done it out of either their own pocket or their own time.

Putnam: There has never been a single federal (U.S.) grant given in this area.

Kluft: Rosalind Schultz, I think is almost a tragic figure in this respect. She has three studies out that have enrolled over 500 MPD patients, by latest count—and she's had to do it out of her own pocket. The computer costs and mailing costs are mind-boggling, to do this kind of stuff. And [when] you try to get past a research committee, and they say "Ha, ha, ha, we're not sure multiple personality exists," and after you go through that a few times and don't get funded—and get reviews that have that kind of attitude— it takes the people of great tenacity to persist. I would think that many of these questions that are being raised are "askable," and there are many models available to exploit. And Mary Jo's study is an excellent example of the application of models that are already established being applied to these phenomena. I think that funding would be very, very nice. I don't think that it will come in the foreseeable future for projects that are direct for MPD.

Kluft: I think the way that this will be approached [successfully] is by people who take it from either a neuropsycho-physiological point of view that sounds respectable or a child abuse, epidemiological point of view that has redeeming social value.

Bower: I think I agree. I'd like to change the topic of conversation, for a minute. We've been on multiples here for a long time. Let's talk about dissociation. I think one of the problems in studying that is how do you produce it experimentally in the laboratory? What you need is a good laboratory model if you want to do analysis of dissociation, dissociative memory. And, is it really a good concept worth a damn, or should we just toss it out? It just means you forget, from one condition to another condition. But that's one of the problems I've been having. You see, the main dissociative conditions you study in the laboratory are post-hypnotic amnesia (and we have the usual problems with that), organic amnesia (as in the classic case of HM)), and then there's some recent work on the so-called dissociation between free-recall and priming.

Klein: And there's also state, and drug dependency.

Bower: Yes. But those effects, let me tell you, Herb [Weingartner] was saying they're fragile—well he's right, they're small and they're fragile. I slipped into my talk the fact that the effects don't always occur.

Bowers: One thing that has occured to me: When you bring a subject into a laboratory, the tendency is for them to play the role of a lab subject. They're vigilant, they're reality oriented to the demands of the situation, and so forth. And the kinds of things that are apt to show up in real life, you know revery states and so forth, things that occur spontaneously that are very hard to capture (like instead of dialing the intended number you dial the more familiar one). It's a very complex motor act . . . action slips like Donald Norman [has described]. One of my favorite examples of a dissociated condition that I've use on many occasions that occurs to everybody, that's a good illustration, because everybody on one level or another can connect with it —and that is that you're reading a book (not a particularly difficult book) but at the bottom of the page, it suddenly occurs to you as you shift to the top of the next one, that nothing had gotten in; you know your eyes have gone down the page but you've been "somewhere else" . . . What's interesting, however, is that if you ask the person what they were thinking about instead of reading there are huge individual differences in the extent to which people can tell you what they were [think]ing—Some people have absolutely no trouble. I've done this informally in classroom demonstrations. Some people will sort of say, "What's the mystery, of course I was thinking about 'this'" and especially if they were embroiled in some sort of controversy—like breaking up with your girlfriend or something like that. But some people can go through these episodes and they haven't a clue what they were thinking about—its sort of just gone.

Bower: Forgotten.

Barresi: . . . I think part of what Hebb [was recommending] is that there's a whole population of multiple personality people to study these kinds of things with. There's a natural dissociative phenomenon. All you have to do is get experimental psychologists to write grants to do research with them, and maybe we'll have more luck than psychiatrists trying to get grant money to do clinical studies.

Bower: We'll get dinged because we're not clinicians.

Kluft: You might consider collaboration!

Barresi: Yes. That's the next step.

REFERENCES

Humphrey, N., & Dennett, D.C. (1991). Speaking for ourselves: An assessment of multiple personality disorder. In D. Kolak & R. Martin (Eds.). *Self and Identity: Contemporary Philosophical Issues.* New York: MacMillan.

McClelland, J.L., & Rumelhart, D.E. (1981). An interactive activation model pf context effect in letter perception: I. An account of basic findings. *Psychological Review, 88,* 375-407.

Putnam, F. W., Guroff, J. J., Silberman, E. K., Barban, L., & Post, R. M. (1986). The clinical phenomenology of multiple personality disorder: Review of 100 recent cases. *Journal of Clinical Psychiatry, 47,* 285-93.

Name Index

Z

Subject Index